D1544530

Household Decision-Making

Household
Decision-Making

CONSUMER BEHAVIOR, VOLUME IV

EDITED BY

NELSON N. FOOTE

 New York University Press 1961

© 1961 by New York University
Library of Congress Catalog Card Number: 54–11984
Manufactured in the United States of America

Acknowledgments

This fourth volume of the Consumer Behavior series owes its existence first of all to Lincoln H. Clark, editor of the first three volumes and indefatigable champion of the view that the study of consumer behavior can and should unite basic research with practical concerns. As Secretary-Treasurer of Consumer Behavior, Inc., Professor Clark assembled the resources to organize the conference from which the book derives, and later to assure its publication. In negotiating the numerous arrangements he was aided, as previously, by Joan B. Carney, Assistant Secretary.

The program committee for the conference, which in effect served also as an editorial committee, consisted of Dr. Orville Brim of the Russell Sage Foundation, Professor Theodore Newcomb of the University of Michigan, Professor Guy Orcutt of Harvard University (now of the University of Wisconsin), and Professor James Tobin of Yale University, under the chairmanship of the editor. All selections of topics and personnel were made by this committee.

Indispensable to the entire project was the support of the Committee on Economic Behavior and the Family of the Social Science Research Council, which was extended through its wise and patient Vice-President, Paul Webbink.

Professor Bernard Farber of the University of Illinois strengthened the volume by expanding his original comments at the conference to constitute a full-dress presentation of a mathematical model of marital interaction. Similarly, Dr. F. Thomas Juster of the National Bureau of Economic Research contributed a substantial postscript which brings the weight of impressive data to the emphasis on the family planning process found throughout the volume. Thanks are also due to the National Bureau of Economic Research for permission to utilize these data.

Its publication may add some deserved reward for the earnest effort of the contributors and critics whose thoughts it records.

NELSON N. FOOTE

Contents

List of Participants

ALDERSON, WROE
  Alderson Associates
  3 Penn Center Plaza
  Philadelphia, Pennsylvania

BECKER, HOWARD S.
  Community Studies, Inc.
  417 East 13
  Kansas City, Missouri

BERNARD, JESSIE
  Department of Sociology
  Pennsylvania State University
  State College, Pennsylvania

BILKEY, WARREN
  Department of Economics
  Notre Dame University
  South Bend, Indiana

BIVENS, GORDON
  Department of Home Management
  Iowa State College
  Ames, Iowa

BRIM, ORVILLE
  Russell Sage Foundation
  New York, New York

BROWN, GEORGE
  Ford Division
  Ford Motor Company
  Dearborn, Michigan

CAHALAN, DON
  ARB Surveys, Inc.
  201 East 57 Street
  New York 22, New York

CARNEY, JOAN
  Consumer Behavior, Inc.
  6 Washington Squarc North
  New York 3, New York

CHAPIN, F. STUART
  President, Consumer Behavior, Inc.
  40 Shorewood Drive
  Asheville, North Carolina

CLAWSON, JOSEPH
  Stanford Research Institute
  South Pasadena, California

DANIERE, ANDRE
  Department of Economics
  Harvard University
  Cambridge, Massachusetts

DAUER, ERNEST
  Household Finance Corporation
  Prudential Plaza
  Chicago 1, Illinois

DIMOND, C. LEIGH
  Bureau of Advertising, American Newspaper Publishers Assn., Inc.
  485 Lexington Avenue
  New York 17, New York

DOYLE, JOSEPH
  General Foods Corporation
  250 North Street
  White Plains, New York
DUBOIS, HAZEL
  Social Science Research Center
  University of Puerto Rico
  Rio Piedras, Puerto Rico
FARBER, BERNARD
  Department of Sociology
  University of Illinois
  Urbana, Illinois
FERBER, ROBERT
  Bureau of Business and Eco-
    nomic Research
  University of Illinois
  Urbana, Illinois
FLEISHMAN, AVROM
  Printers' Ink
  635 Madison Avenue
  New York, New York
FOOTE, NELSON N.
  General Electric Company
  570 Lexington Avenue
  New York 22, New York
GARTNER, JOSEPH
  Department of Economics and
    Sociology
  Iowa State College
  Ames, Iowa
GLICK, PAUL
  Social Statistics Branch
  Population Division
  U. S. Bureau of the Census
  Washington 25, D. C.
HALBERT, MICHAEL
  Operations Research Group
  Case Institute of Technology
  Cleveland 6, Ohio
HILL, REUBEN
  Family Study Center
  University of Minnesota
  Minneapolis 14, Minnesota

JOHN, M. E.
  Department of Agricultural Eco-
    nomics and Rural Sociology
  Pennsylvania State University
  University Park, Pennsylvania
JUSTER, F. THOMAS
  National Bureau of Economic
    Research
  261 Madison Avenue
  New York 17, New York
KATONA, GEORGE
  Survey Research Center
  University of Michigan
  Ann Arbor, Michigan
KENKEL, WILLIAM
  Department of Economics and
    Sociology
  Iowa State College
  Ames, Iowa
KOMAROVSKY, MIRRA
  Barnard College
  Columbia University
  New York, New York
LANSING, JOHN
  Survey Research Center
  University of Michigan
  Ann Arbor, Michigan
LEICHTER, HOPE
  Jewish Family Service
  113 West 57 Street
  New York, New York
LIPPITT, VERNON
  General Electric Company
  1 River Road
  Schenectady, New York
MAHONEY, THOMAS
  Industrial Relations Center
  University of Minnesota
  Minneapolis 14, Minnesota
MAYNES, E. SCOTT
  Department of Economics
  University of Minnesota
  Minneapolis 14, Minnesota

MEYERS, TRIENAH
Market Surveys Section
U. S. Department of Agriculture
Washington, D. C.

MILLER, A. EDWARD
McCall Corporation
230 Park Avenue
New York 17, New York

MILLER, DONALD
Burke Marketing Research, Inc.
2374 Kemper Lane
Cincinnati 6, Ohio

MORGAN, JAMES
Survey Research Center
University of Michigan
Ann Arbor, Michigan

MUELLER, EVA
Survey Research Center
University of Michigan
Ann Arbor, Michigan

ORCUTT, GUY
Department of Economics
University of Wisconsin
Madison 6, Wisconsin

PETER, HOLLIS
Foundation for Research on
Human Behavior
1141 East Catherine Street
Ann Arbor, Michigan

RIVLIN, ALICE
Brookings Institution
722 Jackson Place
Washington 6, D. C.

ROSETT, RICHARD
Department of Economics
University of Rochester
Rochester, New York

SCHMOELDERS, G.
Department of Economics
Koln University
Koln, Germany

SCHLAIFER, ROBERT
Graduate School of Business
Administration
Harvard University
Boston 63, Massachusetts

STANTON, HOWARD
New York School of Social Work
Columbia University
New York, New York

STEINKAMP, STANLEY
Bureau of Business and Eco-
nomic Research
University of Illinois
Champaign, Illinois

STRAUS, MURRAY
Department of Rural Sociology
University of Wisconsin
Madison 6, Wisconsin

THOMAS, EDWIN
Department of Psychology
University of Michigan
Ann Arbor, Michigan

WALLACE, DAVID
Ford Motor Company
Detroit, Michigan

WARNE, COLSTON
Consumers Union of the United
States
Department of Economics
Amherst College
Amherst, Massachusetts

WATTS, HAROLD
Cowles Foundation
Yale University
New Haven, Connecticut

WEST, DONALD
Redbook Magazine
230 Park Avenue
New York, New York

WESTOFF, CHARLES
Department of Sociology
New York University
New York, New York

Household Decision-Making

Introduction

For many years, students of consumer behavior have sought to understand the different outcomes of household decision and action by classifying consumers according to numerous capacities and environmental conditions. The most familiar example of past theories is the one that held that different incomes account for differing quantities of purchases. According to the presumed logic of the scientific experiment, these antecedent capacities and conditions have often been termed independent variables or predictors, whereas the consequent behavior of interest has been termed a dependent variable. It has been further assumed that the route to understanding lies in seeking and finding better predictors—independent variables that fluctuate in closer correlation with specified outcomes. The search for these predictors has been pursued assiduously by means of applying a proliferating arsenal of statistical measures of association. Indeed, "explanation" has been deemed to consist of a number—R^2— between 0 and 1 which stands for that portion of the variance in some independent variable that is "accounted for" by the variance in some independent variable, or several taken in combination— and the higher this number, the better.

The strategy and tactics of the empirical search for better predictors appear to have made substantial progress, sufficient to encourage hope for further progress. Some supposed associations between certain antecedent conditions and specified outcomes have been found unwarranted. On the other hand, by more precise definition and measurement, other independent variables have come to be appreciated as more significant than they were previously thought to be. At the very least, an antiseptic rigor in clarification of concepts has been forced on discourse about consumer behavior, and substantial refinement of understanding has occurred in regard to the relative influences to be attributed to its various antecedents. Moreover, the dependent variables themselves have steadily become objectively quantified. These are worthy gains.

In the brief period since World War II, however, certain disquieting observations have been made, which raise some basic questions about the wisdom of depending exclusively on the strategy and tactics of multivariate analysis for coping with consumer behavior. Most conspicuously, instead of improved predictiveness through further refinements in definition and measurement, income has shown a decline in its power as a predictor. And so have some of the other independent variables on which it had been conventional to rely in the past—age of head of household, education, home ownership, rural or urban residence. If it is not a contradiction in terms, one can say there has been rapid secular deterioration in the predictiveness of the predictors.

Confronted with the dwindling of their principal resource for interpreting consumer behavior, social scientists and applied researchers alike have begun to feel growing concern about the shaken foundations of their arts. Reactions to the disturbance, however, diverge widely. Without going into the logical and methodological controversies that have been engendered, we can summarize them as ranging from complete defense of previous procedures—and even denial that a problem has arisen—to complete rejection—as perhaps might be expected. Even certain hallowed premises of empiricism, not seriously challenged since they were erected by Hume, are being reexamined, such as his view that causation reduces to association of events. Obviously such intellectual ferment pervades circles of discourse far outside the specific area of consumer behavior, and its ramifications there cannot be pursued. On the other hand, if the basic questions that have so manifestly been opened up by recent trends in consumer behavior can be answered here, the answers may apply elsewhere also. Thus the examination of what has been undergoing reformulation in this particular field has basic scientific importance.

Among the scientific reactions to the faltering predictiveness of conventional predictors, perhaps the most constructive have been the efforts of a number of investigators, scattered among a variety of disciplines and employed by a variety of institutions, to penetrate more intensively the connections between the independent and dependent variables of consumer behavior, not merely by refinements in measurement, but by theoretical thinking. Without wasting any previous methodological resource, they have begun to recognize that consumption occurs in or through certain units that possess properties of their own—and, moreover, changing properties—which mediate the relations between antecedents and consequents. In individuals, these intervening variables are taken by psychologists to be motives and attitudes. In households, however, which are the units by which consumer behavior tends to be organized, the intervening variables become such phenomena as authority, influence, and values, as will be seen in the papers of this volume

Because the various investigators who have begun to think theoretically about the household unit of behavior have emerged more or less spontaneously in quite differing settings, and because, despite common problems, they have taken hold of differing concrete data, the officers of Consumer Behavior, Inc., felt that it would be desirable to bring a number of them into direct communication for the exchange of ideas. And because it was recognized that the development of models of household decision-making has basic scientific importance, it seemed wise to ask for the collaboration of the Social Science Research Council, especially its Committee on the Family and Economic Behavior. Such collaboration was readily forthcoming, in the form of sharing both costs and committee members. In the course of preliminary deliberations, it was agreed that in addition to a conference embracing as many of the leading contributors to this vein of thought as could comfortably talk to each other in a single spot, a volume of prepared papers, formal discussions, and spontaneous comments of participants should result. Finally, it was foreseen that, considering the diversity of origins of participants in the conference, some mechanism must be devised for directing the writers of the main papers, at least, to a common target. The mechanism was a "preconference" in January, 1958, at which the joint program committee and the invited writers of the main papers came to terms on what was to be sought at the conference itself, held during the following September at Ann Arbor, Michigan.

The resulting volume, which the reader holds in his hand, thus gives him a unique opportunity to sit in on a meeting of minds attempting an exceedingly timely reformulation of how consumers behave. Of those minds known to the program committee to be having some success in coping with the subtleties and complexities of household decision-making, the only ones absent are persons forced to decline invitations to attend the conference. The audience was as carefully invited as the formal speakers, and because of their interest and previous work in the area, most accepted. Through the medium of this volume, however, it is hoped that many more students of the area than were known to the program committee will be put into touch with each other.

Examining the table of contents, the reader may note in the formal assignments a deliberate pairing of consumption economists with family sociologists. These, obviously, are the two disciplinary subgroups most concerned with the household unit. But in that list of names, he will note exceptions—for example, persons engaged in marketing research. And in the list of other participants, he will note how much wider is the range of affiliations of specialists who have a common interest in plumbing further the nature of household decision-making.

The preconference spent many hours going over what is meant by "model," "household," and "decision-making," a relatively sterile yet probably indispensable academic exercise which the reader is spared. Perhaps it will suffice here to describe a model as a theory of how some unit of behavior operates, stated in a form that will generate quantitative predictions and permit itself to be operationally tested. It may consist of a very elaborate interconnection of hypotheses or component relationships or a very limited set; but, generally speaking, it contains three parts: inputs or independent variables, units or intervening variables, and outputs or dependent variables, with the central part receiving principal attention—in this case, the household.

The household, rather than the family, was taken to be the unit in which consumption occurs. Although it is usually a family that occupies a household, not all writers insist that common residence is required to define a family, whereas by definition a household is where consumption occurs; also, the household is usually the income and spending unit. Households are readily distinguishable from each other.

Decision-making, by contrast, was the slipperiest of the three terms employed in naming the conference. Not only were the ambiguities involved in distinguishing process from product and independent from dependent variable thoroughly gone over, but the difficulties of locating decision-making at some specific point in time were fully exposed in both preconference and conference. Simply as an emphasis to force explicit identification of the phenomena of interest, there was agreement that the postwar focus on decision-making as the proximate nexus between tendency and action is valuable intellectual discipline. Secondly, when arbitrary definitions are made—as they have to be—in formulating research problems, they should at least be plainly advertised. And finally, it was reiterated by speaker after speaker that decision-making occurs over time, that solution of most of the difficulties of predicting—for either practical application or theoretical understanding—will come only by full appreciation of the longitudinal dimension in consumer behavior.

The theme of the longitudinal dimension runs more consistently throughout the papers and discussions than any other aspect of the common model of household decision-making toward which it was originally hoped they would tend. Even before the preconference, it became evident to the program committee that the possibility of developing a single common model through a few days of discussion was as remote as its desirability was debatable. The conference was nonetheless rather optimistically entitled: Conference on Models of Household Decision-Making. Despite the real achievement of the preconference in developing a common object of discourse, it can hardly be claimed that each of the papers presents a model, however minimally defined. The reader will note, however, that certain threads recur. Certain components of an eventual model are probably identifiable by their recurrence in papers emerging from a diverse array of backgrounds and bodies of data. Indeed, because it was decided to cross the spectrum of applications of an eventual model by dividing the papers among areas or products of decision-making, it may perhaps be taken as a test of the essentiality of any element of any future model that it recurs across the whole range of applications. Certainly, the already mentioned passage of time is the outstanding example. Its independent emphasis by each writer and speaker may also be taken as confirmation of the widespread discontent with cross-sectional predictors, which gave rise to the conference in the first place.

The first division of labor imposed on the program was decision-making with regard to the composition of the household itself: How many incomes to earn? How many children to have? Labor-force analysts have moved from cross-sectional aggregates, arranged in time series, to cohort analysis, and finally to foci as pointed as Mahoney's on the wife's decision to join the labor force and Westoff's on the couple's decision to add a third child. But their papers (and the comments thereon) disclose the investigators as seeing themselves no farther than mid-passage in devising a satisfactory model of these events. And the interesting question of whether family composition is best taken as input or unit or output of an eventual model is left for arbitrary specification in future studies.

In the papers and discussions on asset accumulation and financial management in the family that follow, family composition is treated as input, as unit, and as output, first through the medium of the life cycle and intergenerational analysis proposed by Hill, and then through the bold effort of Morgan to interrelate the motives of individuals. As consistently happened throughout the conference, both drew extensively on previous research for insight, although research reports had not been the aim. The reader will find the bibliography appended to the Morgan paper especially informative about the scope of current research.

Houthakker in the next section offers the reader such a balanced and sophisticated appraisal of where consumption economics stands at present, and Lippitt offers such an enlightening summary of the concept of a model that their papers deserve to have stood first in the volume. On the other hand, the progression of thought of the entire audience is already so visible that the reader would have lost more by rearrangement than he would gain. And, furthermore, at midpoint of the conference, the gulf that remains between the economists and sociologists of consumer behavior has been disclosed, even while some real accomplishment in bridging it has rapidly occurred —witness Juster's comments on Kenkel's paper and the ensuing discussion.

In the session on decision-making regarding actual buying behavior, problems of interdisciplinary communication recur, as between an economist and an economist-turned-psychologist. But two even warmer issues emerge around the practical interests awakened by discussions of brand choice, on the one hand, the exigencies of the marketer as against the liberties of the theorist, and on the other, the defense of the consumer against the importunities of the advertiser. Nonetheless, the net movement of the exchanges is toward some convergence, especially in the understanding of husband and wife roles as they vary according to the article being purchased. Both Brown and Clawson illuminate the intricacies of motivation involved when the individual buyer acts for himself and when he acts as an agent for his or her family. The audience itself went on to bring out more fully the importance to the consumer's career of the postpurchase process of assimilation. To the cumulative effect of prior purchases and inventory on current decisions is added the cumulative effect of each succeeding increment of information, experience, learning, and confirmation by others.

It is not, however, until the reading of Becker's paper on occupational career decisions that the longitudinal dimension of consumer behavior is fully crystallized in the concept of the career, which he feels can be as aptly attributed to the consumer as to the producer. He does not win the immediate acceptance of the economists, but they testify eloquently to their interest as do they in the ingenious application by Komarovsky of the sociological concept of class. Gathering together from various studies some anomalous reversals in statistical relationships between family decision-making and husband-wife authority patterns that can be noted as the participants ascend the socioeconomic scale, Komarovsky propounds a master explanatory hypothesis that seems to synthesize successfully many well-verified subhypotheses and many kinds of data. While disclaiming that she has produced a model, she achieves the simplification and generalization of a vast complex of particulars that is sought in a model. Assigned at first only to discuss the Becker and Komarovsky papers, Farber was so persuasive in meeting a challenge put to Becker by the audience—to put his career model into quantifiable form—that he was asked to expand in detail his model of marriage as a pair of intercontingent careers. Thus the conference ended with at least one full-fledged model of household decision-making that contains specified, quantified inputs and components and generates quantitative predictions, which can in turn be checked against ensuing experience.

A portion of the presidential address given to the concurrent meeting of Consumer Behavior, Inc., is appended. It succeeds better than this introduction in shedding historical perspective on the holding of a conference on the topic of models of household decision-making. Dr. Chapin's career, first prominently recognized by virtue of his measurement of socioeconomic status of families by inventorying their possessions, has spanned the whole period from the beginnings of fully quantitative social research to the construction of mathematical models; and his appreciation and understanding of this progression have plainly kept pace.

Finally, as an extraordinary example of how far understanding of cross-sectional data can be enhanced by full comprehension of the longitudinal dimension of household purchasing and product history, Thomas Juster has contributed a second appendix on the acquisition of durables.

Beyond this point, as it always does in research, lies further investigation. Many areas of application of models were not included— decision-making on housing, financing higher education, borrowing and time allocation—all of great timely importance. But enough areas were considered to warrant some confidence that models appropriate to these areas will be found to include most of the essential components disclosed here.

Meanwhile, the reader has the stimulus and most of the material that he needs to reflect upon the basic question which provoked the conference: What has been happening in recent years that has made environmental conditions decline in predictiveness of consumer behavior and developmental patterns of household decision-making increase in importance? Is it simply that constraints have weakened, whereas options have multiplied? Or can it be that some competence in manipulating this environment has been gained by consumers themselves, as suggested by Hill's search for "consumership" or Becker's concept of consumer careers? Has something been learned by consumers themselves, which, if understood, will make them not less predictable, but more so, even if, simultaneously, they have become less controllable by others?

I. Decision-Making Regarding Changes in Family Composition

Influences on Labor-Force Participation of Married Women: A Model for Spending-Unit Decision-Making

THOMAS A. MAHONEY

American social and economic life has undergone considerable change and development during the last half-century of prosperity, depression, and war. One development that underlies and is related to many of these changes is an alteration of the patterns of work and employment in our economy. Today, women provide more of the labor required in industry than ever before. One-third of our labor force is now composed of women as compared with one-fifth at the turn of the century, the number of women workers increasing 400% during this period whereas working males increased only 300%.

This increased supply of womanpower is related to some basic changes in patterns of female work and employment, the labor-force participation rate of women increasing from 20% to 30% while the male participation rate declined from 84% to 79%. Although this trend toward increased female participation can be noted over the entire half-century, it has been particularly noticeable in recent years, women providing 55% of the net increase in labor force during 1940–1949 and 72% of the net increase during 1950–1956 (4, 7, 10).

The change in patterns of work is especially apparent among married women, the group with the largest increase in rate of labor-force participation. Married women today form more than half of the female labor force as compared with 18–20% in 1900. This is not to imply that married women, or even all women, work more or harder than they did fifty years ago. Rather, it represents a shift from work within the home to work outside the home. This shift by married women from housework to industrial employment may have implications that bear upon many aspects of social and economic activity—employment and utilization of labor resources, patterns of family consumption of goods and services, and bearing of children and caring for their education and training. An understanding of the factors influencing decisions to seek employment is important in the prediction of future labor supplies, the identification of potential sources of labor supply, and the design of programs to influence the further entry or exit of wives from the labor force. In a current study of factors that affect labor-force entry by women in the St. Paul labor market, an effort was made to summarize relationships among these factors in a way that can be generalized to other labor markets.

A Model for Decision-Making

The hypotheses offered here in explanation of the labor-force participation of married women can be represented by a model of consumer choice (9). We start with the concept of the spending unit defined as a household of persons who pool their resources and make joint decisions concerning the expenditure of these resources. As a member of the spending unit, the wife contributes her resources of time, energy, and talent. These resources may be expended for the welfare of the spending unit in a variety of employments. The decision for the wife to seek employment outside the household involves making a choice among alternative expenditures of her resources. In this manner, it can be considered a consumption decision of husband-wife spending units.

Two major alternative expenditures of the wife's resources are available to the spending unit. One involves expenditure in the form of household activities, the production of goods and services for direct consumption by the household. Such activities include the traditional maintenance of the household and the rearing of the children. The alternative expenditure involves employment outside the household in income-producing activities to finance a less direct consumption by the spending unit. Historically, the common pattern of expenditure of the wife's resources has been in employment within the household, great value having been attached to this activity and employment outside the household having been viewed as a distinct loss in comparison.

The nature of these alternative employments of the wife has changed considerably in recent years, as have the evaluations of the alternatives. For example, opportunities for the employment of wives outside the household have increased in recent years with the reduction of employment barriers and the physical demands of employment. Earnings available to wives through this employment also have increased, making such employment more attractive. At the same time, changes in the patterns of family living and the nature of traditional household activities of wives have tended to reduce the value of employment of the wife in household activities. Thus, although the alternative of employment of the wife outside the household was not feasible in the majority of spending-unit decisions sixty years ago, it has become a realistic alternative expenditure of the wife's resources today.

The spending unit's decision concerning the expenditure of the wife's resources can be treated as though it were the decision of a single consuming unit, no matter how complicated the actual decision-making process of the spending unit. Whether this decision is made with the active participation of all members of the spending unit or by a single member, the welfare of the entire spending unit is assumed to be the criterion for decision-making. We can assume a spending-unit utility function illustrated by the usual set of indifference curves assumed for individual decision-making. The alternative choices considered in this utility function (U) are earnings of the wife derivable from outside employment (Y) and participation of the wife in household activities (P).

$$U = U\ (Y, P)$$

Both of these alternative choices represent normal goods to the spending unit, both being desired for their contribution to spending-unit utility or welfare. As normal goods, continued additions of the amount of either earnings or household participation of the wife decrease the marginal utility of further additions of this good and increase the marginal utility of additions to the other. Figure I.1 represents the spending-unit indifference map described here. The

FIGURE I.1

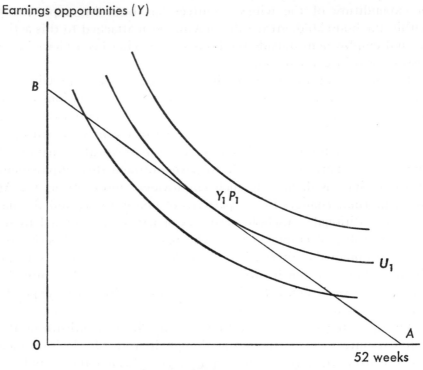

wife's earnings opportunities are measured on the vertical axis, and household participation is measured on the horizontal axis.

Labor-force participation is considered in this formulation as the only alternative to expenditure of the wife's resources in household participation; leisure and volunteer service activities are included in the concept of household participation. With all the wife's activities classified as either labor-force participation or household participation, any change in one causes an automatically compensating change in the other. This classification involves the concept of household participation as a normal good providing utility for the spending unit, whereas labor-force participation is viewed as a disutility. The concepts of utility of household participation and disutility of labor-force participation are merely different ways of looking at the same spending-unit evaluation; changes in the utility of household participation imply related changes in the disutility of labor-force participation. The classification of leisure and volunteer service activities of the wife as household participation is in accord with this formulation because these activities are usually viewed as desirable in themselves, whereas labor-force participation by itself is more often viewed as a disutility. Earnings of the wife through labor-force participation that are viewed as desirable are separated in this formulation from the act of producing earnings and are considered a normal good possessing utility for the spending unit. This concept is illustrated in Figure I.1 by viewing the unit of measurement on the horizontal axis as "number of weeks" varying from 0 to a maximum of 52 weeks in any given year. Household participation is measured from the axis and labor-force participation is automatically indicated in distance from the 52-week measure on the right. Operationally it is much easier to measure the number of weeks of labor-force participation and obtain weeks of household participation through a subtraction from the maximum of 52 weeks.

It would be possible to construct a model in which labor-force participation receives much more direct attention, including, for example, the wife's enjoyment of her job. This is not done because earnings and household participation are viewed as the goods primarily involved in the spending unit's decision. Labor-force participation that does not possess a direct utility for the spending unit does not enter directly into this decision. It is the means of obtaining the earnings desired by the spending unit and is a result of the earnings–household-participation decision.

A constraint is placed upon spending-unit decision possibilities in the form of a limitation upon earnings opportunities available to the wife. This constraint is represented in Figure I.1 by line AB and may be viewed as the rate of earnings available to the wife, or as the rate at which the spending unit may exchange housewife participation for earnings from labor-force participation. Given this constraint, it is assumed that the spending unit selects that combination of housewife participation and earnings which provides the maximum welfare available. This maximum is determined at Y_1P_1 where the rate of earnings, or rate at which household participation can be exchanged for earnings, is equal to the marginal rate of substitution between earnings and household participation.

Rate of earnings opportunities = marginal rate of substitution
$$Y/P = \Delta U_y / \Delta U_p$$

Thus the relative marginal utilities afforded to the spending unit by earnings of the wife and by her household participation, illustrated in the set of indifference curves, as limited by the earnings opportunities available to the wife, are assumed to determine the spending unit's decision concerning labor-force participation of the wife.

Shifts in the earnings opportunities of the wife or changes in the spending-unit utility function may be expected to occasion changes

FIGURE I.2

Earnings opportunities (Y)

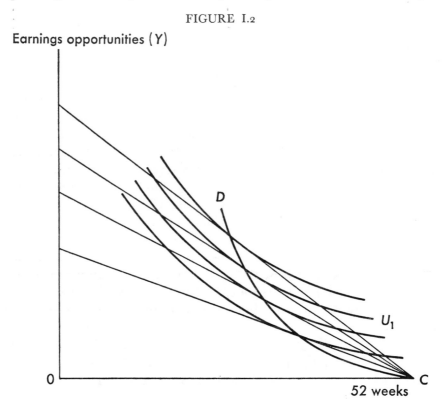

Household participation (P)

in spending-unit decisions and consequent changes in labor-force participation of the wife. Consider, for example, a fixed spending-unit utility function, U_1, and varying earnings opportunities. Each change in the earnings-opportunities constraint represents a change in the market-determined rate of exchange between the goods of household participation and earnings. Given a fixed spending-unit utility function, a shift in the earnings-opportunities constraint changes the point of maximum welfare or utility attainable by the spending unit. The line CD in Figure I.2 connects the varying points of maximum spending-unit utility under these conditions and illustrates the relationship between labor-force participation and earnings, given a fixed utility function. In this illustration, labor-force participation varies directly with changes in earnings opportunities.

Spending-unit decisions are also expected to change as a result of changes in spending-unit preferences for earnings and household participation. Changes in spending-unit preferences involve shifts in the relative desirability and thus the marginal rate of substitution between earnings and household participation. Given a fixed constraint of earnings opportunities, any change in the marginal rate of substitution determines a new combination of these goods which affords the maximum welfare or utility attainable by the spending unit. Thus, decisions concerning labor-force participation may be expected to vary with changes in the spending-unit utility function; Figure I.3 illustrates this relationship. The utility function U_1 in situation A represents a set of preferences such that the marginal utility of earnings is high relative to the marginal utility of household participation or the marginal disutility of labor-force participation; the utility function U_2 represents a set of preferences such that the marginal utility of earnings is low relative to the marginal utility of household participation. Given fixed earnings opportunities, we would expect relatively greater labor-force participation in situation A. We can say that labor-force participation will tend to vary directly with the marginal utility of earnings relative to the marginal utility of household participation.

Hypotheses concerning the labor-force participation of wives are derived from this model of consumer choice. Various variables are hypothesized as influences on labor-force participation through their expected impact upon the major factors of the spending-unit's decision concerning expenditure of the wife's resources, earnings opportunities of the wife and the spending unit's utility function. Positive relationships are hypothesized when variables are expected to raise the earnings opportunities of wives, and negative relationships when they reduce earnings opportunities. Changes in the spending-unit utility function are expected to occur as these hypothesized variables alter the marginal utility of earnings relative to the marginal utility of household participation or the marginal disutility of labor-force participation. Thus, positive relationships are expected when changes in the hypothesized variable are expected to increase the marginal utility of earnings or reduce the marginal utility of household participation or the marginal disutility of labor-force par-

FIGURE I.3

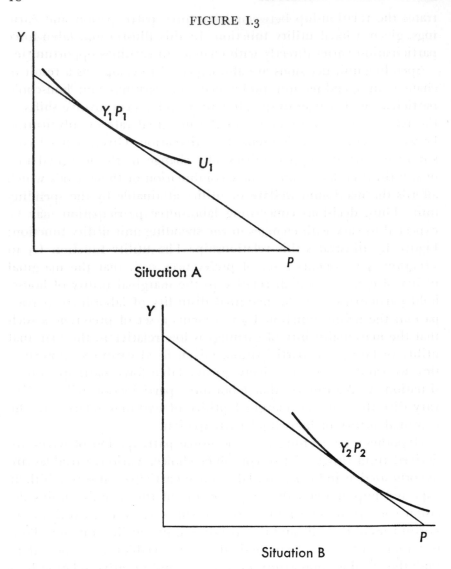

Situation A

Situation B

ticipation, and negative relationships are expected when the reverse is suggested.

EARNINGS INFLUENCES

A positive relationship between earnings opportunities and labor-force participation of wives is suggested in Figure I.2. Earnings opportunities for wives can be expected to vary considerably from one labor market to another and from one time period to another (1).

The industrial composition of the labor market, for example, is a major determinant of both the number of opportunities for the employment of wives and the earnings available through these opportunities. Opportunities for employment and levels of earnings are also influenced by variations in economic activity. Both of these influences on earnings opportunities are held constant in this study through limitation to a single labor market, St. Paul, Minnesota, and through consideration of labor-force participation during a single year, 1957. Another factor influencing earnings opportunities that is held constant in this study is race: only white spending units are considered. Holding constant these particular sources of variation in earnings opportunities does not imply that they are any less important influences on labor-force participation than other factors (3). Rather, this restriction represents the aim of maximum utilization of resources available for the study.

Earnings opportunities also vary among wives within any labor market. These are the earnings opportunities associated with job and occupational requirements. Higher rates of earnings usually are associated with increasing skill requirements of different positions. Thus, we might expect a positive relationship between earnings opportunities and education of the wife, vocational training, and occupational experience (2, 9). Consequently, it is suggested that these factors are positively associated with labor-force participation of wives.

Utility Influences

Other factors are expected to be associated with variations in labor-force participation as a result of their influence upon the marginal utility of earnings relative to the marginal utility of household participation or marginal disutility of labor-force participation. Factors that tend to increase the marginal utility of earnings and/or decrease the marginal utility of household participation (decrease the marginal disutility of labor-force participation) are expected to be positively associated with labor-force participation; those influencing the marginal utility of earnings and/or household participation in the reverse manner are expected to be negatively associated with labor-force participation. It is assumed, for example, that every spending unit desires to achieve some positive net-assets position and that spending-unit debts tend to increase the marginal utility of the wife's earnings, whereas assets tend to reduce the utility of such earnings. Debts also usually constitute a claim upon current income and thus increase the marginal utility of the wife's earnings relative to the utility of household participation. Consequently, spending-unit debts are expected to be positively associated with labor-force participation and assets negatively associated (9).

Much the same reasoning applies to a suggested positive association between spending-unit expenses and labor-force participation. The marginal utility of the wife's earnings is expected to vary directly with the amount of family expenses, tending to shift the spending-unit utility function and lead to an increase in labor-force participation.

Size of the spending unit frequently has been found to be positively associated with labor-force participation. This association might be expected to follow from the direct relationship between economic needs of the spending unit and the number of members in the spending unit, thus increasing the marginal utility of earnings of the wife. Furthermore, increases in the size of the spending unit might be expected to provide additional members who could assume certain of the wife's household responsibilities and thus reduce the marginal utility of household participation by the wife. At the same time, however, increases in the size of the spending unit automatically increase the household responsibilities and tend to increase the marginal utility of household participation. Thus, the relationship between spending-unit size and labor-force participation would appear to be more dependent upon composition of the spending unit than upon mere size. The presence of adults other than the husband and wife is expected to reduce the marginal utility of household participation and thus be positively associated with labor-force participation. At the same time, the presence of children under six years is expected to raise the marginal utility of household participation and to be negatively associated with labor-force participation. The number of children under 18 years tends to increase the value of household participation as household responsibilities are increased and also tends to reduce the value of household participation as older children are available to assume certain of these responsibilities. Previous studies suggest that the net influence is to increase the marginal utility of household participation and lead to reduced labor-force participation (2, 5, 9).

A negative association between labor-force participation and spending-unit income excluding earnings of the wife is suggested for obvious reasons. Increases of spending-unit income tend to reduce the marginal utility of further increases and thus reduce the value of the wife's earnings (2, 6). The major source of spending-unit income will be earnings of the husband, but the variable spending-unit income is used here, because property income and/or earnings of other members of the spending unit would have the same effect as increased earnings of the husband.

The employment status of the head of the spending unit (the husband in this instance) is expected to have a direct influence on the marginal utility of the wife's earnings and thus on her labor-force participation. Unemployment of the husband temporarily reduces spending-unit income, increasing the marginal utility of the wife's earnings, and thus leading to increased labor-force participation (8).

Attitudes of the husband and wife toward employment of wives outside the home are expected to be a factor in labor-force participation. Attitudes toward the role of the wife as a member of the spending unit and toward her responsibilities are thought to affect the spending-unit evaluation of the marginal utility of household participation, and the marginal disutility of labor-force participation. For example, strong attitudes or opinions to the effect that the role of the wife is primarily that of housewife would be associated with a high valuation of household participation because attitudes to the effect that working women take jobs away from males would increase the marginal disutility of labor-force participation. Attitudes favorable to the employment of women are suggested as positively associated with labor-force participation. Attitudes of the wife are measured directly in this study, whereas attitudes of the husband are assumed to correlate with factors such as education and occupation. Higher education and occupational status of the husband are expected to be positively associated with labor-force participation because of their expected positive relationship with attitudes favorable to the employment of wives.

Other factors investigated for association with labor-force participation are believed to be influences on both opportunities for earnings and the spending-unit utility function. Age of the wife is an example. Opportunities for employment and the available levels of earnings tend to decline with the age of the wife, suggesting a negative association with labor-force participation. Furthermore, favorable attitudes of the wife toward employment and helping to meet the economic needs of the family during the early years of marriage are expected to encourage labor-force participation, which will decline with the birth of children. The marginal utility of household participation may be expected to decline with advancing age, when the children are grown and have left home, thus suggesting increased labor-force participation of the wife. A negative association between age and labor-force participation is expected through age 35 and a positive association following age 35 (2). Note also that the hypotheses concerning age of the wife imply relationships between age and such other factors as family formation and childbearing. Interrelationships among other factors investigated are also expected.

Hypotheses concerning the influence of all these factors upon labor-force participation can now be summarized in a regression equation, if these influences are assumed to be linear and additive:

$$LFP = a_0 + a_1Y + a_2O_w + a_3E_w + a_4A + a_5O_h + a_6E_h + a_7At + a_8U + a_9S + a_{10}C + a_{11}K + a_{12}O_1 + a_{13}I + a_{14}W + a_{15}D + a_{16}B$$

where LFP = number of weeks of labor-force participation in 1957
Y = weekly earnings of wife
O_w = occupation of wife
E_w = education of wife
A = wife's age
O_h = husband's occupation
E_h = husband's education
At = attitudes of wife toward employment
U = weeks of unemployment of husband
S = number of members in the spending unit
C = number of children under 18
K = presence of children under 6
O_1 = presence of adults other than husband and wife
I = spending-unit income excluding wife's
W = value of spending-unit assets
D = spending-unit debts
B = monthly expenses of spending unit

and $a_1 > 0$
$a_2 > 0$
$a_3 < 0$ through age 35, $a_3 > 0$ after age 35
$a_4 > 0$

$a_5 > 0$

$a_6 > 0$

$a_7 > 0$

$a_8 > 0$

$a_9 < 0$

$a_{10} < 0$

$a_{11} < 0$

$a_{12} > 0$

$a_{13} < 0$

$a_{14} > 0$

$a_{15} < 0$

$a_{16} > 0$

Certain of the independent variables mentioned above appear to be measuring the same general factor, for example, S, C, and K. It is quite possible that all these variables are closely interrelated and that one of them or a composite measure of them would be most useful in the prediction of labor-force participation. All are included in the design of this study because all have been found, in previous studies, to be related to labor-force participation. The vast majority of these studies were concerned only with single-order relationships, however. The study outlined here is designed to investigate possible interrelationships as well as the relative association of the independent variables with labor-force participation.

Results and Implications

The hypotheses outlined here are being tested in a study of a single labor market, St. Paul, Minnesota. Information obtained through household interviewing of a random sample of 420 white, husband-wife spending units is being used in this analysis. The approach taken here is limited in certain respects, which should be kept in mind in the interpretation of results. The results obtained will describe relationships existing within a single labor market during 1957. Extension of the study to include various labor markets would provide an opportunity to cross-validate results with different samples and also an opportunity to investigate the influence of labor-market characteristics upon labor-force participation of wives. Furthermore, a cross-sectional approach is used here with the obvious need for cross-validation of associations with variables related to the family cycle through a longitudinal study. The present approach consciously ignores the process of spending-unit decision-making and looks instead at results of this decision-making.

Possible implications that may be drawn from the results of this study should contribute to the design of more intensive studies of specific problem areas. For example, results of this study will have obvious implications for problems of prediction and control of labor-force participation. Associations found in this study should also aid in the description and understanding of the spending-unit utility function and thus furnish guides for more intensive study of spending-unit decision-making. Finally, labor-force participation is believed to influence spending-unit consumption behavior and family formation, so results of this study should contribute to increasing knowledge in these areas.

REFERENCES

1. BELLOC, NEDRA BARTLETT. "Labor-Force Participation and Employment Opportunities for Women," *J. Am. Statistical Assoc., 45* (Sept., 1950), 400–410.

2. BUREAU OF THE CENSUS, U. S. Department of Commerce. "Family Characteristics of Working Wives," *Current Population Reports—Labor Force.* Series P-50, No. 81. March, 1958.

3. DORNBUSCH, SANFORD M. "Correlation between Income and Labor Force Participation by Race," *Am. J. Sociology, 61* (Jan., 1956), 340–344.

4. DURAND, JOHN D. *The Labor Force in the United States, 1890–1960.* New York: Social Science Research Council, 1948.

5. LANSING, JOHN B., and JAMES N. MORGAN "Consumer Finances Over the Life Cycle," in Lincoln H. Clark (ed.), *Consumer Behavior,* Vol. II: The Life Cycle in Consumer Behavior. New York: New York University Press, 1955.

6. MILLER, HERMAN P. *Income of the American People.* Census Monograph Series. New York: John Wiley & Sons, 1955.

7. NATIONAL MANPOWER COUNCIL. *Womanpower.* New York: Columbia University Press, 1957.

8. PALMER, GLADYS L. *The Significance of Employment Patterns in Households for Labor Market Analysis.* Special Report No. 8. Industrial Research Department, Wharton School of Finance and Commerce, University of Pennsylvania, Philadelphia, 1942.

9. ROSETT, RICHARD. *Working Wives: An Econometric Study.* Cowles Foundation Discussion Paper No. 35.

10. WOMEN'S BUREAU, U. S. Department of Labor. *Women as Workers . . . A Statistical Guide.* D-65.

Some Aspects of Decision-Making in the Family Growth Process

CHARLES F. WESTOFF

THE VARIABLE OF FERTILITY

The creation of a new human life through conception and birth is simultaneously an everyday, prosaic event in the life of a society and an occurrence with profound, far-reaching consequences for the lives of the parents. Although in recent years each day witnesses, on the average, the births of some 11,000 infants, thereby impressing one with the commonplace regularity of the process, behind each child born there lies an extremely complex pattern of social and psychological antecedents. On the surface, the background of the process may be fairly simple for any given couple; such apparent simplicity vanishes promptly when the criteria of science are applied in attempts to formulate generalizations explaining such individual behavior at the aggregate level.

There are many alternative points of departure for an analysis of human fertility, all legitimate and interrelated. One might be concerned, for example, with the explanation of such phenomena as the course of a society's birth rate, temporal variations in completed family size, the changing incidence of childlessness, patterns of fertility differentials by social class, intelligence, or other characteristics, the interrelations of fertility rates and economic development, and numerous other points of view. Obviously, for the task at hand the problem area must be delimited to be manageable.

Let us exclude, as a first simplification, all aspects of fertility other than completed family size. There have been many studies of the factors affecting the number of children a couple has by the time the reproductive span has drawn to a close. Such studies have ranged from Census Bureau tabulations of national data to more intensive analyses of social and psychological factors affecting family size, represented chiefly by the recent Indianapolis Study (5). Despite the restriction of the problem to predicting completed family size and the considerable resources invested in such research, only a small fraction of the variability has thus far been explained. The Indianapolis Study was, in part, an outgrowth of the recognition that the study of such conventional sociodemographic characteristics as rural-urban residence, occupation, and education had been carried as far as their potential warranted. Although the Indianapolis Study did provide important new insights into the interrelations of socio-economic status with contraceptive practice and with the fertility of couples who had successfully planned all births (for example, it suggested a reversal of the familiar inverse association of socioeco-nomic status with family size when birth control is practiced success-fully), its venture into the more elusive attitudinal and personality domains proved largely unproductive of appreciable increments in explained variation.

Several explanations are possible. The hypotheses may simply have been invalid, the measuring instruments too crude, or possibly the interview survey method unsuited for the problem. It seems prob-able that all these explanations contain some truth. An additional factor of theoretical significance for the general study of decision processes and their outcomes was elicited, however, which seems to be an even more plausible explanation. Is it possible that the variable studied—completed family size in this instance—is still too complex to yield to unidimensional social-psychological variables? Is it not possible that the goals of such research are being set too high? Con-sider the problem: the process of completing a family takes as long as 20 years—at least this is a reasonable estimate of the length of time that an average couple is exposed to the risk of pregnancy during marriage. What is to be explained? Some couples have no children at all, some one, two, three, and so forth. The research problem is defined as isolating the social and psychological factors that account for these differences. Even assuming that fecundity or physiological risk is equal for all, the task of accounting for such differences is considerable when we realize that the objective variance is the net result of a series of five-minute "collusions" over a 20-year period.

Whatever the explanations, a current development of research in this area has been to restrict the objectives to the addition of a child to the family at a given point in the family-building process.[1] The study that has incorporated this design has concentrated on couples all of whom had had their second child at the same time. The principal objective is to account for future variations in the occurrence and timing of the third and subsequent children.

The objective in the following pages is to assess some of the critical considerations in the study of fertility, some of which are based upon reflections generated in analyzing the initial data from this study. Within available time limits, this means a brief survey of some of the leading theoretical issues that seem to be appropriate to this conference rather than intensive consideration of only part of the problem. We shall begin by comparing the fertility process with consumer behavior in general.

Fertility and Consumer Behavior

The decision to have another child is basically different from conventional types of consumer decisions. In the first place, it is an irrevocable decision. Once made, a process is generated that, for all intents and purposes, is irreversible,[2] and its consequences are experienced over a lifetime. Moreover, one buys, so to speak, sight unseen. The sex of the child is indeterminate, and there is always an element of chance about the "product." It requires little capital, and what expenses do accrue in the early years tend to be slight except for initial costs, which are often covered by insurance. Furthermore, the conception of another child does not demand any planning or saving in the same sense that the purchase of a home does—although, in a way, the psychology of "no down payment" may be operative here as well.

Another pertinent difference in the two types of decisions is that a child cannot be considered an economic asset, income-tax deductions notwithstanding. Perhaps in previous generations, a child did

---

[1] A monograph reporting the first phase of this study has been completed and awaits publication: Charles F. Westoff, Robert G. Potter, Jr., Philip C. Sagi, and Elliot G. Mishler: *Family Growth in Metropolitan America.*

[2] Estimates of the incidence of induced abortion in the United States imply an important qualification to this notion.

have a positive economic value and could be considered in some measure the result of rational economic motivation (an unlikely hypothesis at best), but it is abundantly clear that such conditions no longer obtain.

Perceived in terms of outcomes, perhaps the most fundamental difference between fertility behavior and more conventional types of consumer behavior is that the former, having a biological basis, will ordinarily result from the natural course of events, whereas the purchase of a home or automobile, for example, requires the overcoming of some degree of self-imposed resistance or inertia. Thus, fertility is controlled in a negative sense by techniques of prevention; a conception will occur (under optimally planned circumstances) when a decision is made not to prevent its occurrence. The first decision that has to be made, however, is to control conception. The fact that women are much more articulate about the reasons for not wanting another child than they are about why they would want one suggests that this negative aspect of the process may be more susceptible to investigation.

Despite such fundamental differences, there are a number of similarities between having a child and other types of resource outlays. There are many expected and experienced psychological rewards, ranging from a type of creative expression and gratification to the warmth of intimate interpersonal relationships. There is also a sociological function other than the conventional aspects of population replacement that is probably involved, particularly in having the first child. This function might be considered an initiation rite into the society of young parents. Judging from the recent increases in higher order births, the addition of a third, fourth, or even fifth child to the family might almost be regarded as a currently fashionable form of conspicuous consumption. It seems clear that the social climate with respect to family-size norms has changed radically over the past generation. Today, sterility or poor health is probably a more acceptable justification for childlessness than an explanation that children are not wanted for some "personal" reason or other. This climate is particularly evident in the postwar mass housing developments, which were, of course, tailored specifically to the market of young parents. Selective recruiting of residents has undoubtedly reinforced pressures for conformity in the homogeneous neighborhood dominated by topics of children and homemaking.

The basic similarity between adding a child to the family and economic behavior in general is that it means an allocation of resources (time and energy as well as money) that might otherwise be expended or invested in something else. Stated differently, it implies some degree of sacrifice. On the other hand, not having the child also implies a sacrifice of certain rewards. It is this consideration that suggests a conceptualization of the fertility decision process in terms of a configuration of values and interests, some of which compete or conflict with having the child, others of which promote or reinforce the process, and many of which are irrelevant to the problem. Within such a context, the so-called background factors such as occupation, income, and education can be meaningfully interpreted in their association with fertility.

To utilize a value frame of reference, although it appears all-embracing if not suspiciously tautological, means opting for one approach among several alternative social-psychological models. A problem-solving model used in a study of fertility in Puerto Rico, for example, emphasized the nature and extent of communication channels open between husband and wife. These appear to be of critical importance in predicting contraceptive behavior. Such an emphasis would appear to be fruitful in societies where role specification and differentiation are rigid and clear-cut. In urban America, where the roles of the sexes in marriage have become increasingly overlapping, such an approach seems less promising. Another approach, related to the problem-solving model, would view the addition of a child to the family in terms of the capacity of the social structure of the group to absorb adequately the strains resulting from such a change. This approach focuses attention on the division of labor within the family and the patterns of intrafamilial interaction, responsibility, and dominance. A third approach, at the psychological level of personality, would focus on the compatibility of a child with the ego needs of the parents and would include such variables as needs for nurture and succor, generalized anxiety, feelings of inadequacy, and the like.

All these different conceptualizations have been utilized in varying degrees in our own current study of fertility, which adopted an admittedly eclectic approach to the subject.[3] There is, of course, a type of reasoning that would reduce all these seemingly different approaches to the concept of value and, perhaps even more damaging,

---

[3] The conceptual organization outlined in this paper is a modification of that published several years ago (2).

could equate the concept with the criterion, thereby producing a tautology. The research standard of whether or not such a reduction in terms is valid is whether the concept of values is useful in the heuristic sense of providing certain categories of variables that are distinguishably independent of other categories.

FERTILITY PLANNING AND THE DECISION PROCESS

The phrase "decision to add another child to the family" implies an element of deliberate, conscious behavior. Confining attention to factors determining explicit motivation to have or not to have another child would result in limiting the analysis to perhaps less than half of the population who could be classified as planners at some given period of their fertility experience. Ideally, the objective should be a conceptualization of factors leading to the consequence, the observed behavioral result of a birth for the total population at risk. This would open the way for a formulation covering the whole range from irrational, impulsive behavior to the most rational, explicit decision, all of which will have the same biological result.

This dilemma persistently confronts the researcher. On the one hand, there is the image of the couple dispassionately weighing the pros and cons of having a child; at the opposite extreme, the undesired consequence of impulsive sexual behavior. Can these two types of events, similar in outcome but vastly different in apparent cause, be joined in a single unifying frame of reference? Theoretically, the concept of values would permit such integration, although the plausibility of this common denominator is strained. The reasoning would be that the greater the perceived disadvantages of having another child, the more effective will be the contraceptive precautions taken. Thus, the couple having an unplanned pregnancy can be located conceptually as having a balance of values for and against another child midway between the couple who interrupts contraception deliberately in order to conceive and the couple who continues to practice contraception effectively.

Although there is a certain logic to this integration of the two different paths to fertility—the planned and the unplanned—it would appear to contain an implicit assumption of the operation of subconscious motives. Carried to its ridiculous extreme, this logic would negate the very existence of a genuinely accidental pregnancy. To deny the validity of this extreme position does not imply a denial of the operation of subconscious motives. But the fact that some unplanned pregnancies may have been subconsciously motivated does not therefore demand the conclusion that all unplanned pregnancies are so motivated.

One of the sources of difficulty in integrating these two types of experience into a single frame of reference is the fact that there are different kinds of unplanned conceptions. Two main subtypes are (1) conceptions resulting from the failure of the method, due to its intrinsic unreliability, mechanical failure, or, more commonly, ineffective use and (2) conceptions resulting from irregular use. A third type of unplanned pregnancy results from a complete lack of any contraceptive usage, the incidence of which decreases sharply after the first pregnancy. It is the second type that comes closest to the "subconsciously planned" category. An explicit, deliberate decision to have a child exacts certain psychological tolls; occasional and perhaps increasingly frequent interruptions of contraception permit consequent pregnancy without full psychological responsibility for the decision. The event can then be rationalized as the natural consequence of taking a chance.

This type of "semiplanned" pregnancy is not infrequent. In the current Princeton study, some 10–20% of first pregnancies and nearly 20% of second pregnancies were reported to have occurred in such circumstances. Of course, regardless of the circumstances in which an unplanned pregnancy occurs, a great deal of rationalization takes place. Particularly in the case of the clearly accidental pregnancy, the first few months following the realization of the fact are probably often characterized by despair, regret, and perhaps mutual recriminations between husband and wife; the next several months are a period of transition between despair and anticipation, a period that might be described as one of adjustment or resignation to the inevitable; and the last few months before birth are characterized by growing anticipation. This process of rationalization is fortunate from the point of view of the parents and the well-being of the child. From the perspective of the researcher dependent upon interview data, however, it is unfortunate that after several months the conception may now be recalled as planned.

The remaining category of unplanned pregnancies comprises those conceived by couples who do not practice contraception at all. If "planning" is defined as selecting appropriate means to achieve a desired goal, the couple who do not practice any contraception

because they desire another child as soon as possible cannot be classified logically with the nonplanners. The incidence of this type of
behavior diminishes rapidly, however, with increasing birth order.
The most frequent type of complete noncontraceptive practice results from adherence to religious values that proscribe the use of
effective contraception, if they do not more profoundly negate the
whole value system of the rational control of reproduction. Although
there are other reasons for not using contraception—ignorance, su-
perstitious fears, a feeling that it interferes with sexual enjoyment,
assumed difficulty of conceiving later—nonuse for religious reasons
constitutes the major type of nonplanning in this category.

In American society, it is in the main Catholicism that promotes
this set of values. Evidence from current research indicates that this
influence is so fundamental that any analysis of fertility decisions
must be conducted within the context of religion as a controlling
influence. Our findings thus far indicate that different sets of factors
influence both fertility-planning success and the family-size goals of
couples among the three major religious groupings. Even the Protestant and Jewish groups are distinguished from each other as well
as from the Catholics with respect to factors affecting fertility. Although the nominal characteristic is religious preference or affiliation, the relevant factors are more broadly cultural, particularly in
the case of the Jewish group. Although formal Catholic doctrine
provides some basis for predicting fertility, a knowledge of formal
Judaism or the tenets of most contemporary Protestant sects does
not, yet adherence to these groups makes for significant differences
in behavior. Although there is some communality of factors in the
fertility process that distinguish American couples from couples
elsewhere, no research design should fail to treat these subcultures
separately.

To a lesser extent, the same arguments could be advanced for the
factor of social class. The key variable here is the concept of style
of life or pattern of consumption considered compatible with the
socioeconomic level and aspirations of the couple. To what extent,
if at all, are these values affected by the addition of another child
to the family? What are the points of conflict between class and religious values for the Catholic couple as they impinge on fertility?
How does the emphasis on educational values that is so much a part
of Jewish culture relate to family-size preferences? Are mobility aspirations among Protestants inconsistent with additional children?

These questions are simply illustrative of the proposition that two principal dimensions of the sociocultural environment must be included in the analysis of differential fertility.

FAMILY ORGANIZATION

It has almost become a cliché in fertility research to emphasize the fact that fertility is the consequence of the behavior of two persons of opposite sex. This reaction has been prompted by surveys in which only the wife was interviewed or by separate statistical analyses of the characteristics of each spouse. The criticism has been extended to suggest that the structure of wife-husband authority or dominance relationships might prove to be a fruitful avenue of investigation with respect to channels of information about contraception, as well as the formulation of family-size ideals. Unfortunately, the measurement of influence patterns within the family is extremely difficult. The question of who in the family actually makes the decision is, in the majority of cases of planned fertility, probably impossible to determine. Tracing the sources of contraceptive information and the origins of family-size orientations is perhaps less difficult. The important question, however, is whether a focus on the patterns of social interaction within the family is the most strategic approach to the study of fertility. This question, for the most part, cannot be answered positively on the grounds of empirical evidence (apart from theoretical plausibility). There is little evidence thus far that indicates any appreciable improvement in the prediction of fertility from the separate value orientations of the husband or from measures of intrafamilial patterns of authority in various decision-making areas. It should be emphasized that this lack of evidence refers exclusively to the analysis of the fertility process in urban American society and not to many other societies where sharp differences in patterns of familial authority may exist.

To minimize the authority aspect of family structure does not exclude consideration of other features of the family. The factor of family composition rather than family organization would appear more productive. This distinction between concepts may be objected to, but it seems useful to group such characteristics of the family and its members as age, number of siblings, age differences between children, and sex of children under "composition," differentiating them from such organizational features as patterns of hus-

band-wife dominance, division of responsibility or role allocations
in various areas of family activities, and patterns of help available
to the mother. These structural characteristics describe the configuration of social relationships within the family, which may vary
within the same composition.

From a knowledge of the sex composition of children already in
the family, for example, certain probabilities can be attached to
whether an additional child will be wanted. Thus, couples with two
children of the same sex will be more likely to want another child;
this is particularly true where the children are both girls, although
the husband is somewhat more likely to react to the cultural value
of the male child than is the wife.

FAMILY-SIZE PREFERENCES

Although there is a substantial association between the number
of children desired by the wife and by the husband, it is necessary
to evaluate family-size preferences both conceptually and in terms
of empirical validity. In connection with the latter criterion, an
analogue exists in the more conventional studies of consumer preferences and the same question is appropriate: are preferences expressed at one point in time valid predictors of subsequent behavior?
Since the measure of validity is a relative consideration, the question
might be posed more precisely as one of degree of association—how
well do preferences predict behavior at the individual level?

The answer to this question, at least in the study of fertility, must
still be stated in the form of an hypothesis. The only completed
empirical study of the subject (3, 4) indicates that family-size preferences stated before marriage did correlate significantly with achieved
fertility over a 20-year period of marriage, but the degree of association left over 90% of the variance of actual fertility unexplained.
What should the verdict on validity be in such a situation? It depends wholly on one's point of view. Although one could dismiss
preferences, in this case, as of only negligible predictive utility,[4] re-

---

[4] This low correlation is particularly interesting in view of the fact that the average
number of children born to these couples was only about 3% different from the average number desired before marriage. This close correspondence in the aggregate prediction is due to the particular composition of that sample with respect to fertility-
planning success. The number of children born to completely successful planners was
20% below the number desired by that group of couples originally; the number of
children born to couples who reported one or more unplanned pregnancies was 20%
greater than the number desired initially. The sampling artifact that these two categories each composed 50% of the total produced the close over-all correspondence.

stricting the comparison to couples who reported no unplanned pregnancies increased the controlled variation to about 25%. This estimate of validity is more reasonable, since one cannot expect preferences for a desired family size to account also for variations in the effectiveness of contraceptive practice.[5] Moreover, these particular findings are an acid test of the validity of the hypothesis: the question was asked of these couples while they were engaged to be married, whereas achieved fertility was assessed after approximately 20 years of marriage. It is not unreasonable to assume that the predictive validity of preferences would increase substantially after a few years of marriage and following the experience of having one or two children.

The evaluation of evidence accumulated to date is thus susceptible to conflicting interpretation. It is significant to note that, although a subsequent analysis of the predictive capacity of a battery of sociological and psychological variables from the same study revealed that a number of different variables collectively accounted for more of the variance of fertility, only one other variable (number of wife's siblings) singly did as well as family-size preferences. *Moreover, among the completely successful planners, preferences were clearly the best single predictor.*

The current thinking on the validity of the preference variable (although disagreement exists) is that these expressions of desire or preference are sufficiently relevant over the short range to be regarded as a main dependent variable. This assessment has been made by two different large-scale studies of American fertility: a national survey under the direction of Freedman, Whelpton and Campbell (1), and the Princeton Study of the Future Fertility of Two-Child Families. In the former study, the family-size plans of couples of different ages and varying marriage durations are to be utilized for the improvement of population forecasts. In the Princeton Study, the total number of children desired by couples (all of whom had recently had their second child), in conjunction with measures of fertility-planning success and previous birth intervals, is treated as a dependent variable in the analysis of values, family-structure variables, and personality characteristics. As such, the presumption is that the statement of family-size aspirations is not only an attitudinal expression of legitimate interest in its own right but an index of the probability and spacing of the third birth. More con-

---

[5] Only about 4% of the variance of completed fertility was controlled for the group which reported one or more unplanned pregnancies.

fidence is attached to this assumption when the behavioral indices of the spacing of the previous two births and the successfulness of past contraceptive practice are also taken into account. In both these studies, different types of validity checks will be possible. The Freedman-Whelpton-Campbell assumptions will be tested ultimately by the accuracy of their estimates of future fertility rates, whereas the Princeton Study features a longitudinal design of reinterviews over a period of 36 months with the same couples, thereby permitting an empirical check on their performance.

SUMMARY

The discussion thus far has emphasized the complex nature of the dependent variable—fertility—laying particular stress on the psychological diversity of its motivational antecedents. The concept of the "decision process" with regard to fertility must be radically expanded to incorporate behavior that has unintended consequences. *Any model that excludes all but purposive, rational fertility-planning, probably excludes the most typical experience.* Thus, the process of decision must include the decision to use or not to use contraception. When this occurs in its clearest form, it reflects the decision not to conceive. But as has been described, there are several types of unplanned pregnancies, the circumstances of which can be reconciled with the concept of decision-making only by including within it the disposition, either implicit or explicit (more pertinently, the behavior itself) to take or not to take a chance.

This chance-taking behavior, whether it involves employing no contraceptive precaution at all or risking conception through the use of ineffective methods, can be interpreted as the consequence of the competition of different values. If the values opposing the conception of another child are strong, whether they center around mobility aspirations, aspirations to send children to college, or feelings of economic insecurity, presumably chance-taking will then be less. Two major sociological categories—religion and social class, but the former particularly—have been suggested as subcultural dimensions within which different sets of values are relevant to the fertility process. Family-size preferences cannot be considered a decision at any point in the process except in the negative sense of a decision not to have any more children. Undoubtedly, there are couples who formulate a clear-cut family-size goal early in marriage and proceed to achieve that goal in a systematic manner, but such couples are probably the exception. The more typical example is the couple who have a general notion that they would like at least two children and possibly another, depending perhaps on the sex of the first two or on their financial circumstances at the time. For most couples, desired family size is therefore more accurately classified as an attitude or orientation with certain degrees of freedom. This variable might almost be viewed as the psychological analogue of fecundity. Even among planners, the tendency is to think more in terms of whether another child is compatible with their life interests and circumstances at the time. Mothers are much more articulate about why they would like to have the next child 12, 18, or 24 months from now than they are about why they would like another child at all.

The foregoing description of the fertility process has deliberately excluded substantive theory. The components of some of the main variables have been described, but hypotheses connecting these with alternative value systems and the rationales for such connections have not been developed in this paper. The reason for such an exclusion is obvious. Many of the hypotheses are derived from rather lengthy theories, including speculation about the processes of social change over a long period of history, and space simply does not permit any such formulation.

The primary objective of this paper has been to elucidate some of the leading theoretical problems in the study of social and psychological factors affecting fertility that might have some relevance for studies of consumer decision-making in general. No attempt has been made to develop an integrated model for the study of fertility. Whether the kinds of problems arising in this area and the theoretical and research solutions to these problems are relevant for the social scientist concerned with other areas of decision-making is a question appropriate to the objectives of this conference. The converse of this question is equally significant.

REFERENCES

1. FREEDMAN, RONALD, P. K. WHELPTON, and ARTHUR A. CAMPBELL. *Family Planning, Sterility, and Population Growth.* New York: McGraw-Hill, 1959.
2. MISHLER, ELLIOT G., and CHARLES F. WESTOFF. "A Proposal for Research on Social Psychological Factors Affecting Fertility: Concepts and Hypotheses," in *Current Research in Human Fertility.* New York: Milbank Memorial Fund, 1954.

3. WESTOFF, CHARLES F., ELLIOT G. MISHLER, and E. LOWELL KELLY. "Preferences in Size of Family and Eventual Fertility Twenty Years After," *Am. J. Sociology, 62* (March, 1957), 491–97.
4. ——, PHILIP C. SAGI, and E. LOWELL KELLY. "Fertility through Twenty Years of Marriage," *Am. Sociological Rev., 23* (Oct., 1958), 549–56.
5. WHELPTON, P. K., and CLYDE V. KISER (eds.). *Social and Psychological Factors Affecting Fertility*. 4 vols. New York: Milbank Memorial Fund, 1946, 1950, 1952, 1954.

Discussion

ALICE M. RIVLIN

These papers represent a very encouraging trend in consumer-behavior studies. The consumer economist has traditionally addressed himself to the problem of how the consumer allocates a fixed income among various spending and saving alternatives, leaving the size of the family and the number of income earners as independent variables to be explained by somebody else—presumably the demographer and the labor economist. Recognizing that consuming units also make decisions about who will work and how many children they want and that these decisions *cannot* be isolated from spending and saving decisions gives promise of realistic and useful results. Being a woman, I am especially interested in how joint income affects consumption.

Let me start with some observations on Mahoney's paper on the labor-force participation of married women. I have some reservations about his indifference curves and, indeed, about the general usefulness of the indifference-curve model in formulating hypotheses in this area. The decision facing a married woman is more complicated than that facing a man—or at least it seems so in theory. For a man, the alternative to working is always assumed to be leisure, and additional leisure is always assumed to have positive utility. Hence, the man's alternatives can be represented on the traditional two-dimensional indifference map with income on one axis and leisure on the other, and with utility increasing toward the northeast corner of the

39

map. But, as every woman knows, the wife's alternative is not leisure but what Mahoney calls "household participation," i.e., some combination of leisure with the production of goods and services for the home that would otherwise have to be bought or done without. Now, Mahoney assumes that additional household participation, like additional leisure, has positive utility. But this is a purely masculine point of view! The actual housework—scrubbing floors and ironing shirts—certainly has disutility. For some women, housework may have more disutility than the same amount of paid employment. The married woman's indifference map should have more than two dimensions. Mahoney is justified in reducing it to two dimensions and assuming that the utility of increased household participation is always positive *only* if he makes some further explicit assumptions about the rate at which the utility of the wife's services increases relative to the disutility of housework and the disutility of paid employment. Changes in any of these will, of course, change the wife's indifference map.

My point here is that I question whether much can be said *a priori* about the typical woman's indifference map, or about the influence of other variables (e.g., her husband's income, her education, his attitude) on that map. Might it not be more efficient simply to formulate some hypotheses about the influence of these variables on the wife's labor-force participation and proceed to test them, rather than to infer these hypotheses from speculation about the influence of the variables on her indifference curves and the influence of changes in these curves on her behavior?

At this point, Mahoney would be quite justified in reminding me that he was asked for a model of consumer decision-making, not a model of consumer behavior. This raises a rather philosophical question, which I shall not attempt to answer; namely, is a model of consumer decision-making an end in itself, or is it useful only to the extent that it enables us to formulate testable hypotheses about consumer behavior?

Turning to Mahoney's specific hypotheses, I have several questions, some of which are only requests for clarification and definition. For example, how are "assets" to be defined? Are these liquid assets? The fact that it is not possible to measure assets at the time the woman enters the labor force may cause problems. The role of assets in predicting labor-force participation may be similar to the role of assets in predicting savings behavior; i.e., the spending unit may have acquired assets *because* the wife was working (or because they were "savers"). This may be true even when income is held constant, if the wife's income is regarded as a special or temporary income to be saved for a particular purpose.

How are "expenses" defined? If "expenses" are the same as total expenditures of the spending unit, then the expected positive association between "expenses" and labor-force participation may have either of two explanations: the wife goes to work because expenses are high, or the family spends more because the wife is working. These last two points emphasize a fundamental difficulty in the model; namely, I think Mahoney would like to be asking the question, "What influences a married woman to enter or leave the labor force?" whereas his data only permits him to ask, "What factors determine whether or not a married woman is currently in the labor force?" These two questions are related, but they are not the same. Answering the first one would require data on the same women in successive time periods and, incidentally, would also necessitate taking a much larger sample.

How is the income tax going to be treated? It should be remembered that a progressive income tax coupled with joint returns for husband and wife greatly reinforces the hypothesis of a negative association between the husband's income and the wife's labor-force participation. Because the wife's income is always regarded as marginal (and hence taxed at the highest bracket), her income after taxes will actually fall if her husband's income increases while hers remains the same. This involves nothing so esoteric as the diminishing marginal utility of income; it represents actually diminishing income after taxes for the wife.

I shall be curious to see Mahoney's statistical results when he finishes. Meanwhile a few cautionary questions about the statistical model may be in order, although I am sure they have already occurred to Mahoney: (1) Can all the included variables (age, for example) be assumed to be linearly related to labor-force participation? (2) How is the significance of the regression coefficients to be tested in view of the fact that labor-force participation does *not* show a normal distribution? (3) Can reliable coefficients be estimated when so many of the independent variables are sure to be closely correlated with each other?

Turning to Westoff's paper, I agree that there are many similarities between the decision to have a child and other consumer decisions and that it will probably prove fruitful to consider them within the same general framework. In fact, even some of the characteristics of the offspring decision that Westoff believes distinguish it from other consumer decisions are not without counterparts in the area of purchase decisions. Many purchase decisions are largely irrevocable, and there is often "an element of chance about the product." A child may not be an economic asset, but neither is last month's vacation, which you may still be paying for but which you cannot possibly sell to someone else. Even the distinction between planned, semiplanned, and accidental pregnancies, so important in fertility analysis, is not without analogue in the area of expenditures —witness the growing literature on impulse buying. A major purchase made "on impulse" has considerable similarity to a semiplanned pregnancy, and the genuinely accidental pregnancy is not unlike the unwanted expenditures forced on the consumer by illness, accident, fire, or flood.

With respect to the usefulness of family-size preferences in predicting fertility, I wonder if Westoff is not overly pessimistic. He refers to an interesting study in which he participated in which engaged couples were asked about the number of children they wanted. Twenty years later the preferences, although significant, were found to be very little help in predicting how many children each couple actually had. The fact that *on the average* these couples had almost exactly the same number of children that they said they wanted is dismissed in a footnote as accidental, but this is because Westoff has focused his attention exclusively on predicting individual performance. If an improved version of this study were repeated at intervals over a period of years, it might well turn out that average preferences bore some constant relationship to average performance—a fact that would be tremendously helpful to those of us who are more interested in predicting aggregates than in predicting individual behavior. In a more representative sample, one would expect the ratio of average family size to average preference to be somewhat less than one. Moreover, even if this ratio should show wide fluctuations, it might still prove useful if the fluctuations themselves were found to be closely related to income, employment, or some other variable. The experience of the Survey Research Center and others with consumer purchase expectations seems to have indicated that, while these data may not be very useful in predicting individual behavior even in the short run, they often prove useful in predicting aggregates.[1] One might hope for similar (or better) results in the demographic field.

Westoff suggests that the planning horizon of most couples is quite short; i.e., they are more sure about whether they want another child in the next year or two than about how many children they ultimately want to have. I am not quite certain whether he means that their short-run preferences are more definite at the time of questioning or that they are better correlated with performance than are longer-run preferences. If he means the latter, then he is questioning whether it is valid to interpret fluctuations in the birth rate in terms of couples "advancing," "postponing," and "making-up" births in response to short-run fluctuations in economic conditions, draft legislation, and the like. This sort of interpretation of the birth rates of the 1930's and 1940's (associated with the name of Whelpton, among others) implies that most couples have fairly fixed ideas about ultimate family size, but that they change the timing of births in response to short-run conditions. Personally, I would suggest the not very startling hypothesis that there is some truth in both positions and that the best correlations between preferences and performance may be found for periods of intermediate length (e.g., three to six years), rather than for very long or very short periods.

Finally, I would like to take exception to one rather incidental point near the end of Westoff's paper. In support of the proposition that the planning horizon for fertility is short, he offers this evidence: "Mothers are much more articulate about why they would like to have the next child 12, 18, or 24 months from now than they are about why they would like another child at all" (p. 37). I doubt that articulateness about motives is evidence of firmness of plan. If you ask a woman why she wants to have children, you are asking an emotion-fraught question about her fundamental values, asking her to put the motherhood urge into words for a strange interviewer. But if you ask her why she would rather have a baby next year than this year, you are asking a relatively superficial question, which demands much less soul-searching and to which I would certainly expect a more articulate answer. Actually, I would expect an even *more* articulate response to "Why do you need a new washing machine?" But I would not conclude that the plan to buy the

[1] See, for example, the papers of Lansing and Withey and Schweiger in Conference on Research in Income and Wealth: "Short-term Economic Forecasting," *Studies in Income and Wealth*, *17*, Princeton, N. J., Princeton University Press, 1955.

washing machine was more important or less subject to change than the plan to have a baby.

In sum, both these papers seem to me valuable and stimulating contributions to the field of consumer behavior, broadly considered. Mahoney, by having the audacity to present a very specific model, complete with testable hypotheses, has invited rather specific criticism and has certainly aroused interest in seeing his empirical results. Westoff has presented a much more general framework, within which I hope it will be possible for him and others to formulate models as specific as Mahoney's.

Discussion

HOWARD S. STANTON

In the main, I want to bring out some aspects of how the decision-making process may be studied. Both papers dealt with areas of interest and very pervasive change in family life. One of the primary reasons for the interest in these kinds of decisions is their substantial change in our culture during recent generations. Another is the predictability of their change in underdeveloped areas as they industrialize. Birth rates have gone or are going down, and rates of married women workers have gone or are going up almost everywhere. However, this is not the central concern today. Both Mahoney and Westoff have focused on the factors influencing the decisions as made within each family taken individually.

Mahoney has indicated a number of variables that are found to be related to the decision for or against the wife's gainful employment, and he has related these variables to each other as part of a model and as part of a study in progress. Westoff has similarly commented on a number of variables that have been used in research attempting to account for decisions for or against the use of birth control. It is striking and convenient for the discussion to note the extent to which these two decision areas are structurally similar. The working of wives and the using of birth control are both joint decisions involving a family, or at least a couple, rather than an individual. Both decisions involve immediate acts, as well as going beyond these acts to definitions of the kind of family in which one is going to live.

With respect to both decisions, there is a group of "antis" (non-working wives or nonusers of birth control), for whom any decision would mean saying yes or no to the family's involvement in a new set of problems and skills, beginning with the wife's applying for a job or a diaphragm and continuing through the integration of the new with the old family ways. This is a decision situation very different from that facing what we might call the "semis" (sometime workers or sometime users), for whom a decision means a tentative rebalancing of conflicting pressures between already familiar alternatives. Still another kind of decision problem is that faced by the "pros" (the established workers or users), for whom a decision means quitting an established practice at least temporarily. From the subjective point of view, the decision process of a nonuser considering birth control is probably very different from the process of a user considering stopping to have another child.

Can these three types—pros, semis, and antis—be treated linearly? Mahoney, working more objectively, treats these three groups as arranged along a single quantitative scale of number of weeks worked. He hopes to predict the position of any given family on this scale by summing the strength of pushes and pulls toward and away from the wife's working. These pushes and pulls are organized in terms of a model in which outside work is treated as uniformly undesirable except for the money earned. Some variables may make outside work less undesirable—e.g., a family composition with fewer persons to be cared for or more persons to share the tasks. Other variables may make the wife's salary more tempting—e.g., higher earnings opportunities, or a poorer family financial position.

This plan has a number of promising features. There is value in a study that includes most of the variables thus far found to be related to the decision. Even more valuable is the relating of the variables to each other through a relatively simple, clearly stated model. This, I think, is a step forward. It should be pointed out, however, that the correlation coefficient derived from the data will in no way prove or disprove the model. The variables are already known to correlate when taken separately, and the multiple correlation can be no lower than the highest of those. The model, at this point in Mahoney's research, is little more than an heuristic classification of empirical correlations. Nor will the size of the coefficient itself be an important finding. With 16 variables, a fairly high correlation may be expected—but it is the nature of multiple correlation to capitalize on the idiosyncrasies of the given case. On any new sample, the previous coefficient would probably be reduced considerably. The most interesting finding will be the weights assigned to the different variables in the regression equation. But, as Mahoney recognizes, these may not have much significance beyond the market studied—St. Paul, 1957.

Westoff, working in a more thoroughly researched area, is able to go beyond the summarizing of relationships between unidimensional variables. He has much to say about the actual processes of decision-making with respect to birth control. Rather than treating "number of children" or "frequency of use of birth-control devices" as a single variable comparable to "number of weeks worked," he advocates separating out the "antis"—the nonusers. These he would try to account for through some combination of values, such as religion and social-class aspirations. The remaining families—including the "sometimes" and "always" users—vary in number of children, and this variation is in places talked of in terms of preference, modified somehow by family composition. To say the same thing even more simply: some families have values that oppose the use of birth control—they are expected to have large families. Those who approve of use will have a large or a small family depending on how many they want.

It is quite possible that an explanation as simple as this would account for more of the variation in number of children than would a multiple-correlation type of index—and it might hold over a wider range of cultures. The difference between the two approaches is the simple plausibility of the one as against the additive empirical model of the other. This simple plausibility of Westoff's paper is, of course, deceptive. It is a result, rather than a forerunner, of the kind of empirical work Mahoney has described in his paper.

Discussion

BRIM (CHAIRMAN): The plan is not to have retorts by the givers of papers to their discussants, but comments by the audience. The writers of the papers will write a rejoinder to remarks by both discussants and the audience.

KENKEL (to MAHONEY): Have you considered using the variable "family life cycle" to help explain the difference between women who do and do not work outside the home? It seems to me, for example, that knowing whether a child under six or 18 years of age is the first or last child of a family would be as important as knowing simply that there is a child of this age.

MAHONEY: We considered this but did not settle it. We can see the value, but it may be included in the other variables, and we have not worked this out yet. Since we have much data, ample for handling by five or six models, we may be able to work this treatment out specifically later. We did use age of youngest child.

JOHN (to MAHONEY): You include as a variable the attitude of the housewife toward working. Why not consider other members of the family also, especially the attitude of the husband? This is important, because the culture says he is the provider and this view is challenged by her working.

MAHONEY: I agree about its importance, but the study was restricted to data got from the wife. We tried obtaining the wife's perception of her husband's attitude, but found it so perfectly correlated with her own that the question was discarded.

HILL (to MAHONEY): You may have a high correlation but still should not throw away such data, because wherever you do have a discrepancy between the wife's perception of her husband's attitude and her own attitude, you may have a highly illuminating index of stress, which would be useful in predicting how long she would work.

BERNARD: Are we looking at a model of consumer behavior or at the household decision process? There may be many utility functions; the consuming unit may be a composite of disparate functions. Taking the group factor into account, we may ask if her friends work. Similarly, pregnancies are influenced by group behavior. In a model of the wife's behavior in the game situation, uncertainty and the risk of such disutilities as hurting her marriage or children must be included.

GLICK (to WESTOFF): In studies of complex behavior, such as predictions of family size, the percentage of variance explained is often disappointingly small. How much of the variance must be explained for the researcher (and his sponsor) to feel that the study has been successful?

WESTOFF: We have lowered our sights. You can only maintain a comparative point of view—how well have you done in the past? The answer can only be empirical. You might want to look at our forthcoming article in the *American Sociological Review* (see reference above).

ORCUTT: R squared as an explanation of variance is not a satisfactory test. The degree of correlation is not as relevant as its stability over time. But I wonder what Westoff wants to predict *for*. What is the importance of predicting the individual?

WESTOFF: We are not trying to predict for practical application. We are trying to determine what the differences are among families that have two, three, four, or five children.

ORCUTT: Isn't there an average behavior? You don't care to predict individuals, do you?

WESTOFF: Variability in average fertility is very low, so you won't get far in understanding changes in the aggregate without breaking it down as we do.

HALBERT: Isn't there a possibility of evaluating research by how much insight it gives? Some research tells you what you are going to research next.

Two questions are being discussed here, what the value of R^2 is, and how good this research is. How high R squared must be to have good research depends on whether it is "action" research or "conceptualization" research. In action research, the value can be determined by using an operations research model of the alternative courses of action and the values of their outcomes. The R^2 sufficient for a decision depends on the cost and value of better prediction. In conceptual research, the value depends on how far the conceptual model seems to be verified by the data. It is important to distinguish these two criteria of good research. If your purpose is understanding a process, this would make R^2 less important.

DANIERE: All research is action research. We want a high R^2 because it will give success in a large number of actions, whether these are specified now or not. If you feel the probabilities will change over time, you will want to introduce more explanatory variables; but that there is greater difficulty in predicting behavior and that this makes prediction a different test are not correct. The future of your research, however, is affected by the view you take, as in the decision what to do or not do regarding having a child, planning versus submitting to chance.

HILL: The attempt to explain fertility planning may well be rendered more manageable by breaking families down into the three categories suggested by Stanton, anti-use, semi-use, and pro-use, using these as the dependent variables. In Puerto Rico, we found it easy to predict the fertility of the first group of never-users. It was more difficult to differentiate among the semis and the pros, and to distinguish within the pros which were successful users with low incidence of accidents. The irregular users were often "inconsistents" who would alternate between large and small family preference and who were, moreover, experimental, shifting from one method to another. In terms of the concept of risk-taking, the irregulars had less to lose—unplanned children were not disasters—and their propensity to experiment was thus more pronounced. Some pros risk great loss if they fail. Some of the experimentally minded semis, showing high empathy and communication, moved from failing method to failing method to sterilization.

Westoff should seek further to explain the relative success of failure of fertility control among the planning group. It is within this group that the factors making for competence in decision-making will be illuminated.

WESTOFF: We did do some preliminary wondering about the stability of the distribution of such types over time. During recent history, births have gone up and stayed up, while the techniques of contraception became more available. One interpretation of this trend might be that people want more children. However, the correct interpretation might be that the improved economic situation has made risk-taking less disastrous.

GARTNER (to MAHONEY): You indicated that, as assets increase, marginal utility of earning declines. Might we not be faced with a kinked utility function? Marginal utility might actually increase over some range of increase in assets; aspirations could go up faster than the level of living. Also, are you attempting to estimate the slope of the indifference curves?

MAHONEY: We may find such a kink. We are not seeking the slope of the composite indifference curve.

MAYNES: Do you attempt to estimate the costs of women's entrance into the labor force? For example, additional durable goods may be required in the household inventory. How do such anticipated costs affect participation?

MAHONEY: We are not trying to measure cost. We gave this much consideration at first and also considered the net return after subtracting that cost. In our pilot work, we found a few who considered this important, but we could not get at it objectively; people did not formulate their costs.

CLAWSON: Why didn't you attempt to get a measure of the indifference curves of the respondents?

MAHONEY: Because it was too big a measurement problem.

DuBois: You have categorized working outside the home as disutility and home participation as utility. Women work for positive values other than money, however, for stimulation and improved mental health. Would removing volunteer work and work not for pay from home participation affect your model?

MAHONEY: We have held the wife's labor-force participation to her contribution toward the spending unit. If the wide's attitude is positive toward her work, we assumed it would affect the spending unit too. We could not measure the husband's attitude directly, because we dealt only with her, but we assumed that the attitudes of others affected her attitudes.

FERBER: The best way to resolve this would be to separate the utility factor from empirical questions. More categories could be used, breaking household participation apart from nonwork and nonhousehold participation from nonwork, but this would be another study.

HALBERT: Perhaps the point at issue here might be cleared up a bit if we remember that when the dependent variable, the outcome, is quite complex, as it is here, the researcher has the option of simplifying it by putting part of it on the other side of the equation. DuBois is concerned that the positive attitude toward the wife working—the value to her of getting out of the house—is not included in the variable being predicted. But Mahoney has included at least the wife's attitudes by making them a part of the predictor. This is always the researcher's decision, and in this case a wise one. The husband's attitude is also included, registered indirectly by his age and education.

HILL: How does your dependent variable behave when you break it into categories of no work, part-time work, and full-time work? When the decision to work is made in the family, these three categories appear, rather than the continuous variable, number of weeks the wife shall work.

MAHONEY: Full-time work and no work are characteristic; part-time work is exceptional.

HILL: Is not this the choice, instead of number of weeks? Would there not be a difference in your results if it were used? And would not number of hours per week also be more important in the decision than the number of weeks worked per year?

MAHONEY: Further analysis, perhaps including number of days per week, is planned, but part-time work has played a small part so far.

We did get discrimination by the way we did it; the differences were not obscured.

KOMAROVSKY: Have you done a correlation of husband's earnings and wife's employment? In the recently published *Womanpower* study, the relation was found to be curvilinear.

MAHONEY: This has not been completed yet, but the relation does seem to vary irregularly, for example, in part of the range, negative between categories while positive within. There are numerous other studies touching on this matter. We have found them to be about equally divided between finding a negative and a positive relation.

ORCUTT: I wonder if using number of weeks increases the influence of the availability of jobs. On the other hand, is availability or opportunity so different from the utility of working? Some jobs that are technically available are not acceptable.

PETER: Are household participation and working really substitutable? Might there not be a real difference between women who are employed full-time with few or no household duties to perform and women who carry on considerable household production activity in addition to full-time employment? Employment may not be an alternative to household activity, but some kind of overtime combination. If you have data on this matter, how do they relate to decisions by husband and wife on her working?

FOOTE: Carrying that point further, how much of her household work does the husband take over when she goes to work? His actions may be a truer sign of his attitude than her report of it. If you could find them out from her, you might solve the field problem of getting from her a more valid account of his attitude.

WESTOFF: We have much data available in our study on this matter and could supply it.

BRIM (CHAIRMAN): One purpose of this conference is to make the work of each researcher better known to the others, but we cannot pursue all the leads opened up by this discussion.

DIMOND (to MAHONEY): In calculating participation by weeks per year, how do you treat women involuntarily relieved of their jobs?

MAHONEY: According to Census definition, anyone seeking work is counted in the labor force for as many weeks as she may seek it.

FOOTE: The point made earlier (by Orcutt) can be generalized to other lines of consumer behavior; the available alternatives may not be acceptable, but the person is in the market.

WESTOFF: Fortunately that is not a problem in studying fertility. (*Overheard*): That could be argued.

WESTOFF: I should like to thank both Rivlin and Stanton for their thoughtful critiques. I have no quarrel with most of their observations. I accept Rivlin's criticism that there exist other types of consumer decisions that in common with fertility contain elements of irrevocability and chance. I believe she may be stretching the similarities a little in comparing the genuinely accidental pregnancy with "unwanted expenditures forced on the consumer by illness, accident, fire, or flood." But this is minor in comparison with the more important question of whether such a transfer of concepts from consumer economics to social demography is useful for research purposes. In my judgment, this remains to be demonstrated, although some further effort has since been made in this direction.[1] The probable outcome will be that some concepts will prove useful, such as perhaps the indifference-curve model, while others will not.

The differences in micro and macro perspectives have been aired frequently, and there is nothing new that we can add here. They simply relate to different choices of research interests and different levels of "explanation." Personally, I would have much more confidence in the validity of aggregate forecasts if validity at the individual level could be demonstrated. But I recognize that this point of view does not obviate the usefulness of aggregate predictions.

Rivlin's observation that articulateness is no necessary indication of stability of plans is well taken, and I accept her correction.

In his discussion, Stanton interestingly compares decisions about the use of contraception and fertility with decisions about the wife's participation in the labor force. I think that there are numerous similarities in the decision process, and his observations are suggestive.

In conclusion, I would like to note that the first phase of our large-scale, longitudinal study of the decision process in connection with family size has just been completed. It contains many tests of some of the ideas advanced in this paper.

[1] See Gary S. Becker's "Economic Aspects of Fertility," a paper presented at a National Bureau of Economic Research meeting and to be published in its proceedings, *Demographic and Economic Change in Developed Countries.*

II. Decision-Making Regarding Saving and Borrowing

Patterns of Decision-Making and the Accumulation of Family Assets

REUBEN HILL

At the orientation sessions held prior to the conference, the economists in the group expressed an interest in extending the range of variables beyond the familiar economic and demographic categories presently used to explain the variance in saving and borrowing behavior. New conceptual frameworks were sought which would be more theoretically appropriate to the study of household behavior than the present approach of economic theory. I have accordingly attempted to present the concepts and tools of my own discipline, providing for you a case description of a family sociologist attacking the special problem of family asset accumulation.[1]

Because we are in the data-gathering stage of the study that furnishes this example, the emphasis will be on problem formulation and research design rather than on findings. My objectives are threefold: (1) to demonstrate the range of conceptual approaches from family sociology that can be brought to bear on the problem of asset accumulation; (2) to build a theoretical model based on the approach chosen, identifying crucial analytic categories and their relationships with the dependent variables chosen for study; and (3) to render the theoretical model researchable, specifying in the research design the methods of sampling, data collection, and analysis proposed.

[1] I wish to acknowledge help in preparing this paper from my colleagues Roy Francis, E. Scott Maynes, and Roy H. Rodgers of the University of Minnesota.

CONCEPTUAL APPROACH AND FOCUS

A first issue in the formulation of a research problem is the question of the optimum unit of study. In studies of consumer behavior, the individual consumer is often the behaving unit studied. Heads of households, the household at the time of the study, the nuclear family (defined as husband, wife, and immediate offspring living under the same roof) and the extended family (made up of all immediate blood kin) are other possible units of study. The criteria of selection we employed can be stated as questions: (1) What is the accumulating unit? (2) What is the choice-making and decision-making unit? (3) How accessible is the unit for study? (4) About which of these units do we have the most theory?

The nuclear family meets all four of these requirements better than any other units suggested. Let us consider its advantages: (1) The inventory of acquisitions over time is the property of a nuclear family. (2) The nuclear family is the decision-making unit in asset accumulation. Many choices and decisions are made by family heads, to be sure, but they are made *for* the family and often involve some participation from children.[2] (3) The nuclear family is more accessible for study than the extended family, and more easily definable for purposes of study, than is the household, which may include roomers and servants who have little part in family acquisitions. Only the individual consumer is more accessible. (4) Finally, the nuclear family serves as a referent in several conceptual systems of theory and has been subject to greater study than most of the other suggested units. By these criteria, the nuclear family is clearly the optimum unit of study.

Alternative Conceptual Frameworks

The nuclear family having been selected as the unit for study, a number of alternative conceptual approaches may be considered. Sociology, cultural anthropology, psychology, and consumption economics have developed approaches that differ almost as much as the proverbial blind men's perceptions of the elephant. I have earlier identified seven such conceptual frameworks from analysis of several hundred pieces of research on marriage and the family, primarily in the United States, using as criteria for classification the definitions

[2] A number of studies could be cited to support this assertion (e.g., 12).

of the family implied, the key concepts and their interrelationships, and the peculiar subject-matter foci employed (5). Generalizations arising from these different approaches cannot always be added to each other to form cumulative theories, and students who learn the concepts and techniques of only one approach are often handicapped in making sense out of writings based on other approaches.

Table II.1 provides a list of these competing frameworks for family study, with the disciplines which originated and elaborated them, and the names of men whose research best exemplifies them. Of these seven conceptual approaches, the institutional-historical may be eliminated at once as a possibility for this research problem because of its macroscopic scope and institutional focus. The situational approach suffers from too great specificity, although it is relevant to study of family discussions. The learning-theory approach is unable to handle the plurality of actors involved in family acquisitions and focuses too narrowly on the personality development of children. The household-economics approach is also ineligible by virtue of its focus on the household as a firm, its close alliance with farm-management concepts, and its lack of concepts of family organization. The household-economics framework is essentially a balance-sheet approach, relating the resources of time, money, and energy to various outputs. It is probably inappropriate, therefore, for a study of decision-making and choice-making. It is essentially a normative, efficiency-oriented approach seeking to prescribe rules that, if followed, would enable consumers to maximize their satisfactions.

The three approaches that survive our scrutiny all deal with the nuclear family as the focus of interest. They bring to the research rich concepts and theories that will be useful to consider: the structure-function, the symbolic-interactionist, and the family-development approaches.

The structure-function approach, which views the family as a social system, has its roots in anthropology and sociology and is rapidly winning adherents in the United States and Europe. Elaborated in the United States in more recent years by Harvard and Columbia sociologists (notably Talcott Parsons, Kingsley Davis, Robert Merton, George Homans, and Marion Levy), it has been profitably applied to the family at several levels from broad macroanalysis to intensive microanalysis: in the interplay between changes in the family and society in changing China (9), in the strains induced between

TABLE II. 1

APPROACHES TO THE STUDY OF THE FAMILY COMPETING FOR ADHERENTS IN AMERICA *

Conceptual Framework	Originating in Disciplines of:	Exemplified in Researches by:
The institutional-historical approach	Sociology and Historical Sociology	C. C. Zimmerman and associates
The structure-function or social-system approach	Sociology and Social Anthropology	K. Davis, C. McGuire, G. Murdock, T. Parsons, L. Simmons, L. Warner, and others
The symbolic-interactionist approach	Sociology and Social Psychology	R. C. Angell, E. W. Burgess, R. Cavan, L. S. Cottrell, T. D. Eliot, N. Foote, R. Hill, M. Komarovsky, E. Koos, E. T. Krueger, H. Mowrer, W. Waller, and Paul Wallin
The situational-psychological habitat approach	Developed independently by Sociology and Psychology	J. H. S. Bossard and associates; R. Blood; R. G. Barker and H. F. Wright
The learning-theory-developmental approach	Psychology	R. Sears and John Whiting; Arnold Gesell and associates; A. Davis and R. Havighurst
The household-economics approach	Consumption Economics and Home Economics	H. Kyrk, J. Morgan, L. Gordon, P. Nickell, and Margaret Reid
The family-development or family-life-cycle approach	Interdisciplinary, borrowing from Rural Sociology, Child Psychology, Human Development, and Sociology	No research completed as yet, approximations seen in work of R. Faris, P. Glick, J. Lansing, J. Morgan, M. Sussman, L. Stott and in writings of R. Cavan, E. Duvall, R. Foster, R. Hill, and L. D. Rockwood

* Developed by Reuben Hill and associates in family research seminars from careful analysis of the definitions of the family implied, the key concepts used, and the peculiar foci employed in more than 200 pieces of research on marriage and the family during the last 20 years. This listing of approaches to the study of the family obviously does not do justice to the various approaches to consumer behavior except as caught by the household-economics approach. Excluded are, for example, the distinctive Gestalt psychological framework of Katona and associates and the Lewinian approach of Bilkey.

the occupational structure's demands of the family farm on the farm family (4), in the analysis of power allocation among families of four differently oriented cultural groups (11, pp. 468–73), and in the analysis of relative stress of economic deprivation and political terrorism among families of political refugees (3). This conceptual framework has the advantage of providing descriptive categories within a scope wide enough to encompass the interplay between the family system and larger systems like the community and the society; the interplay between the family and collateral systems like the school, the occupational world, and the marketplace; and the transactions between the family and its smaller subgroups—the husband-wife dyad, the sibling cliques, and the individual personality systems of family members.

The symbolic-interactionist approach, first developed in sociology and social psychology, has been the most frequently employed in the past 20 years in American family sociology. The approach was a direct outgrowth of the work of George Herbert Mead and the University of Chicago group of symbolic interactionists, of which Ernest W. Burgess was a prominent member. He first suggested the feasibility of viewing the family as an interacting entity in 1928. Subsequent studies have gradually refined the interactional conceptual framework. It assumes the family to be a relatively closed system of interaction. It is thus narrower in scope than the structure-function approach, which, as Homans in *The Human Group* indicates, has both an internal system for regulating relations within the family and an external system for dealing with the transactions between the family and nonfamily agencies and events. The scope of the interactional approach corresponds roughly to the internal system of the structure-function schema. As a consequence, it has stimulated hundreds of inner-oriented studies of marriage and the family but has not spawned many family-community studies. Three orders of concepts are illustrative: (a) status and interstatus relations, which become the bases for authority patterns and initiative-taking; (b) role, role conception, role expectation, and role differentiation; and (c) processes of communication, conflict, compromise, and consensus, and of problem-solving, decision-making, and action-taking.

The family-development approach emphasizes the time dimension but it is not precisely a competing framework because it attempts to transcend the boundaries of present approaches through incorporation of the compatible sections of several approaches into one unified scheme. From rural sociologists, it has borrowed the concept of stages of the family life cycle. From child psychology and human development have come the concepts of developmental needs and tasks. From the sociologists engaged in work on the sociology of the professions have been borrowed the concept of career and the view of the family as a convergence of intercontingent careers of husband and wife, later of children. From the structure-function and interactional schools have been borrowed the concepts of age and sex roles, plurality patterns, and the many concepts associated with the family as a system of interacting persons. The resulting frame of reference furnishes an opportunity for the accretion of generalizations about the internal development of families from their formation in the engagement and wedding to their dissolution in divorce and death. An integration of the scattered writings on family development has recently been completed by Duvall (1). This approach to family study implies use of the longitudinal method of research, which because of its expense and slow yield has seen limited use in family research to date.

In quick summary, these three approaches are both appropriate and suggestive of concepts and ideas for our research problem. The symbolic-interaction approach is rich in concepts related to decision-making and goal-setting and offers help especially in relating internal family organization to success in making family acquisitions. The family-as-a-social-system approach (structure-function) offers leads about the transactional behavior of the nuclear family unit with outside agencies like the school, the church, and the marketplace. Transactional concepts will be important in the exchanges between the nuclear family and kinship extensions in studying intergenerational transfers, gift giving and receiving, styles of conspicuous consumption, and living up to or down to the Joneses. The family development approach offers us the widest scope. Indeed, to take full advantage of this framework, we should follow the families we study over their entire life span. This is prohibitively expensive financially and organizationally, and I doubt if I would live to see the study completed. As an approach, however, family development has the advantage of incorporating most of the relevant concepts about the family from both the interactional and social system frameworks while adding the dimension of family growth over time, coping as it does with the orderly and predictable changes that occur over the family's life cycle. Of the seven approaches we have considered, it offers the most for this research.

The family-development approach views the family as a small-group system, intricately organized internally into paired positions of husband-father, wife-mother, son-brother, and daughter-sister. Norms prescribing the appropriate role behavior for each of these positions specify how reciprocal relations are to be maintained, as well as how role behavior may change with changing ages of the occupants of these positions. This intimate small group has a predictable natural history, designated by stages beginning with the simple husband-wife pair and becoming more and more complex as members are launched into jobs and marriage and the group once again contracts in size to the husband-wife pair. As the age composition of the family changes, so do the expectations for occupants of the positions in the family, and so does the quality of interaction among family members.

Viewed social psychologically and developmentally, the family is an arena of interacting personalities, each striving to obtain the satisfaction of his desires. Parents often defer their own needs, however, in building complementary roles between themselves and their children. At some stages of development, parents and children are good company; at other stages, their diverse developmental strivings may be strikingly incompatible. There can be identified, by the use of these concepts, seven stages of the family life cycle, each with its own peculiar sources of conflict and solidarity. Each of these stages may be seen in three dimensions of increasing complexity: (1) the changing developmental tasks and role expectations of the children; (2) the changing developmental tasks and role expectations of the parents, both mother and father, in their capacities as providers, homemakers, spouses, and persons; and (3) the developmental tasks of the *family as family*, which flow from the cultural imperatives laid upon it at each stage of growth, and the implications for the family of the personal developmental requirements of each child and parent.

Coping with the demands of the community and of family members, families may develop policies that not only help in making choices in the present but give direction and structure to the future. As the family develops in stature and competence from wedding day on, it builds a history of problem solutions, a pattern of decision-making, and a set of rudimentary family policies by which choices can be made involving children and the family's future and by which actions can be judged. These policies, moreover, include the family's time schedule for reaching important goals and objectives—owning a home, completing the family, launching children into jobs and marriage, and retirement. These are the contents of the family culture which, if we knew them, would make family behavior more or less predictable.

Scope and Focus of the Research Problem

With the choice of the nuclear family as the unit of study and the family-development approach as the conceptual framework within which to work, the research problem can be more readily delineated. If we are to join fruitfully with economists doing the bulk of the research on savings and asset accumulation, the dependent variable must, however, be translatable into their terms.

We have been studying quite directly family exchange behavior, both acquisitive and transmissive. The behaving units are nuclear families with variable histories and at differing stages of their careers. The extent and quality of acquisitions vary greatly by stage of the family cycle. At any given stage, the acquisitions achieved should be related to the effectiveness with which the family to date has managed its many resources. This suggests a possible bridging variable between the many explanatory variables from sociology that we shall be using and the strictly economic variable of assets and liabilities, namely, family effectiveness in long-range planning. Moreover, effective planfulness is not only an intervening variable presumably correlated with the inventory of family acquisitions, but is a thoroughly defensible alternative dependent variable in its own right.

Using the lenses provided by family-development concepts, variables are suggested that may be expected to account for the success or failure of families in managing resources and moving toward their objectives. Beginning with the assumption that the family is a purposive system and that its members are goal-oriented, we hypothesize that motivation toward planfulness, the accompanying knowledge and skill in manipulating the means of planning, and good group organization for action comprise the essentials for effective long-range planning.

Motivationally, families will vary in their valuing of planfulness as a mode of living. Most families will fall between the extremes of Benjamin Franklin's type of prudence and the fatalistic acceptance of one's lot in life characteristic of depressed families. Furthermore, families will vary in the degree to which they value services, travel, and education more than such durable goods as houses, cars, and appliances. Additionally, we expect families to vary greatly in their orientation to time, some looking to the past, many to the present, and some to the future for the good life. It will be interesting to correlate these orientations toward time with planning effectiveness and asset accumulation.

Knowledge about methods of problem-solving or rational decision-making may be expected to be unevenly distributed among families. The skills of management may be transmitted, as are other aspects of the culture, from the parental families. The analysis should explore the possibility that knowledge about the procedures of problem-solving runs in families like speech forms and techniques of table etiquette. Intergenerational comparisons will be extremely useful here.

By now those who know our work on fertility planning in Puerto Rico will recognize the close parallel between the problem of accounting for fertility-planning effectiveness and effectiveness in long-range financial planning. Families in Puerto Rico who were highly motivated, possessed a knowledge of the means of fertility control, and were internally well organized to act upon this knowledge were more likely than others to be regular, effective users of birth-control methods (6).

To be efficient and effective in stewarding resources, a family must be a well-organized team, the relations between spouses being especially important. How effective, for example, is the family as a group in perceiving, discussing, and arriving at consensus about what to do in vital areas of family planning? Families may be expected to vary in their power structure, in the openness of the channels of communication within the family, in the adequacy of communication among members, and in the accuracy of perception of the wishes and desires of other members. These are illustrative of the action potentials that are brought to bear when the family is viewed as an organization for meeting problems and taking action.

Finally, the family-development approach suggests the great gain to be obtained from a historical-longitudinal view of family success and failure in coping with major problems. Just as scholastic success in college can best be predicted from high-school scholastic achievement, marital success best predicted by the pair's success in engagement adjustment, and parole behavior best predicted by the prisoner's criminal career, so also can a family's effectiveness in long-range planning be best anticipated by an analysis of its past successes in management, as represented by the family's residential history, its income and wealth curves, and the occupational and educational careers of the breadwinners.

The outlines of a theoretical model of analytic categories that will be useful in explaining both family effectiveness in long-range planning and the accumulation of family assets have begun to shape up from our discussion of the contributions of family-development thinking to the problem at hand. The advantages of the framework will be even clearer as we complete the theoretical model and indicate the methods suggested by the framework for rendering it researchable.

A Theoretical Model of Analytic Categories

In the schema of analytic categories that we have prepared (Chart II.1), the demographic background variables used by the economist are placed on the extreme left and the dependent variables of effectiveness of planning and of asset accumulation on the extreme right. Intervening between these two major blocks are categories of explanatory variables that become increasingly specific and dimensionally similar to the dependent variables as we move from left to right. From this rudimentary model, we would argue that the economic variable of asset accumulation will be explained best in most families by the effectiveness with which the family has planned and carried out long-range decisions rationally. It is this latter variable that I, as a family sociologist, would like to predict, and it constitutes the chief dependent variable of the present study.

As we look at the categories of explanatory variables on the left of the dependent variables, Block G and Block H, we identify in Block E, Family Action Potentials, and Block F, Cumulative Career Patterns, conceptual categories that should have high predictive value. Block E reflects the adequacy of internal organization for action in problem-solving, including measures of husband-wife communication, marital empathy, and marital consensus, plus a measure of competence in decision-making with respect to parent-child problems. Block F involves typologies and career profiles cumulating the family's history in choice-making with respect to such issues as where to live, what jobs to keep or leave, and how much education to provide for one's children. The resulting profiles should predict planning effectiveness with more accuracy than measures of family attributes alone could ever do.

Block C, Family Goals, Policies, and Life Styles, taps the propensities to act—latent action sets that subsequently are manifested as behavior in the dependent variables of long-range planning and asset accumulation. They are to be distinguished from Block B, General Value Orientations, which reflects much more general attitudes toward life and nature. Block C includes those policies, developed over time, that govern choice and timing of expenditures and determine the choice of means for asset accumulation, e.g., policies of paying with cash or using credit. The style of life toward which the family is striving is broadly sought in this analytic category.[3]

Block D, Family Structure and Organization, is a more general and theoretical category of variables than Block E. It would have greater theoretical usefulness than some of the more specifically relevant variables in Block E, if our research shows it predicts planning effectiveness. How do size of family, age, composition, and stage of the life cycle, for example, relate to planning? How do families with a restrictive type of organization, highly centralized in power structure and possessing a rigidly segregated sex division of labor, compare with families with open, permissive organization, characterized by egalitarian distribution of power and high sharing of duties and responsibilities within the family? In Puerto Rico, restrictiveness of family organization, indicated by high husband dominance and restrictions on the wife's working and participating socially, was found negatively related to success in fertility planning (6).

Block A, Social Placement-Situational Category, has been widely used to explain economic behavior of families but has meager relevance to any body of middle-range theory. These demographic background variables reflect the vagaries of life conditions and the environmental limitations under which families operate. They become meaningful theoretically in our model when they are translated into the values that families of similar situational circumstances share, shown in the schema as Block B, General Value Orientations. People

[3] This may on first glance appear vague and hard to elicit from respondents, but our pretests tell us that families talk quite freely about the style of life to which they would like to become accustomed, and if they have developed policies, they verbalize well about the policies that govern their choices of major expenditures.

CHART II.I

Schema of Analytic Categories Specifying Interrelations Anticipated in Family Inventory Study

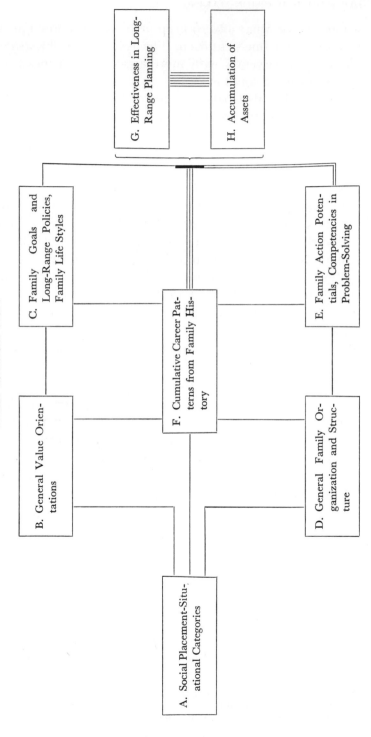

A. *Social Placement-Situational Categories*
  1. Index of social position (Hollingshead)
  2. Education
  3. Occupation
  4. Residence
  5. Income-financial status

B. *General Value Orientations*
  1. Traditional-modernism (Brim *et al.* Cognitive Values Scale)
  2. Conceptions of parenthood (Blood)
  3. Time orientations (Cognitive Values Scale)

C. *Family Goals, Policies, and Life Styles*
  1. Propensity to invest in present consumption vs. future (intergenerational transfer test)
  2. Work and leisure policies, investment in time-savers and time-fillers (from history)
  3. Upward mobile, conformers, or upgraders growth- and talent-oriented (from history)
  4. Cash-, credit-, or gift-oriented (from history)
  5. Services vs. things (from inventory and history)
  6. Liquidity policy (from inventory)

D. *Family Organization and Structure*
  1. Size
  2. Age composition and life-cycle stage
  3. Power structure
  4. Role allocation pattern
  5. Marital integration (Farber)

E. *Family Action Potentials*
  1. Adequacy of husband-wife communication
  2. Marital consensus
  3. Marital empathy
  4. General competency in decision-making and problem-solving (Brim Decision-Process Test)

F. *Career Patterns*
  1. Occupational mobility and career profile
  2. Residential mobility and upgrading profile
  3. Financial status profile
  4. Class mobility
  5. Education profile

G. *Planning Effectiveness*
  1. Proportion of purchases preceded by discussion, information-seeking, conferring (inventory history)
  2. Discrepancies between number of purchase plans and plans fulfilled, 15-month period
  3. Effectiveness of decision-making over 15-month period based on criteria of effective planning, rated by interviewers, 15-month period
  4. Satisfaction with items purchased, 15-month period

H. *Accumulation of Family Assets*
  1. Inventory of family possessions (tangible durable assets)
  2. Inventory of savings and other financial assets

reared in the open country share a set of values that will be somewhat more traditional, fatalistic, and magical than will people reared
in a metropolitan environment. It is not the country air but the
country associations which differentiate rural from urban residents.
Likewise, education and occupation are social-placement variables
which, when used to classify families, segregate those who are restrictive and severe in their disciplinary practices and conceptions
of parenthood from those who are permissive and developmental.
By combining education, occupation, and area of city lived in, an
Index of Social Position can be computed, which segregates families
into social classes sharing a common subculture (see, e.g., 7). Our
schema will permit the testing of the relationships between Block A
and Block B variables to ascertain whether or not the predictive
value of the former lies largely in the value orientations of families
rather than in the happenstances of social placement in the community.

The schema in Chart II.1 allows for historical and cross-sectional
analysis, because the conceptual categories provide both time-depth
variables and contemporary-attribute variables. It is possible to undertake both "discerning" analysis—through progressive cross-classi-
fication of variables—and factorial analysis. The model, finally,
permits the testing of our basic formula that high motivation,
acquaintance with means, and adequate organization to take action
are necessary for effectiveness in long-range planning.

RENDERING THE MODEL RESEARCHABLE: A RESEARCH DESIGN

Let us again phrase the research problem. We have, basically, a
problem in explanation leading to prediction, rather than, merely
description. *We wish to account for the success or failure of families
in structuring and controlling the future* as this is reflected in long-
run consumption and asset accumulation. The main subject matter
will be longitudinal patterns of earning, saving, spending, buying,
and financial planning; the basic data are sequential rather than
cross-sectional in character. The dimensions of time and timing are
crucial to the understanding of family planning; postponement of
expenditures is as important to predict as purchases. Our research
design needed to make possible long-run observations of families
through history-taking and shorter-run observations forward in time
through waves of interviews with a panel of families. To accomplish

this objective required appropriate decisions on sampling, methods of data collection, and schemes for analysis. Without making problem subordinate to method, it is nonetheless true that the theoretical design of an inquiry must be disciplined by its practical feasibility.

Who Is Being Studied?

Within the limitations of our budget, a number of possibilities for research populations occurred to us: (1) a cross-sectional sample of families at all stages of family development broadly representative of Minnesota, (2) a sample of metropolitan Twin Cities families encompassing two or more generations but unrelated, (3) an intergenerational sample of intact three-generation families representative of Minneapolis–St. Paul.

Although we recognized the possibility of undue residential stability in the third alternative, the advantages it offered for our family development framework were substantial. The population of families could be regionally homogeneous, largely urban, and intergenerationally linked, thus holding constant the variables of region, urbanity, and variations in private family culture. Moreover, it would offer depth historically and permit the type of intergenerational comparison that no study had yet undertaken.

We were fortunate in being able, through the generous co-operation of the Research Department of the *Minneapolis Star and Tribune,* to tap a series of area-probability samples of families in the Twin Cities. In surveys undertaken during the period of our tooling up, respondents were asked about their membership in three-generation families. Roughly 4% of 3,000 opinion-poll respondents reported such three-generation linkages, with their kin resident within a 50-mile radius of the Twin Cities. This has made it possible to identify 360 nuclear families linked in threes, 120 grandparent families, 120 parent families, and 120 young married children families.

Through this device of three-generation families, it is believed that the excessive cost and awkwardness of a truly longitudinal study, which would try to follow families for an entire generation, can be avoided without sacrificing more than a few of the benefits of a longitudinal study.[4]

---

[4] Other trials and tribulations of longitudinal studies which we are avoiding through the three-generation device can be noted in the recent evaluation of the longitudinal method in child development and physical growth research. See Dankward Kodlin and Donovan J. Thompson (8).

By means of intergenerational comparisons, continuity in the transmission of family culture can be noted. Such data also permit us to take into account changes due to historical circumstances such as wars, depressions, and periods of inflation. Patterns of family spending and consumption change over time, partly because family members grow older and partly because historical circumstances shift. From intergenerational data it is hoped that we can distinguish the continuities and changes that can be generalized as part of life-cycle development from those that are adventitious or due to historical circumstances.

The sample is weighted by residentially stable families, because if the generations had moved outside the area, they would not be represented. Yet, when plotted on a map, the families are ecologically dispersed among all major neighborhoods of the metropolitan area. Since the respondent families were originally obtained through surveys that included basic demographic information, it will be possible to compare our sample of three-generation families with the pool from which they were selected for whatever bias has been introduced by our method of selection.

How Will Families Be Studied?

A number of strategies were open to us in the choice of methods of data collection. Interviews, tests, questionnaires, diaries, records, and projectives had all been suggested. Choice of informant was an issue, whether to use husband or wife, or both in joint interviews. Panel interviews, poll type interviews, or depth interviews constituted still another dimension to consider.

We decided that our chief reliance in technique would be on standard semistructured interviewing procedures. Respondents would be interviewed in their own homes, where interviewers could obtain the data necessary for interviewer ratings from direct observations at the same time that they conducted formal interviews. A sequential system of interviews seemed indicated. Families are being interviewed in five waves, once every three months, covering a 15-month period. One purpose of repeated interviewing for the period of a year is to encompass a complete annual cycle, thus accounting for seasonal variations in routine. The repeated interviewing also enables us to conform to the principles of a longitudinal study for the year of data-gathering. To supplement this year's data with retrospective history-taking, we shall have to rely for the past on respondents' memories and powers of verbalization, as assisted and checked by the testimony of the prior and succeeding generations.

Interview content for successive waves of interviews is designated in Chart II.2. The chart indicates that content will divide into a part that is repeated at each wave and a part that is different; the former will deal primarily with recent and immediately prospective purchase plans, or other changes in status, and their fulfillment or modification, whereas the latter will deal with the intergenerational history of the family and its long-range financial goals and commitments. At each interview, data about family attributes (termed cross-sectional explanatory variables in the chart) are elicited by pencil-paper tests or questionnaires.

During each wave after the initial one, one-fourth of the families will be seen in a joint interview with both husband and wife present, during which they will discuss their family goals and policies, questions of authority, decision-making, division of labor, and those items, such as the financial aspects, on which the husband is likely to be the more expert informant. From the joint interview, the interviewer will observe husband-wife interaction directly on a number of issues requiring reconciliation of differences, to give him the basis for rating the adequacy of communication between husband and wife, the degree of consensus they demonstrate, the locus of initiative-taking, and the locus of power in decision-making in the family.

With the exception of this joint interview, the wife will be the spokesman for the family. Previous studies have verified the high reliability of the wife as informant for the family. Most recently, Elizabeth Wolgast has found the wife equally well informed, and more accurate in predicting the fulfillment of purchase plans than the husband (12). From the standpoint of expediency, the wife is by far the most accessible family informant for repeated interviews.

Beginning with the first interview, the history of each status variable is taken one at a time, with residential status in the first meeting and supportive services in the fifth wave. Expected changes in each of the five statuses are noted to be checked in subsequent waves. Thus, in five waves a life-cycle pattern for each family on residential mobility, family composition, occupational careers, financial growth, and supportive-services use will have been elicited.

The dependent variable data are gathered longitudinally by interview exclusively, by obtaining in the first wave the inventory of

CHART II.2

PROPOSED CONTENT OF INTERVIEWS AND TESTS FOR FIVE WAVES

FAMILY INVENTORY STUDY

Type of Variables Treated	Wave 1	Wave 2	Wave 3	Wave 4	Wave 5
Cross-sectional Explanatory Variables					
a. self-reporting	a. (1) role allocation (2) power structure	a. (1) BGL cognitive values (2) Blood conceptions of parenthood	a. (1) communication-empathy (2) social participation	a. (1) BGL decision-making test	a. (1) family living style—diet, vacations (2) marital integration test
b. observer rating (based on joint interview)		b. ¼ of sample joint interview (1) Foote test of decision-making demonstration of affection role allocation (2) family goals—progress	b. ¼ joint interview (1) ditto (2) ditto	b. ¼ joint interview (1) ditto (2) ditto	b. ¼ joint interview (1) ditto (2) ditto
Historical Environmental Variables	1. Residential Status and History	1. checking changes and reasons for changes with generation once removed	1. changes in residential status	1. changes in residential status	1. changes in residential status
	2. family composition status	2. Family Composition, History and Changes In	2. checking family comp., history and changes	2. changes in family comp.	2. changes in family comp.

3.		occupational and educational status	Employment, History and Changes In	checking job changes with generation once removed and changes	changes in job status
4.		financial status	changes in financial status	Financial History and Changes In	checking financial history and changes in
5.		supportive services status	changes in supportive services	changes in supportive services	Supportive Services, History and Changes In
Longitudinal Dependent Variables — 1.	inventory of durable possessions	changes in inventory since Wave I (outcome) (a) confrontation of discrepancies (b) what happened?	changes in past 3 mos. (a) ditto (b) ditto (c) impact of interview on plans	changes in past 3 mos. (a) ditto (b) ditto (c) impact of interview on plans	changes in past 3 mos. (a) ditto (b) ditto (c) impact of interview
2.	one-fifth of history of inventory	second fifth of history of inventory	third fifth of inventory history	fourth fifth of inventory history	completion of history of inventory
3.	expectations of purchases next 3 mos.	expectations or purchases	expected changes	expected changes	satisfaction test on items acquired over period
4.		interviewer rating of decision-making effectiveness	interviewer rating of decision-making	interviewer rating	interviewer's over-all rating for entire period

durable possessions and making a beginning on the history of each possession. The inventory is a selected sample of the durable items listed by the LIFE study and includes items from the categories of labor-savers, comforts, time-fillers, and status indicators. At each wave, expectations of purchases during the next three months are elicited and the extent of commitment to the expenditure probed. On the second and subsequent waves, changes in the inventory are noted and discrepancies between expectations and outcomes discussed. An account of the reasons for postponement, the change in importance now ascribed to the expected but postponed purchase, and the interplay of members about the purchase or failure to buy will be obtained.

This concentration on *what happens between waves* distinguishes this longitudinal study of decision-making from most panel studies, which merely observe changes in opinion on issues at different points in time or collect evidence of fulfillment or nonfulfillment of purchase plans at specified points in time. The advantage of taking soundings at different points of time is lost unless linkages of a process nature are made *in between* to account for change or non-change, wherever this is discrepant with expectations.

At the end of each confrontation interview in which discrepancies between plans and fulfillments are discussed, the interviewer will make a rating on the decision-making effectiveness of the family for the period covered. This procedure will be followed for the last four waves, ending with an over-all rating by the interviewer of the planning effectiveness of the family over the 15-month period. These ratings will be an attempt to evaluate what might be called the "consumership" of the family. They will take into account the planfulness, judgment shown, adequacy of information on which decisions are based, and extent to which long-range and short-range outcomes are considered in arriving at decisions. Advance training in rating from role-playing skits will be provided interviewers.

The hazard of *attrition* is grave for this study, since every family we lose for whatever reason represents a total loss of 15 interviews. We feel keenly the importance of minimizing panel attrition. Our initial contact with the families is a letter from the Director of the Minnesota Family Study Center of the University of Minnesota telling them of the purpose of the study and its importance. Much is made of the facts that this is a pioneering study of three-generation families, that such families are hard to find, and that they are rare and important people. Interviewers so far have found the doors open when they arrive and have been able to move ahead quickly to obtain commitments to participate, through the high interest of these families in intergenerational comparisons.

Interviewers themselves have been carefully selected and trained. They have been exposed to much more difficult stress situations than they are likely to encounter in the field. Taped interviews with tricky responses have been used to develop skill in probing for clarification and in accurate recording. An important part of interviewer training has been the involvement and commitment of the interviewers to the research idea, which has been made possible by their participation in the final stages of constructing and pretesting the original interview schedules. Interviewers are expected to develop high rapport with their families, since they will remain with the same families for 15 months, barring unforeseen contingencies. A supervisor operates as troubleshooter when emergencies arise, to follow up on reluctant families. We cannot afford and do not anticipate the amount of attrition experienced by the Ferber panel in Illinois (2, pp. 10–12).

An equally serious problem with our type of research design is the possible reflexive or practice effect of being interviewed over the 15 months on the planning effectiveness of the families. This problem of conditioning panel families has not been given the attention it deserves, but a beginning has been made. Sandage found no marked evidence of bias developing in panel members either in beliefs or information about co-operatives and chain stores as a consequence of prolonged membership of up to seven years in a consumer panel of farm families, when compared with newly added panel members (10). Ferber, however, found his more frequently interviewed panel members purchased more and were more accurate as a consequence of being studied. He has no measures to indicate that they also became more planful or that they became more effective in fulfilling their purchase plans (2, p. 11). We will be able to make the same tests of reflexivity that Ferber did, but hope to go further. As part of each interview after the first wave, we expect to ask the respondent if any discussions in the family between waves made mention of the interview or the interviewer and what difference, if any, this made in the plans arrived at.

Problems of operationalizing conceptual variables are great for certain parts of the theoretic model depicted in Chart II.1. Many of the self-reporting items among the cross-sectional variables in the top row of Chart II.2 can be collected by tests and scales already used in other studies, and employing them will further standardize their use. Two tests devised by Orville Brim and colleagues, the Cognitive Values test and the Decision Process test, are particularly appropriate to our study. We have also utilized previously developed tests for power structure, role allocation, conceptions of parenthood, social participation, communication-empathy, marital integration, and marital consensus.

We are less fortunate with other categories of variables and will be undertaking the operationalizing of concepts, measurement of which will be shaky at best. The measures of planning effectiveness are subject to such criticism, because they will be based on interviewer ratings of consumership or effective planning and decision-making over a 15-month period, on a satisfaction test covering items purchased over the 15-month period, and on the discrepancies between purchase plans made and purchase plans fulfilled over the same period. An over-all index of planning effectiveness will be constructed from these scores to make up our chief dependent variable.

How Will the Data Be Analyzed?

The possibilities for data analysis are enormous. There will be rich materials for sheer description of the processes of family planning and decision-making, comparing three generations of the same family line. Descriptive analysis should make clear the types of issues and problems that families have been most planful about, what they leave to chance, and what they tend to handle impulsively. The major sources of influence in setting long-term goals can also be identified through descriptive analysis—immediate family, kin, neighbors, age peers, mass media, or professionals. Descriptive analysis of the retrospective data should reveal patterns of family policy formation, how long a family takes to develop a consistent set of family policies with respect to housing, education, health, and possessions, and whether such policies are transmitted from generation to generation or are developed afresh by families from considerable trial-and-error experience.

At the more analytic level, the schema depicted in Chart II.1 provides a model for factor analysis by blocks of variables and for multiple and partial correlation analysis of the variance in the dependent variables explained by all blocks of explanatory variables. Covariance analysis of the longitudinal scores appears indicated when measures over the five waves are placed in juxtaposition.

The systematic construction of typologies from career pattern data in the family history offers still another mode of explaining variation in planning effectiveness. Similarly, intergenerational analysis can be undertaken in comparing the patterns of purchasing, planning horizons, use of savings and credit, and patterns of family acquisition by generations for the same stages of the family cycle.

The research design also permits comparing the predictive value of *self-reported* data with *direct observations* by interviewers. Similarly, the comparative value of cross-sectional data, historical data, intergenerational data, and longitudinal data for prediction of planning effectiveness can also be tested.

IMPLICATIONS FOR FURTHER INVESTIGATIONS OF CONSUMER BEHAVIOR

The longitudinal dimension of consumer behavior has been consciously but reluctantly neglected by previous investigators because of the high cost entailed, yet all authorities agree on the desirability of such studies. By joining the theoretical interest of sociology in family development with its methodological interest in intergenerational comparisons, we have provided a device for obtaining the benefits of longitudinal study without having to follow families for 20 or more years. By comparing generations of the same lineal families over their histories from marriage to the present, and by observing their consumption behavior over 15 months, an effective compromise or synthesis of the several considerations involved has been achieved. Our research should open up the way for long-range planning by producers of consumer products to become more fully co-ordinated with long-range planning by their customers. Illumination of the various patterns by which families cope with the years-long problem of financing major purchases (houses, cars, children, major appliances, education, retirement) should prove of strategic usefulness in contemplating how demand might be stabilized or how credit costs might be lowered without reducing purchases.

If the study furnishes better predictors of consumer purchases than are now available, these will also have implications (1) for determining what differentiations in consumer buying styles or policies should be matched by differentiations in products or modes of distribution (choice of clientele), (2) for regulating rates of obsolescence and innovation, and (3) for gauging how business should respond to secular trends in consumer preferences for leisure and services as opposed to goods.

If the intercorrelations of these sequences of family acquisition and development can be illuminated, these will have implications for understanding some of the stabilities and instabilities of consumer decision-making, the potentialities for upgrading consumership, and the dynamics of investment by families of varying portions of their income.

Finally, if the solutions to the field and analysis problems encountered prove sound, a path will have been broken for future longitudinal studies more within the limits of existing resources, much existing cross-sectional data will become more meaningful, and some of the errors deriving from inadequacies of cross-sectional data may be detected. Some light should be shed on the ever-vexing problem of how to assess the predictiveness or validity of statements of consumer intentions against later behavior, a check that can obviously be applied only longitudinally. Progressively a better answer can be given to the question of what differences among cross-sectional, panel, and longitudinal studies determine when each is most appropriate.

REFERENCES

1. DUVALL, EVELYN M. *Family Development*. Chicago: Lippincott, 1957.
2. FERBER, ROBERT. *Factors Influencing Durable Goods Purchases*. Urbana, Illinois: Bureau of Economic and Business Research, 1955.
3. GEIGER, KENT. "Deprivation and Solidarity in the Soviet Urban Family," *Am. Sociological Rev., 20* (Jan., 1955), 57–68.
4. GODFREY, ELEANOR. *A Construction of Family Typologies and Their Initial Verification*. Cambridge, Massachusetts: Radcliffe College, 1951.
5. HILL, REUBEN. *Sociology of Marriage and Family Behavior, 1945–56*. London: International Sociological Association and UNESCO, 1958. Published also as Vol. VII, No. 1 of *Current Sociology*.
6. ———, J. MAYONE STYCOS, and KURT W. BACK. *The Family and Population Control*. Chapel Hill: University of North Carolina Press, 1958.
7. HOLLINGSHEAD, AUGUST B., and FREDERICK C. REDLICH. *Social Class and Mental Illness*. New York: Wiley, 1958.
8. KODLIN, DANKWARD, and DONOVAN J. THOMPSON. *An Appraisal of the Longitudinal Approach to Studies of Growth and Development*. Lafayette, Indiana: Society for Research in Child Development, 1958.
9. LEVY, MARION. *The Family Revolution in Modern China*. Cambridge, Massachusetts: Harvard University Press, 1949.
10. SANDAGE, C. H. "Do Research Panels Wear Out?" *J. Marketing xx*, 5 (April, 1956), 399–401.
11. STRODTBECK, FRED L. "Husband-Wife Interaction over Revealed Differences," *Am. Sociological Rev., 16* (Aug., 1951), 468–73.
12. WOLGAST, ELIZABETH H. "Do Husbands or Wives Make the Purchasing Decisions?" *J. Marketing, 23* (Oct., 1958), 151–58.

Household Decision-Making

‖

JAMES N. MORGAN

The purposes of this paper are to formulate a rather general theory about household decision-making in areas of decision of major importance to the family in our own culture, and then briefly to relate this theory to research already done and to propose a design for future research. The theory is an eclectic one that attempts to make use of variables at several different levels of abstraction, including some from personality psychology. Its major innovation is an attempt to separate the forces affecting an individual into two parts—those relevant to the decision as such (a bachelor theory), and those relevant to the individual's relationships with the rest of the family.

Restrictions to a Class of Decisions and Culture

If a theory is to be useful in research, it usually has to be somewhat less than universal; or at least one must select the aspects of behavior relevant to the problems to be studied. Both the level at which one operates (basic causes, intervening variables) and the limited set of variables one selects to measure and test depend on the researcher's judgment about how to develop an operational theory for the problem at hand. In laboratory situations where one can keep some variables constant, this is obvious. In less controlled situations, decisions about which variables to measure and use are difficult at best even if one deals only with a narrow class of actions.

Originally I intended to try to spell out the over-all outlines of a general theory of household decision-making in two stages, one at the individual level and the other at the level where the individual preferences were combined to come to a family decision. It soon became obvious that this was too ambitious an effort, and I intend to limit my responsibility somewhat in the following ways:

1. Only decisions that are salient and important to more than one member are to be considered: (a) Although there may be some role differentiation within the family even on these decisions, the final decision is one not likely to be delegated to a single member. (b) There should be only minor reliance on habit, cues from similar situations, what others do, or what the advertiser suggests. The individual's motives and insights should be important. (c) These decisions are also those of economic importance to society—the decisions that determine changes in consumer saving and spending and changes in consumer assets and debts.

2. Patterns of decision-making that are unusual and infrequent in society as a whole will be neglected. Compulsive patterns that do not adjust to changing situations, e.g., the use of spending-saving decisions to satisfy pathological aggressions, are assumed to be infrequent and will be neglected.

3. I shall not discuss situations in which the individual really has no freedom of action because laws or social regulation or his own previous decisions have predetermined what he "must" do. This is not an absolutely clear distinction, but a predetermined decision may be thought of as one in which an action has only very inferior competing alternatives involving a lot of trouble, e.g., mortgage payments are made in most cases.

4. Our attention will be concentrated on the present-day United States, leaving intercultural differences and long-term changes in behavior patterns to others more expert in these areas. (a) This is an affluent society, where there is much opportunity for social-psychological motives as well as physiological needs to affect behavior of consumers. (b) There are culturally accepted roles and patterns of behavior that affect household decision-making and that we can take for granted as long as we are building a theory to explain behavior only within the culture. (c) Specifically, there is evidence in our culture of a tendency for husband and wife to do things together and to make decisions jointly, rather than any of the three other possible patterns delineated by Herbst: father domination, mother

domination, or division of authority into separate realms of influence. This tendency is particularly strong for the salient decisions I intend to discuss. Even simple questions as to who makes the final decision (which are somewhat biased toward getting answers in terms of a division of power) generally result in answers that the decision is made jointly (48, 14, 11, 6, 4, 62). Differences appear mostly in decision areas where the culture assumes some greater interest or responsibility of husband or wife, e.g., the car for the husband, certain child-rearing or home-care decisions for the wife, or in minor personal purchases. Furthermore, most research as to who is the more reliable respondent on past behavior, plans to buy, or even attitudes finds that either husband or wife gives about the same results and of roughly equal reliability (62, 53, 16, 14).

Having thus set aside what may well be, for many, some of the more interesting problems and some of the more easily researchable ones, such as role differentiation in the family, intercultural differences, pathological conflict within the family, or pathological individual behavior, we turn to an examination of the decision-making in reasonably normal families in contemporary Western capitalistic society when the decisions have to do with things of some importance to more than one family member.

While the *process* of decision-making and the differentiated roles of husband, wife, and others in this process are interesting and important (54, 55, 10, 65, 20), it seems to me that we must first go back and ask what motivates the individuals in a family, before we can have a theory of how they interact to make decisions. Otherwise, we shall be in the position of bringing in individual motives piecemeal and somewhat *ad hoc,* to explain, for instance, why one person mostly makes affective supportive contributions to family decision-making and another person concentrates on problem-solving, marshaling facts or making suggestions, or why one person seems to exert more power and to make decisions that change others' behavior in the family. Although there may be culturally determined roles that individuals play in the family and interesting differences from culture to culture, we submit that there are other variables affecting family decision-making and we need to start with a theory that includes them.

Our problem then is how we can (1) develop an adequate theory of individual preferences and contributions to a group decision, (2) add a compatible theory of group decision-making in the family, and

(3) make both theories operational by selecting and quantifying only the most important variables and designing methods of testing, particularly in dynamic situations.

THE INDIVIDUAL

There is no time or space to spell out in full a theory of individual motivation and personality, but some broad outlines may suffice. What determines whether an individual feels that a particular course of action is urgent, acceptable, or strenuously to be opposed? Somewhere between the magnificent complexity of the clinician's answer and the absurd deductive simplicity of the economist's indifference surface, there must be a workable theoretical structure with which we can start.

A first contribution of the economist to this problem is his insistence that any decision to act is a choice between alternative courses of action and that there may be more than two alternatives. If one could think of "saving" as a decision, there are many desires that call for spending, and we must either generalize and combine them under some general rubric like the "marginal utility of money spent now" or select only the most promising alternative (the most urgent and appealing purchase or expenditure) for comparison. In order to keep things simple, we choose the latter alternative, i.e., to consider an individual deciding between a course of action and its most appealing alternative. As other alternatives occur and attract his attention, we must repeat our analysis.

Finally, since the attractiveness of any course involves the same sort of analysis, we can end up considering what it is that makes any one course of action attractive or repellent or uninteresting, keeping in mind that this process will have to be repeated not only for each alternative, but again for every change in the situation, or in the individual's information or his insights.

Attractiveness of a Course of Action to an Individual

Let us now focus on the individual's assessment of a single course of action, remembering that the same assessment must be made of its alternatives (including the alternative of doing nothing, which in consumer decisions often means saving the money temporarily).

We must now start using words which, even more than some we have already employed, are used differently in different social sciences and even by different individuals within disciplines. If the reader will assume in any case that a given term is *not* being used in the way customarily accepted in his own field, misunderstanding will be less likely. In the words of Humpty-Dumpty, "When I use a word, it means just what I choose it to mean—neither more nor less."

A. Each individual has certain stable characteristics that affect his decisions or preferences. These can be classified as physical and social needs, but within each group there are serious problems about the degree of detail in which to classify them. We certainly do not want to invent a new "need" to explain each action, particularly if we must then devise methods of measuring and quantifying each of these.

At the physical level, where the economist has traditionally operated, we can think of an individual needing and enjoying food, shelter, clothing, sex, and the arts (creatively or as pleasurable input stimuli) in degrees that are determined both by his physiology and by his education in appreciation. In a dynamic world, future needs require some present economic security as well, e.g., through saving.

At the "social level," where the personality psychologist has concentrated, we can think of an individual as attaching importance to things for reasons other than their physical impact on him, even though in translation this may affect his desires for the physical pleasures. Let us list a few which seem to be the most important, and which have been investigated: *Achievement*—a disposition to overcome obstacles by one's own efforts, to solve problems, to get ahead, in order to experience pride in the successful exercise of talent. Atkinson, McClelland, and others have done a great deal with this, first in laboratory situations, and second in some intercultural comparisons. It would appear a most crucial variable in theories of business behavior as well as consumer behavior. *Affiliation*—the disposition to belong, to be loved by others. To the extent that one wants to "belong" to groups in society and does so voluntarily, this would appear to be what the sociologist means by "perceived role" or "reference group" behavior. In other words, one acts as he is expected to or as some valued group does, in order to gain their acceptance and affection, or perhaps just to express this affection without thought of return. As we shall see later, however, when we look at the family as a group, this motive would appear also to be the major path through which the desires of others in the family would become a part of the desires of each individual in it. Hence, the motive enters at two stages and perhaps with different effects. *Power* —the disposition to influence others and to resist being subject to their wills. Upward mobility and drives toward social status may be an expression of the need for power, but they may also result from a need for achievement. Again, this motive comes in not only here but later within the family, if dominating others in the family is seen by the individual as an expression of power. This would, of course, lead to some conflict in the family, to be resolved by compromise, division of spheres of influence, or a pattern of dominance if others feel that other needs (physical wants, affiliation) satisfied by keeping the family together are more important to them.

These basic personality dispositions may well not be conscious desires or, if conscious desires, may not be expressed in verbalized attitudes. Also, one cannot tell from observing an act just which personality needs are being satisfied, and there may be several different acts that are functionally equivalent in satisfying a particular need. Attitude scales such as those for authoritarianism may well be related, say, to the need for power, but there is some evidence that verbally expressed attitudes and values differ from measures of needs derived from imaginative creations like those in the Thematic Apperception Test. Methods of assessing these three motives or personality dispositions quantitatively have been developed and tested in the laboratory for their predictive ability (1). They have also been used in national field surveys without major difficulties and hence offer promise of providing motivational data more basic than expressed attitudes and yet measurable even in personal interview surveys on large populations.

How many more motives need to be added? Or should we insist on incorporating other needs under these three rubrics? One other motive frequently mentioned is curiosity—the disposition to want to try new things, explore, make sure one's past experience is still relevant. This seems likely to be important in such minor decisions as which brand to buy, but it may also affect willingness to try a new product, to move, to change jobs.

At any rate, the individual is seen as having stable, basic, physical and social needs that result from his physiological make-up and his early childhood experiences and training. There may be more basic things, like anality, behind them, and they may express themselves in more specific values or even more specific attitudes, but they represent one important level of variables.

If the economist would admit social as well as physical wants into the picture, the "indifference surface" of Pareto and of modern consumption theory becomes a conceptualization of the individual's need structure. The social needs are even more likely than the physiological to vary from individual to individual, of course.

B. At any point in time, these needs become relevant only as they are perceived to be involved in the outcome of a path of action being considered. How much any act will be seen as contributing to the satisfaction of some basic need will depend on the situation at the moment. Atkinson calls this the "incentive value" of an outcome. One's experience tells him that a certain outcome gives him a sense of achievement or affiliation or power or physical well-being, or he may infer it from the actions or reports of others. In the physical area, the distinction between a basic need and the incentive value of a particular outcome is analogous to the distinction between the position of food in a preference function (marginal utility curve) and the expected marginal utility (added satisfaction) from eating one more piece of apple pie just now. The latter clearly depends on how one ranks apple pie as a food and how many pieces of apple pie one has had recently. One achievement depreciates the future incentive value of that particular success and induces one to want to succeed in the future at harder tasks. We can think, then, of basic personality characteristics combining with the facts of the present situation to produce expected subjective utilities of the outcome expected from some action or decision.

C. In this world, we must always add the element of uncertainty. Of many decisions we are not quite sure just what the outcome will be or that the expected satisfactions will really result from it. We have subjective probabilities but no certainty. In practice, these expectations will be affected by information, particularly information that leads one to expect certain outcomes. Generalization from previous experience or from decisions made in similar situations in the past will affect the strength of these expectations or subjective probabilities. Even when the objective facts are the same, as in the laboratory when individuals are told their chances of winning are 50–50, there may be individual differences in the expectancies or subjective probabilities held by the individuals. We dodge for the moment the problem of whether they are uncertainties or probabilities and are somehow measurable.

Our model, which we have really taken from personality theory, then says that an individual confronts a particular decision as it contributes in various measure to his basic needs, the contribution depending on the current situation and its uncertainties as well as the relative importance of the stable needs. Given the constraints of the situation, and perhaps certain decision-making characteristics of the individual, the evaluation of a course of action and of its closest rivals should lead to some decision or choice or, in the family, to a pattern of negotiation and discussion with others in the family. (See Chart II.3) One should not neglect the importance of experience and of habit as factors influencing preferences among alternatives. Recent experience affects the incentives and the subjective probabilities, whereas habit and inertia may well operate to produce resist-

CHART II.3

INDIVIDUAL PREFERENCE FOR ALTERNATIVE "A" PER SE

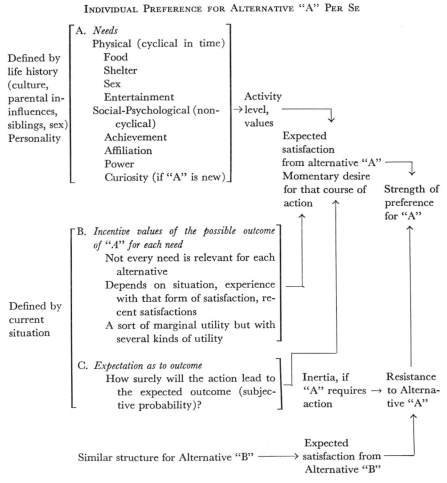

ance to an alternative if it requires an active decision. One might argue, however, that curiosity and habit-inertia are two ends of the same personality scale.

In some situations, at least, these forces may well result in expected satisfactions and even felt desires that can be elicited directly by questioning individuals. However, if our major purpose is to examine the process of decision-making in the family, reliance on such expressions may prove quite dangerous, as we shall see. We turn now to consideration of the way in which individual preferences related to individual satisfactions expected from the course of action combine with other considerations when the family must make a decision.

COMBINING INDIVIDUAL PREFERENCES INTO A FAMILY DECISION

If one wants to investigate the process of decision-making in the family, it is not enough to measure the intensity with which each individual feels a desire for a particular action for its own sake, and his power in the family. We need to know also the degree to which he or she is concerned (a) with the desires and feelings of others in the family, or (b) with exerting power over the family, independently of the content of the particular decision. Concern for what others in the family want clearly can arise from a need for affiliation, as an expression of affection freely given or given in the hope of receiving affection in return. It might also arise from more mundane necessities for keeping the family together as a mechanism for satisfying physical wants. Such a concern might lead to supportive statements in family discussions, but these are only one possible form of expression.

The desire to exert power over others in the family arises from the strength of a basic personality disposition, but the exercise of power presumably depends also on the way the situation is perceived by the individual and on his ability to exert power. Some have hypothesized that ability to exert power depends on one's contribution (economic or other) to the group, but it may also depend on the degree to which others have opposing preferences, one's expertise, culturally determined roles, and the extent to which others value affiliation rather than power in the family (61, 24, 5, 17).

In other words, we see each family decision as a two-stage process. Each individual has his own needs and preferences, his information and expectations, some of which concern the decision *per se,* others, his relation to others in the family. When decisions are made, whether ostensibly by an individual or "by the family," some explicit or implicit process is involved by which the resultant desires of each member of the family are taken into account. If overt discussion is involved, individuals may actually learn more about the feelings of others, or about the situation, and hence may change their own expressed preferences. In an ongoing group like a family, there is a vast reservoir of experiences on which to base judgments about what others want and why, so that, particularly among older couples, very little discussion may be required, and there may appear to be much division of labor in deciding or doing things. At the moment of decision, however, there must be some process by which the desires of the individuals combine to determine the outcome.

The model of individuals thinking only of themselves leads to a power-structure interpretation of the family that seems most unrealistic. The other extreme, where everyone thinks *only* of what the others want, leads to the situation delightfully pictured in C. S. Lewis' *Screwtape Letters:*

> In discussing any joint action, it becomes obligatory that A should argue in favor of B's supposed wishes and against his own, while B does the opposite. It is often impossible to find out either party's real wishes; with luck, they end by doing something that neither wants, while each feels a glow of selfrighteousness and harbours a secret claim to preferential treatment for the unselfishness shown and a secret grudge against the other for the ease with which the sacrifice has been accepted. Later on you can venture on what may be called the Generous Conflict Illusion. This game is best played with more than two players, in a family with grown-up children for example. Something quite trivial, like having tea in the garden, is proposed. One member takes care to make it quite clear (though not in so many words) that he would rather not but is, of course, prepared to do so out of "Unselfishness." The others instantly withdraw their proposal, ostensibly through their "Unselfishness," but really because they don't want to be used as a sort of lay figure on which the first speaker practices petty altruisms. But he is not going to be done out of his debauch of Unselfishness either. He insists on doing "what the others want." They insist on doing what he wants. Passions are roused. Soon someone is saying, "Very well then, I won't have any tea at all," and a real quarrel ensues with bitter resentment on both sides (34, pp. 133–34).

A more interesting and probably more frequent class of cases is that in which there is some conflict still to be resolved within the family, and/or some uncertainty about the facts of the situation or the feelings of other members of the family. In this type of situation, some sort of communication presumably takes place both so that each may learn more and so that some resolution, perhaps temporary, of the conflict takes place.

We come back then to the problem how each individual can take into account in his own preference function the desires of others in the family (which he values because he feels a need for "affiliation" and perhaps also because of more mundane necessities for keeping the family together) and yet communicate his own feelings so as not to fall into the trap pictured in the *Screwtape Letters*. A second problem is how each individual's desire for power and influence can receive some attention without making the family a battleground or an authoritarian power structure complete with one or a series of "pecking orders" for various classes of decisions.

First in simplicity, but last in time, is the final instant of making the decision manifest. One could argue that each individual has a strength of preference for a particular alternative depending on his own needs, including his desire to exert power and his desire to give and receive affection by doing what others desire, and that this is weighted by some index of his "power" in the family. The alternative with the most "weighted preference" would then win.

Some have argued that such pure power in the family depends on one's contributions to the family, in an analogy to the economic system where marginal productivity determines income, which in turn becomes a measure of the demands one can put on the system for goods and services (61). There are difficulties, however, in separating such power from the way in which one person's desires win because they are strong and because others in the family prefer to keep the family a united and happy one rather than to win decisions. We have already built in the desire to exert power at two stages: those relevant to the actual alternatives, and those relevant to the power implications for an individual, if the family chooses what he wants rather than what others want. French and Raven distinguish five different sources of power over another person, with different bases and different potential effects. These five agree roughly with the factors on the diagram.

Chart II.4 pictures the way in which the individual preference for a course of action "A" is combined with other motivation stemming from his relationships with the others in his family, to produce whatever actions or expressions he makes during the decision-making process.

Even more than in Chart II.3, we appear to be dealing with a situation in which it may be easier to measure more variables at more basic levels rather than the somewhat fewer intermediate resultant variables. In other words, while one might be able to measure whether or not an individual knew what others in the family preferred and whether he had a high need for affiliation and a perception that paying attention to the needs of others in the family would lead to an affectionate return from them, it would be most difficult to measure by direct questions the degree to which an individual "voted" for one course in family discussions because he felt

CHART II.4

THE INDIVIDUAL "X" CONTRIBUTES TO A FAMILY
DECISION ABOUT ALTERNATIVE "A"

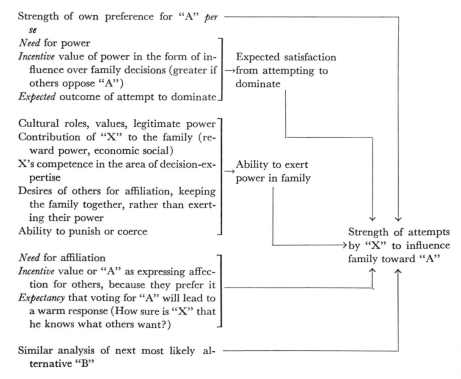

it was what the others preferred. It would appear to be even more difficult to get individuals to report a desire to exert power over other members of the family by dominating a decision, without regard to the specific content of the decision. Finally, as French and Raven point out, power and influence are not the same thing. Power is only *potential* influence.

Making Theory Researchable

There has been some research directly on family decision-making, and a great deal of research on *ad hoc* groups that is only indirectly relevant. There has been a tendency to restrict explanatory variables to easily measured demographic facts like age, sex, and social class, which intersect with the variables of our theory in a complex way difficult to unravel. The dependent variables have been numerous but generally not completely satisfactory, and they have given inconclusive and at times apparently contradictory results. The following dependent variables have been used:

1. Direct questions as to how conflicts are resolved in the family, i.e., who gives in? (62, 18).

2. Questions as to who usually decides, for each of a selected list of decisions, usually purchase decisions. Sometimes these questions are asked of children, sometimes of parents (48, 62, 3, 61, 14, 58, 23).

3. Questions as to what has been purchased, to see who remembers what things and forgets what things (16).

4. Questions about purchase plans to see who plans what type of purchases or ascribes such plans to spouse (62).

5. Attitudes about family roles (24, 29, 30).

6. Analysis from reinterviews as to whose plans or reports predict best what the family actually does (62).

7. Questions on who decides and also on who carries out the action, power being measured by deciding on things that someone else in the family does (24).

8. Observation and quantification of the discussion process in making family decisions in imaginary problems posed by the experimenter, measuring the types of contributions to the discussion (56, 57, 20).

9. Similar observation of family decision processes, measuring influence or power by the proportion of purchases suggested by an in-

dividual which is finally agreed upon, and the amounts of money the family agrees to spend on them (30).

There are a number of problems with these measures, not the least of which stems from the problem of whether we are merely trying to measure dominance or power, or whether we want some understanding of the process and the motives involved and even of the learning that takes place during the decision-making process.

One person may do most of the talking because he or she verbalizes well and knows best what others in the family want. One person may do the actual buying because this (limited) authority is delegated as a matter of division of labor in the family. Information-getting or initiation of discussion may also be delegated to individuals with more direct concern in a particular area, or more ability, or more time, without any real exertion of power by that individual over the decision.

Even more important, there may be wide differences dependent on the particular decision at stake (14). The decision whether or not to buy a car is probably less likely to be delegated even in part than the decision what make to buy, or what color, or from what dealer. This problem becomes even more serious when one attempts to compare cultures, or even subcultures (63).

Verbal reports as to who did what or who generally does what, much less why, are subject to inaccuracies and distortions. Indeed reports of lack of correlation have already appeared (18, 29, 30) when a general question on influence is compared with questions about specific decisions, or with quantified observations of the family decision-making processes. On the other hand, the direct observation of family decision-making avoids reporting errors by the respondents at the expense of focusing on decisions that are imaginary or *ad hoc* and may well be neither salient nor representative and may be affected by the observer's presence.

The research on *ad hoc* groups (mostly sophomores) has the additional difficulty that these groups start with no common experience, no patterns of behavior, no cohesion, no knowledge of the others' desires, and no prospect or need for a continuous future together. This makes the research cleaner and easier, but less directly relevant to the family (20).

Some studies have been concerned solely with showing tendencies in cultures or subcultures for husband or wife to play certain roles

in the family, both as to types of activity and amount of power exerted. There may, of course, be real differences in authority (power)
of individuals in the family either because the culture demands it or
because of the competence of the individual or his need for power
(17).

The important question here as in all ascription of behavior to
perceived role is how and why this becomes the role. It makes a
good deal of difference whether the decision-making role in a particular area is taken by the wife, say, because the culture is matriarchal, because she is competent, because the husband is not
interested in those decisions, because that area has been "traded" for
another where the husband makes the decisions, or because she is so
perceptive of the needs of the family and concerned with the welfare
of the whole family that her decisions are those which would result
from family discussion and negotiation in any case. What appears
most lacking in discussions of roles and power in the family is any
admission that anyone might be concerned with the desires of the
others in the family.

There is evidence in scattered places about differentiation of roles;
it is particularly persuasive in the cases in which it is argued that
the wife tends more to conduct the social and affective relations of
the family, within and without. A recent study of social long-distance
calls found by a multiple regression analysis that the wife's reported
feelings of affection while calling and whether or not she had relatives at a distance were significantly related to the family frequency
of long-distance calls, but that the husband's having relatives at a
distance and his feelings while calling did not seem to affect the call
rates of the family (7). While later refinement of the measures may
change the findings, preliminary data at the Survey Research Center
appear to indicate that women rate higher on needs for achievement
and affiliation, and men higher on need for power. A study of a small
group of injured female workers, mostly blue collar, in Michigan
found these working women rated high on power and achievement
and low on affiliation.

It seems wise, however, before going too far with such generalizations, to ask whether such needs by individuals should be considered as the explanatory variables, rather than sex or the culture
with which they may happen to be related. It is possible, for instance, that women with "male type" need structures do not get married, or at least do not become housewives.

Perhaps the most relevant to our discussion is the question asked in the Detroit Area Study: "When you and your husband differ about something, do you usually give in and do it your husband's way, or does he usually come around to your point of view?"

When Detroit housewives were asked this, 34% said they usually or always gave in, 24% said their husbands gave in, 2% could not answer, and the other 40% gave egalitarian responses indicating that they worked things out jointly somehow. Even this underestimates the amount of joint discussion, because many said they agreed on most things but answered this question in terms of marginal disagreement.

When an index of the relative power of the husband versus wife was made from replies on the same study as to who finally decided about eight things, it proved to be uncorrelated with answers to the single questions above (18). Furthermore, there were no differences in the index between such cultural subgroups in Detroit as immigrants, older people, uneducated, Catholics, or Michigan farmers. On the other hand, there were differences depending on education, education differentials of head and wife, whether the wife worked, and participation in outside organizations. Blood and Wolfe conclude:

> Under these circumstances power in American marriages is not so much a matter of brute coercion and unwilling defeat as a mutual recognition of individual skills in particular areas of competence and of the partners' dual stake in areas of joint concern. Given such a natural working out of particular decisions under varying circumstances, it is no wonder that most wives cannot say *why* they make decisions at home the way they do (5).

In spite of questions that may tend to induce people to say one person decides, past studies reveal a good deal of joint decision-making, even in areas where one member of the family may be more interested and report that he made the final brand selection. Automobiles are presumably the man's province, yet when one asks who in the family can report more accurately whether or not the family will buy a car, reinterview studies show that the wife is as accurate as the husband (62). Perhaps she is more reality-oriented, but certainly she is not often surprised by her husband bringing home the keys to a new car.

Proposed Research

It would appear that what is needed is some "proof of the pudding," some direct observation of what actually happens in the family, in situations in which the family is making an actual decision of some importance and the crucial exploratory variables can be measured. The kind of research that seems most promising would either follow a family through some actual, current decision process or would force some really important decision on the family and investigate how it was made.

One potential design that appears most promising would be to discuss with each member of the family what the next major purchase plans were seen to be, then ask the family à la Strodtbeck to resolve these plans into a set of priorities. Some time later, one would reinterview each member separately as to what was actually done and why and have the family get together and agree as to why they did what they did. Various perceptions and misperceptions as to who wanted what and who exercised power in the family would be revealed in this way. Measures of the basic motive strengths (and their perceived relevance to the decisions) would also be taken for each member of the family.

What would be important is not so much who could predict what the family would do, or whose wishes seem to prevail, as the motives of the various members, the degree to which they really know what the others feel about the situation before the decision is made, the extent to which they are concerned with what the others want and with harmony in the family. With such data, one might be able to understand *why* one person's desires seemed to prevail, if they did.

Such a research design should also indicate whether there are other less idyllic resolutions of conflict in the family, such as the carving out of separate realms of power, smoldering resentment by some members, or a sort of bargaining atmosphere where votes were traded. The Bales-Strodtbeck measures from their two family studies as to individual contributions categorized as "attempts to exercise power" or "making supportive statements" could then be related to personality measures of the need for power or affiliation and perceptions relevant for the arousal of these motives in the family discussions. The three factors isolated by Carter, for instance, sound like expressions of the need for power, affiliation, and achievement (8).

The degree to which learning, both of facts and of their relationships (insights), during the course of time could also be investigated with such data. One could also tell to what extent individuals still did not communicate with one another sufficiently to know what the others wanted or felt. Some observers of the English scene point out that the wife is frequently kept in ignorance of her husband's income (37).

AGGREGATE DYNAMICS

We have addressed ourselves to the problem of how decisions are made in the family. For many economic problems, however, only changes over time in aggregate behavior of families are of real importance. For explaining and predicting such aggregate changes, a limited subset of the variables we have discussed may suffice.

It might be possible to derive and test hypotheses about the effect of changes in situations on changes in behavior, particularly in decisions where similar choices are repeated or in general decisions, such as whether to spend on current consumption, invest in consumer durables, or save. Katona has persuasively argued that changes in the current incentive value of the security feelings that come from saving may result from changed events (war, unemployment, price changes, etc.) and affect consumer willingness to spend on discretionary items like durables. One can test such a hypothesis and work with it without going back to the detailed theoretical structure. If the results are good, one assumes that the basic theory, the derived simplification, and the measurement of the variables are all adequate.

SUMMARY

We have attempted to spell out, in some detail, a theory of family decision-making and to indicate ways in which we might test the theory. It became apparent that the problem is much more complex than many have thought in the past and that thorough investigation would require going behind verbal expressions of attitudes and reasons and preferences, as well as dealing with salient family decisions in a dynamic way. The possibility that motives may operate both with respect to the decision as such and with respect to one's relationships with the rest of the family make both the theory and the research complex.

It remains possible that for many problems, such complexity need not be crippling. Particularly in our culture, where there appears to be a great deal of joint decision-making and much communication between husband and wife, one may treat the family as a unit with a single spokesman for many purposes. And if one is concerned with changes over time in aggregate behavior, it may well be possible to concentrate attention only on the situations and perceptions of them that change, neglecting the personality variables, and still be able to predict aggregate behavior.

But if we are to understand decision-making in the family, a great deal of research needs to be done, to ascertain which variables can safely be neglected and how the crucial variables remaining can be expected to operate. The innate complexity cannot be denied, but it may thus be got around, in a satisfactory model.

References and Supplemental Studies

1. Atkinson, John, ed. *Motives in Fantasy, Action and Society.* New York: D. Van Nostrand, 1958.
2. Bales, R. F., and P. E. Slater. "Role Differentiation in Small Decision-Making Groups," in *Small Groups*, eds. Hare, Borgatta, and Bales. New York: Knopf, 1955.
3. Blood, Robert. "The Division of Labor in City and Farm Families," *Marriage and Family Living*, 20 (May, 1958), 170–74.
4. ———. "The Effect of the Wife's Employment on Family Power Structure," *Social Forces*, 36 (1958), 347–52.
5. Blood, Robert, and Donald M. Wolfe. *Husbands and Wives in America: Dynamics of Married Life.* Glencoe, Illinois: Free Press, 1960.
6. Bott, Elizabeth. "Urban Families: Conjugal Roles and Social Networks," *Human Relations*, 8 (1955), 345–84.
7. Cannell, Charles, and John Lansing. "A Study of Social Long Distance Telephone Calls," forthcoming.
8. Carter, Launor F. "Evaluating the Performance of Individuals as Members of Small Groups," *Personnel Psychology*, 7 (Winter, 1954), 477–84.
9. Cartwright, Dorwin, ed. *Studies in Social Power.* Ann Arbor: Research Center for Group Dynamics, 1958.
10. Chastian, Elijah D., Jr. *An Empirical Study of the Decision-Making Process in Farm Management.* Ph.D. thesis, Purdue University, 1956.
11. Converse, Paul, and Merle Crawford. "Buying Habits in the Home," *Advertising Age* (Feb., 1950), 46–47, 144–50.
12. Dix, Louise Carter. *Decision Making in the Farm Family.* Master's thesis, Cornell University, 1957.

13. DYER, EVERETT DIXON. *Roles and Role Expectations in the Two-Income Family.* Ph.D. thesis, University of Wisconsin, 1955.

14. FAWCETT PUBLICATIONS, INC. *Male vs. Female Influence in Buying and Brand Selection.* New York: Fawcett Publications, 1958.

15. FELDT, BEATRICE LORENE. *Disagreements Between Girls and Their Parents in One Illinois High School.* Master's thesis, Iowa State College, 1957.

16. FERBER, ROBERT. "On the Reliability of Responses Secured in Sample Surveys," *J. of Am. Statistical Assoc., 50* (Sept., 1955), 788–810.

17. FRENCH, JOHN R. P., and BERTRAM RAVEN. "The Bases of Social Power," in *Studies in Social Power,* ed. Dorwin Cartwright. Ann Arbor: Research Center for Group Dynamics, 1958.

18. GOLD, MARTIN, and CAROL SLATER. "Office, Factory, Store—and Family: A Study of Integration Setting," *Am. Sociological Rev., 23* (Feb., 1958), 64–74.

19. GRIGGS, JANE. *A Study of Attitudes of "Successful" and Unsuccessful Mothers from Three Broad Socio-Economic Levels.* Master's thesis, University of Minnesota, 1957.

20. HARE, A. P., E. F. BORGATTA, and R. F. BALES, eds. *Small Groups: Studies in Social Interaction.* New York: Knopf, 1955.

21. HAYNES, ORENA. *Preferences, Practices, and Satisfactions of Husbands and Wives in the Selection, Acquisition, and Serviceability of Specific Items of the Husband's Clothing.* Master's thesis, Ohio State University, 1957.

22. HEER, DAVID M. "Dominance and the Working Wife," *Social Forces, 36* (1958), 341–47.

23. HERBST, P. G. "The Measurement of Family Relationships," *Human Relations, 5* (Feb., 1952), 3–36.

24. HOFFMAN, LOIS W. "Effects of the Employment of Mothers on Parental Power Relations and the Division of Household Tasks," *Marriage and Family Living, 22* (1960).

25. ———. *Some Effects of the Employment of Mothers on Family Structure.* Ph.D. thesis, University of Michigan, 1958.

26. HONEY, RUTH R., VIRGINIA BRITTON, and A. S. HOTCHKISS. *Decision Making in the Use of Family Financial Resources in a Rural Pennsylvania Community.* Agricultural Experiment Station Bulletin 643. University Park, Pennsylvania State University, March, 1959.

27. HUEPENBACKER, AGATHA LOUISE. *Factors that Influence Mothers and Sons in the Selection of Boys' Slacks and Shirts.* Master's thesis, Iowa State College, 1956.

28. JACOBSON, A. H. "Conflict of Attitudes Toward the Roles of the Husband and Wife in Marriage," *Am. Sociological Rev., 17* (April, 1952), 146–50.

29. KENKEL, WILLIAM F. "Influence Differentiation in Family Decision Making," *Sociology and Social Research, 42* (Sept.–Oct., 1957), 18–25.

30. KENKEL, WILLIAM F., and DEAN K. HOFFMAN. "Real and Conceived Roles in Family Decision Making," *Marriage and Family Living, 18* (Nov., 1956), 311–16.

31. KLEIN, VIOLA. *Working Wives.* Occasional Papers No. 15. London: Institute of Personnel Management, 1959.

32. KNOLL, MARJORIE M. *Economic Contributions Given to and Received from Individual Members of Families and Households in Relation to Their Financial Situations.* Ph.D. thesis, Cornell University, 1954.

33. LEVINE, DANIEL B. *Men's Preferences for Cotton, Wool and Other Fibers in Selected Clothing Items.* U. S. Department of Agriculture, AMS, Marketing Research Report No. 244. Washington, D. C.: G.P.O., 1958.

34. LEWIS, C. S. *Screwtape Letters.* New York: Macmillan, 1944.

35. LOCKE, H. J., and MURIEL MACKEPRANG. "Marital Adjustment and the Employed Wife," *Am. J. Sociology, 54* (1948–49), 536–38.

36. LONG, MARY ZOE. *Responsibilities Which Teen Agers Assume and Those Which Their Parents Would Like Them to Assume in the Care of Their Younger Siblings.* Master's thesis, Pennsylvania State University, 1957.

37. MADGE, CHARLES. *War-Time Pattern of Saving and Spending.* Cambridge, England: Cambridge University Press, 1943.

38. MARCH, C. PAUL, and A. LEE COLEMAN. "The Relationship of Kinship, Exchanging Work, and Visiting to the Adoption of Recommended Farm Practices," *Rural Sociology, 19* (Sept., 1954).

39. MOTZ, A. B. "Conceptions of Marital Roles by Status Groups," *Marriage and Family Living, 12* (1950), 136–62.

40. MUELLER, EVA, and GEORGE KATONA. "A Study of Purchase Decisions," in *Consumer Behavior,* Vol. I, ed. L. H. Clark. New York: New York University Press, 1954.

41. MURDOCK, GEORGE P. *Social Structure.* New York: Macmillan, 1949.

42. NEUGARTEN, BERNICE L. "Kansas City Study of Adult Life," in *Potentialities of Women in the Middle Years,* ed. Irma Gross. East Lansing, Michigan: Michigan State University Press, 1956.

43. OGBURN, W. F., and M. F. NIMKOFF. *Technology and the Changing Family.* Boston: Houghton Mifflin, 1955.

44. ORGANISATION FOR EUROPEAN ECONOMIC CO-OPERATION, *The Consumer's Food Buying Habits.* Paris: O.E.E.C., May, 1958.

45. POWELL, EDNA HAYNIE. *Family Relationships as Viewed by High School Youth.* Master's thesis, Florida State University, 1957.

46. RADKE, M. J. "The Relation of Parental Authority to Children's Behavior and Attitudes," *Institute of Child Welfare Monographs, 22* (1946).

47. SCHEINFELD, AMRAM. *Women and Men.* New York: Harcourt Brace, 1944.

48. SHARP, HARRY and PAUL MOTT. "Consumer Decisions in the Metropolitan Family," *J. Marketing, 21* (Oct., 1956), 149–56.

49. SHERWOOD, PAUL MILTON. *Student and Family Attitudes Toward Financing the College Experience.* PhD. thesis, University of Pittsburgh, 1956.

50. SHORT, ELSIE PHILLIPS. *Home Management Problems of Farm Families with Particular Reference to Spending Patterns.* Master's thesis, Texas Women's University, 1957.

51. SLATER, P. E. "Role Differentiation in Small Groups," *Am. Sociological Rev., 20* (1955), 300–10.

52. SMARDAN, LAURENCE E. *An Exploratory Study of Interspousal Verbal Communication Relationships.* Ph.D. thesis, Cornell University, 1957.

53. STAR, SHIRLEY A. "Obtaining Household Opinions from a Single Respondent," *Public Opinion Q., 27* (Fall, 1953), 386–91.

54. STECKLE, JEAN M. *Five Techniques Tested to Study Family Decisions in Household Processes.* Master's thesis, Cornell University, 1957.

55. STRODTBECK, FRED L. "Husband-Wife Interaction Over Revealed Differences," *Am. Sociological Rev., 26* (Aug., 1951), 468–73.

56. ———. "The Family as a Three-Person Group," *Am. Sociological Rev., 29* (Feb., 1954), 23–29.

57. ——— and R. D. MANN. "Sex Role Differentiation in Jury Deliberation," *Sociometry, 29* (March, 1956), 3–11.

58. U. S. DEPARTMENT OF AGRICULTURE, Bureau of Agricultural Economics, *Men's Preferences Among Selected Clothing Items.* Misc. Pub. 706, Washington, D. C.: G.P.O., 1949.

59. VIDICH, ARTHUR J. "Methodological Problems in the Observation of Husband-Wife Interaction," *Marriage and Family Living, 18* (1956), 355–60.
60. WILKENING, EUGENE A. "Change in Farm Technology as Related to Familism, Family Decision Making and Family Integration," *Am. Sociological Rev., 29* (Feb., 1954), 29–37.
61. WOLFE, DONALD M. "Power and Authority in the Family," in *Studies in Social Power,* ed. Cartwright (q.v.).
62. WOLGAST, ELIZABETH H. "Economic Decisions in the Family," *J. Marketing, 23* (Oct. 1958).
63. YAMAMURA, DOUGLAS S., and MAYER ZALD. "A Note on the Usefulness and Validity of the Herbst Family Questionnaire," *Human Relations, 9* (1956), 217–21.
64. YOUNG, MICHAEL. "Distribution of Income Within the Family," *British J. Sociology, 3* (Dec., 1952), 305–21.
65. ZELDITCH, MORRIS, JR. "Role Differentiation in the Nuclear Family," in *Family, Socialization and Interaction Process,* ed. Parsons and Bales. Glencoe, Illinois: Free Press, 1955.

Discussion

EDWIN J. THOMAS

Hill's paper presents a bold and creative approach to the problem of asset accumulation and family decision-making. An analytic scheme has been formulated that contains a set of numerous independent and intervening variables. The six blocks of such variables, which by my count contain reference to some 30 variables—and I am sure there are more if one were to look more searchingly—appear to be comprehensive. The array of variables is impressive, indeed staggering, when one considers the possible interrelationships among them and their relationships to the dependent variables of effectiveness in long-range planning and patterns of asset accumulation. The research scheme that was designed to gather information about these variables calls for five successive waves of interviews with a sample of 360 families characterized by ties covering three generations. The data from the interviews, the ratings of the interviewers, and tests to be administered to the families should reveal much that is not now known about what Hill has called "consumership" and about family decision-making.

This approach to the problem at hand, however, cannot properly be called a model of decision-making about the accumulation of family assets. From the scheme as it is presently conceived we can say little about how decisions in general are made. No clear-cut predictions or deviations can be made from the scheme, because it contains *no postulates or hypotheses which, when combined appro-*

priately, lead to logically consistent statements about family decisions bearing upon saving and spending.

It is correct that a central assumption has guided the research; this assumption, one recalls, was that long-range effectiveness of planning may be accounted for by motivation for planfulness, knowledge and skill in manipulating the means of planning, and the adequacy of the group organization for planning. I have little doubt that the research will corroborate this assumption, for failure to find support for it calls into question the concepts on which it is based. Let me illustrate with the concept of motivation to be planful. If motivation to be planful does not generally result in planning, when other conditions are propitious for planning, then something is wrong with the conception of motivation. Analogously, to find support for the relationship between planning and motivation to be planful serves to validate the conception of motivation. The act of planning, when an individual is in a state of drive that is linked to the goal of planfulness, i.e., is motivated to be planful, is the goal-directed behavior implicitly following from the conception of this kind of motivation. To state that a person or family who *wants* to be planful *will* be planful, when no barriers to planning are present, is perhaps something more than common sense will tell us; but my guess is that it is no more than a statement, which if true, validates the concept on which it is based.

These comments were not intended so much to be critical of Hill's analytic scheme as they were to place in perspective what it is and what it is not. Rather than being a theory or set of hypotheses, the analytic scheme, along with the research design, is a method of discovering how decisions about asset accumulation are made in the family. The scheme does not have predictive power as it is, but, as Hill has pointed out, it has great predictive potential. As such, it may be viewed as a method of discovery and may be evaluated most appropriately thus.

One criterion for evaluating the adequacy of a particular method of discovery is in terms of whether the relevant and promising independent variables have been selected for study. The likelihood of discovering what one is looking for clearly depends in part upon the most promising possible predictive variables. In general, it is my impression, as suggested by my earlier comments, that Hill's scheme is fairly comprehensive in this respect. I wondered, however, why variables of individual motivation, such as individual motives and preferences, were not included. Some of those discussed in Morgan's paper appear to be worthwhile candidates. Moreover, individual motives and preferences, as well as those that are already to be found in the analytic scheme, would seem to be called for in particular by the assumption about the importance of motivation and planning behavior. If I understand correctly the approach of family development presented by Hill, it is sufficiently eclectic to include individual variables as well as group, economic, and developmental ones.

Another way to evaluate Hill's approach is by whether the dependent variable is clearly conceived and adequately measured. The paper suggests that at least two criteria for effectiveness are employed. One concerns what might be termed the rationality of the decisions, which seems to include such matters as the amount of information gathered, the extent of discussing and conferring that precedes purchases, and whether purchase plans are in fact fulfilled. The other involves something apparently quite different: the satisfaction of the family with the items purchased. I am curious about how the variables of the two criteria are expected to be related and about why they are expected to be associated with the accumulation of family assets, as claimed. I would have benefited from a more detailed discussion of these questions in the paper.

Judging from the paper's discussion of method, it appears that interviewer ratings will be relied upon heavily in measuring the components of planning effectiveness. Ratings are generally useful for measuring variables that cannot be measured in any other way. Some of the components of planfulness in Hill's study are no doubt difficult to measure more precisely. For some of them, however, I suspect that more reliable and more precise alternative measures could be devised. For example, instead of rating the adequacy of information on which a decision seems to be based, one could rely solely on objective measures developed to learn about the information that the family members had at different points in time preceding the purchases in question. Also, the use of quasi-experimental tests in the field situation might have promise.

A particular hazard arising from the repeated interviews with the families is what Hill has referred to as reflexivity—the effect on planning and purchasing of being interviewed repeatedly about these matters over a 15-month period. This is no small problem, as Hill has pointed out. The technique of confronting families with discrepancies between plans and purchases is by no means a neutral method of obtaining data. Repeated confrontation interviews, coupled with extensive questioning relating to many aspects of family planning, attain the stature of methods of social influence that could result in variable and unknown consequences. Because the method of obtaining information may itself be an independent variable affecting planning effectiveness, some attempt to understand its effects might be desirable. The use in the field of an extended control-group design, as proposed by Solomon, is one solution to the problem of sorting out the interaction of the method of measurement and the phenomena being measured.

Morgan's paper differs from Hill's essentially in its focus on explanatory variables that derive largely from the theory of subjective utility and motivational psychology, and in its treatment of these variables. Morgan discussed most extensively the variables that influence the individual's preference for a given alternative and those that affect his contribution to the family decision. Some powerful rules for combining variables are suggested that take us beyond the blend of ideas from decision theory and motivation that is the basis of the scheme. A number of predictions may be generated from Morgan's ideas by rendering explicitly some of the assumptions relating variables to one another. Even though the paper is more at the level of what is termed general theory, a great deal of specific theory is to be found in it.

It was probably wise nonetheless to cast the theory at a more general level because some of the theoretical issues at the more specific level have yet to be worked out. For example, it is not clear at present how best theoretically to combine needs, incentive values, and expected outcomes to predict expected satisfaction from a given alternative. The multiplicative combining of these variables that has been suggested by John Atkinson and others raises questions about the weighting to be given to the variables. Is each to be weighted equally, or are some more predictive than others and thus deserving of heavier weights? Even more complex is the question of how to combine all factors affecting an individual's preference for a given alternative, taking into account both the variables contributing to a positive preference for the alternative and the resistances to that alternative.

Assuming that we had a workable formula for expressing an individual's preference for a given alternative that contained the variables Morgan has given us, we would have only taken one small step toward predicting a group decision with respect to that alternative. Morgan's model requires also that all alternatives must be similarly evaluated and that the preference of each individual for a given alternative be assessed. With this information at hand, the next part of Morgan's model may be employed to obtain the individual's contribution to the family decision. But at this point, another crop of variables emerges, such as the need for power and the value of the alternative for gratifying the need, which require us to weigh variables and write another formula for combination to come up with the expressed preferences in the family.

Group decision-making cannot yet be predicted with the model, however, because group influences have not been taken into consideration. Morgan recognizes the importance of group variables, but considers the findings from small-group research on decision-making of little use in his tentative effort to round out the model by the inclusion of group variables. Even though much needs to be learned about group problem-solving, especially in enduring groups like the nuclear family, past research on small groups suggests two conclusions that relate directly to the question of the adequacy of a model that, like Morgan's, places such heavy emphasis on individual preferences and individual contributions to family decisions.

One conclusion, which is supported by a number of small-group studies, is that an individual's preference, attitude, or opinion may be greatly modified by the group in which he finds himself. The group exercises its influence in at least two ways. The first is the more passive type of influence wherein the individual changes merely by reflecting upon what others will think of his individual contribution. The individual takes the role of the others in the group and reacts in terms of what he knows the norms are. This type of influence generally changes the individual's contribution in the direction of the group standard or of his perception of that standard. Thus, individual preferences in groups become less extreme when expressed, private opinions become public opinions, and attitudes become more or less affectively invested and may even change their sign. The more active type of group influence is probably the most potent of the two kinds, for through it strong attempts to influence members are often exerted. If an individual's contribution is different from the others, he may be actively made to conform, depending upon such factors as the extent of his deviation, the strength of pressures toward uniformity, and the goal of the group.

A second conclusion from studies on small groups is that the contributions of the individual members often do not combine in any simple manner to produce a group product or decision. The type of task, the norms, the division of labor, the cohesiveness of the group, the group's size, are among the potential influences upon how final decisions are reached. It is probably safe to state that there are few decision-making situations in which a group decision may be predicted from knowledge merely of the individual contributions; the individual contributions are generally nonadditive with respect to final group products.

If these conclusions are sound, it follows that decision-making about asset accumulation, or probably about most other areas of group decision, may be predicted more effectively by group variables than by individual preferences and contributions to the group. The preference of the individual and his contribution to the group should not be excluded, certainly. But these variables are probably secondary at best when considered along with the group variables that modify individual preferences and psychological states even before they are expressed publicly in the group, and with the group variables that result in the vigorous exertion of pressures on individuals to change.

Discussion

HAROLD WATTS

The two papers presented in this session are clearly interdisciplinary. On the one hand, we have an economist concerning himself with the interaction among family members in the decision-making process, and on the other, a sociologist working on the problems of explaining actual economic decisions of households. Both papers were very interesting to me, and, if they are a fair sample of what co-operation among social scientists can produce, then I certainly look forward to more of it.

Since my own training is in economics, I cannot fairly judge how well an economist does the sociologist's job. My remarks on Morgan's paper, therefore, will be quite specific. My handicap for making judgments on the opposite situation is not quite so great, so I will deal with Hill's paper in a more wholesale fashion.

My comments on Morgan's paper can all be centered on the two diagrams he uses to illustrate the formation of individual preferences and contributions to family decisions by the individual. In the first chart, where individual preferences are formed from more basic concepts, I have a question about the lines that connect the boxes. It appears to me that the set of needs which emerges from A should be an input to B, where the individual's situation and experience are added to produce incentive values. These incentive values, in turn, should go to C, where the effects of uncertainty are introduced. I would suggest that A, B, and C be connected in series with a final

output of expected satisfaction, rather than having all three contributing in a parallel fashion to the formation of expected satisfaction.

To look now at the second diagram, a point that could be explicitly treated here is that a part of the uncertainty that exists for
the individual is removed before the final resolution of the decision
—namely, the uncertainty about the position of each of the other
members of the family. The position of the other members is needed,
of course, to evaluate the potential power-utility or affection-utility
of the alternative courses of action. Perhaps it could be shown more
clearly in the diagram that the individual commences the interaction
phase of the decision-making process with uncertain estimates of
those two kinds of utilities but that at its conclusion he knows what
each alternative offers.

The reference I have just made to two kinds of utility leads me
to another comment. Utility has for some time been a general and,
if you will pardon the expression, a utilitarian concept. It is a standard measure by which all stimuli to the human organism can be
compared. We are now asked to accept a differentiated product; one
kind of utility to measure food for the body and one kind to measure food for the ego. Although it has not been mentioned, it seems
clear that some kind of summary utility is required now for comparing the several special varieties. I simply do not see what is served
by fragmenting the utility concept. It may be advisable to allow a
broader range of motivation to be incorporated in a single utility
function than has been traditional in economics. I am not aware
of any reluctance to do so except that which accompanies any movement into unfamiliar territory. This problem of extending the basis
for utility functions is, by the way, probably a good example of an
area where only the joint efforts of sociologists, psychologists, and
economists can make headway.

I have one final remark to make on Morgan's use of the utility
theory. I would question the necessity of complicating matters on
the general theory level by working with incentive values that are
placed on individual discrete events. Why not define the utility
function in terms of rates of flows of commodities and services and
let the discrete decisions refer to changes in those rates? This avoids
the need for treating separately "absolute" preferences, depreciation
rates on past satisfaction, and the history of past satisfactions. There
is, of course, no way of completely avoiding the problems of dis-

creteness in the objects of consumption, but I feel that in the interest of simplicity those problems can and should be left out of a theory at this level of abstraction.

Turning now to Hill's paper, let me say at the outset that he has, in my opinion, succeeded in accomplishing his aim of extending the range of variables relevant to household economic decisions. It is very interesting for an economist to find out which concepts a sociologist views as important in asset-debt decisions, and it is also helpful to discover that progress has been and is being made in the measurement of these concepts. My reservations about the theory do not have to do with the variables it employs. I think they are all promising with the qualification explicitly noted by Hill: some may be redundant. I am more concerned, as an economist, with the form of the model.

If there is one basic notion that an economist can contribute to the study of household economic decisions, it is that a household tends to maximize its collective satisfaction within the limits of all resources available to it. Whether in an absurdly simple form or in a highly tricked-up version, I must confess some partiality to models that explicitly use this idea. A theory built around this notion can incorporate all the variables mentioned by Hill and add something by way of meaningful interrelations among them.

Let me be a little more specific. First of all, review the statement of the notion. I would first emphasize the word "tends." Only a tendency to maximize satisfaction is being claimed here, rather than an immediate and precise adjustment. There may be lags and/or friction involved in the adjustment. The next term to concentrate on is "collective satisfaction." Here it is assumed that the processes that are discussed by Morgan have resulted somehow in a collective utility function that can be evaluated whenever a decision is to be made. I would also like to make clear that I am here considering satisfaction in its broadest sense, not merely physical satisfaction. Finally I would call attention to the notion of "all available resources" in order to point out that these do not need to be material resources but may be mental or physical in nature. This is surely not a very strong assumption to make about households. To an economist, it appears completely innocuous, but perhaps this is due to familiarity. Now consider its use as a basis for more specific hypotheses.

The variation of behavior that is observed among households is to be explained in terms of differing utility functions or differing resource endowments. Looking first for reasons for variation in the utility function, an economist thinks first of need. I personally would favor limiting this concept to basic physiological necessities, which are fairly constant on a per capita basis. The interfamily variation on the basis of needs can be largely accounted for by family size and age composition variables.

Acquisition and consumption of assets beyond the necessities, whether they be convenience, comfort, or luxury items, are based mainly on the general values maintained by the household. Variation in values is probably the main reason for variation in utility functions. There are many possible indicators of the value system of a household, and many, if not most, of them are pointed out by Hill. The sociologist has devised some relatively direct methods of measuring these values, whereas the economist has usually used demographic and environmental variables in an attempt to achieve the same result.

Another reason for variation in utility functions is differences in knowledge of what is available in the market. A household cannot evaluate the utility of an item with which it is completely unfamiliar. Knowledge, therefore, has a bearing on the dimensionality of the utility function. I cannot say how important this consideration is, but it is at least a possibility worth considering.

A final candidate for explaining utility functions is suggested in Morgan's paper. The power structure of the family apparently can affect the collective utility of a specific alternative. Two families with identical needs, values, and knowledge could differ in their preferences solely because of different proportions of would-be Indians and would-be chiefs.

Now consider the limits on the maximization process. First and most obvious are the limits of material resources—the income and wealth of the household. The use of income and financial status by economists in this connection is surely commonplace and requires no further elaboration.

Less obvious, but perhaps more interesting, is the idea that decision-making capacity is a scarce resource for the household. This capacity to make decisions is a combination of individual skills, family organization, and time, each of which is in limited supply. It is true that close attention to changing external circumstances and a constant adjustment to them can yield a net increase in satisfaction from a given endowment of material resources if we can assume the cost of such vigilance is zero. But it should be recognized that time and energy spent in deciding and maximizing might be used instead to increase material resources through work or be converted into satisfaction directly by leisure activities.

This idea is interesting first because it provides an additional reason for variation in household behavior. The skills of family members in solving problems and in evaluating each other's preferences undoubtedly vary among households; likewise, the internal organization of the family as represented by the various husband-wife measures can be expected to vary. It is also interesting because it provides an explanation for such phenomena as long-range policies and role differentiation. In the structure I am suggesting, these things appear as means of economizing on scarce decision-making capacity. In the case of policies, a general, blanket decision can be made to cover a class of situations that would otherwise require individual attention. The role differentiation that has been perceived may be a result of delegation of certain policies to specific individuals for execution. Alternatively the delegation of authority may permit more discretion on account of family confidence in an individual's ability to make correct decisions.

Finally, the notion of decision-making capacity makes a place for the planning effectiveness variable suggested by Hill. The formulation of feasible plans and the careful execution of them implies a combination of ability in decision-making and time spent in making use of it. If a family is low on this kind of ability, or if it has other highly valued uses for its time, then this hypothesis would suggest that its planning effectiveness would be low.

I have tried to show how the variables that Hill has proposed as the relevant ones can be fitted into an alternative framework, one that is probably more acceptable and certainly more familiar to economists.

I would like to add one final comment, a compliment actually, on the research design outlined by Hill. It strikes me as a very ingenious method for obtaining a kind of information that has been needed for some time.

Discussion

FLEISHMAN (to MORGAN): I wish you had continued with your quotation from *Through the Looking-Glass,* for when Humpty-Dumpty declares that words mean whatever he wants them to mean, Alice says, "The question is . . . whether you can make words mean so many different things." To which Humpty-Dumpty replies, "The question is which is to be master—that's all!"

My question about your paper is not with your choice of words or variables, but whether they have mastered the model or the model has mastered them. My question breaks down into four aspects:

Are not the psychological motives that you have chosen to include among the more rational and traditional in economics, and in so choosing, have you not too strictly ruled out what you call abnormal behavior? The behavior that deviates from the normal may yet lie in a continuum with normal behavior, and may therefore be a measurable part of normal behavior.

Do the three or four motives that you have included constitute a model of a personality whole, or are they simply needs—extrapolations for convenience? What is the theoretical value of using *some* motives in a model of the role of personality in decision-making? Should not a theory, at least in theory, be as complete as possible? Lest this be construed as constructive criticism, may I say that it would be better to use *all* known personality motives in an economic or sociological model, whether this entails a deviation into the realm of psychology or even psychoanalytic theory.

MORGAN: We are aware of deeper motivations, but are trying to exclude the pathological. We need to go behind the demographic variables, and the intent is to go beyond the verbalized reactions to a situation. But we have selected a limited subset because these are quantifiable and particularly relevant to *these* decisions. Others may freely suggest others.

KATONA (to HILL): There is much which is fascinating and promising in the research plan of Reuben Hill. We at the Survey Research Center have found successive interviews with identical people, concerned with what has happened between waves, to be a most useful research tool, especially in studying highly variable behavior. Yet the dependent variables chosen by Hill are not of a type that change rapidly among individual consumers. This is clearly true of effectiveness in long-range planning: within a 15-month period, it can only be studied with the help of historical data subject to memory errors. (In addition, I must confess I do not understand the term "effectiveness." Is "effectiveness" from the observer's or actor's viewpoint?)

The other dependent variable is entitled "accumulation of assets" and suggests additions to and withdrawals from financial assets (liquid saving). It has been revealed in later parts of Hill's paper as meaning accumulation of inventories of durable household goods. Only by jointly considering durable-goods purchases and saving do we introduce problems of choice and conflict, as between spending and saving. The repeated-interview method is better applied to choice than to consumption, so the addition of savings data is suggested.

Moreover, by studying both activities, the probable bias resulting from panel studies, namely, overconcern of respondents with the subject matter of the study, can be reduced. This technique influences respondents, particularly in long-range planning. Also, differences between three generations would be much more interesting regarding saving and borrowing than regarding consumption.

I would also suggest that Hill extend the interval between successive waves from three to six months. Few buy durables within a three-month period, and many of these buy without planning.

HILL: We do include changes in financial status, which will allow observation of saving and spending in dollar terms. And we shall be checking actual against anticipated spending.

But we feel insecure regarding our other dependent variable. We are seeking cumulative theory about competence in the family to deal with a wide variety of problems, that is, serious and recurrent issues for decision. Although we have used competence as a variable in our previous Eddyville and Puerto Rican studies, our operational indices are not yet satisfactory. We may yet need to include some motivational variables.

RIVLIN (to HILL): Have you given any thought to what the restriction of the sample to three-generation families living in the same area may do to the representativeness of the sample? These families are obviously less mobile than others. Do they differ also in other respects? Might you not get overweighted at the high and low ends of the income distribution?

HILL: You tell me. Migrants may be at the high and low ends.

KENKEL: Let me add a point to that question. In your third generation, you are using one child in what may have been a family of many children. What about the others? Can we not assume that children who have moved away differ in important ways from those who have remained? You may get the least intelligent siblings, who move least.

HILL: There is no striking evidence of distortion in the ecological distribution of the families on the map of the area. We have a continuous age distribution, not a trimodality. The first half of the sample was well distributed by education. By definition, our families are more stable residentially and more subject to intergenerational influence. But should we try to generalize to all other families?

GLICK: In view of the variability among characteristics of children within specific families, would you not expect to get different results depending on which sibling is chosen to represent a given generation? My two boys differ.

HILL: The required combination of three generations of a family line was so scarce we had no cases in which such a choice had to be made.

BRIM: In support of Reuben Hill's sample design, his focus is on the relations among variables, not on their distribution. Although the data pertain to perhaps a limited group in the population, the fact is that he is looking for empirical relations among variables, not descriptive data, and there is no reason to expect that the relations he finds would be different for different samples.

Thus, for example, in studying a sample of children who range in intelligence quotient from 85 to 100, it is true that the mean would be below the national average, but the relation of intelligence to school performance would remain linear and similar to the relation found for any other sample. You are working within a segment of a distribution.

Also, I would point out that there are many three-generation families in the United States, and it is of importance to study them. So the questions about sample and universe may not be as critical as they seem.

BERNARD (to HILL): Will you take account of such outside forces as inflation in order to account for savings and expenditures? Do people increase their savings to ensure adequate future income, or do they spend faster in order not to be caught with dollars of reduced value? In European countries facing drastic inflation, people have often invested in almost anything to have goods rather than money.

HILL: Our history-taking maximizes attention to circumstances. We shall be guided by how powerfully such influences come through in accounting for their plans.

DANIERE (to WATTS): In regard to your reformulation of Hill's design according to a utility model, you conceive decision-making as maximizing resources. For example, the resource of time might be maximized for effectiveness in decision-making. Is it really helpful to think about decision-making in this way? Whatever you do, you can say you are maximizing utility. To conform with others would be to maximize. Does it help to formulate such an abstract model? Is it not better to concentrate on sociological factors, to stick to products and services, to specific resources and constraints?

WATTS: It depends. Are your social constraints rigid or loose? If they are loose, it helps to treat choices as utility functions.

CAHALAN (to MORGAN): In view of the conference theme, perhaps it would be well to emphasize that decision is an abstract notion. You may wish to comment on this, because the conference is in need of a clear definition.

One illustration of the artificiality of the concept of decision is the "decisions" made by default or by pressure on the family from the outside milieu. Thus perhaps it is more a decision to do the unusual or deviant. Another illustration is the paradox found in surveys where families who have made important purchases like autos insist they "decided" on the spur of the moment.

Unless we exercise considerable caution, do we not risk confounding the final consummation of a purchase with the really crucial series of events and decisions made prior to that act?

MORGAN: A good point. There may be no thought process regarding alternatives or regarding the decision to do nothing. Although decisions are constantly being made, most are not attended to by the person or are irrelevant to our purposes. I want to deal only with salient, important decisions that involve clear choice, where the alternatives may be equally appealing.

CLAWSON (to MORGAN): With regard to our crucial dependent variables, we have to know what actually happens. Then we need to find independent variables which contribute to the variance in the dependent, just sorting these out to determine how much they matter. Then we have to go back and find out how much they interact with each other. Of course, we try to find out as fast as possible how to get rid of as many of these operations as possible, but back of our selection of the more influential variables lies that kind of process.

MAYNES (to HILL): Hill's dependent variable needs more specification. He should consider getting the money value of the asset inventory and should include short-term saving as a reciprocal of buying. Then he could observe intergenerational differences more reliably over five- and ten-year periods, compare the ratios of debt to gross assets, and compare time patterns in the accumulation of assets.

HILL: We cannot do everything.

MILLER: If the speakers will forgive a crass commercial note, advertising—commercial communications generally—is a ten-billion-dollar industry devoted to influencing the decisions and desires of consumers. Do either of you plan to measure the influence of advertising in decision-making? How important is it?

MORGAN: No, I would like to, but I cannot think of any easy or hard way of doing it.

HILL: In a limited way, by confronting our respondents with the question of accounting for the timing of purchases and the fulfillment or nonfulfillment of plans, we may find that they indicate influence of the mass media. But this influence may be predisposing rather than decisive.

LIPPITT (to MORGAN): I am interested in the usefulness of a model for forecasting as well as explaining. Suppose a usable explanation of the economic decisions of a family could be derived, based on the underlying variables in your model rather than on the more superficial "proxy" variables such as family characteristics. How then could your kind of information be used for forecasting consumer behavior in the future, either individually or aggregatively? Can the distribution of families by these underlying explanatory variables itself be forecast?

MORGAN: To measure and predict, you need to determine which are crucial. The connections between motives and these other factors may change over time. If we can find the motives, we then can find out their connections with family characteristics through further research.

HILL: The conference is indebted to Watts for the trouble he has taken to translate my schema of analytic categories drawn from the family-development approach to family research into terms more familiar to economists. The not so "innocuous assumption" that he must make to order the concepts of household, collective satisfaction, scarce resources, decision-making, utility functions, and effectiveness of planning meaningfully into a utility model should be tested empirically by the present study rather than accepted as a basic premise. The advantage of the "accounting model" that I have developed is that it is unburdened with *a priori* assumptions about either the rationality of the decision process or the maximization of collective satisfaction. We will thus be as well prepared for the transmission of poverty patterns from one generation to another as for the transmission of the notion of maximizing utility.

Thomas has performed a service in distinguishing between the different usages of the term "theoretical model," which permits us to view my schema of analytic categories as a framework for discovery rather than a unified theoretical scheme from which a series of hypotheses are to be derived and tested. I have argued elsewhere that theory can be used at every stage of research, in selecting the problem to be studied, in setting the scope to be covered, and in suggesting questions to explore, giving thereby descriptive order and analytic meaning to the materials collected. In this study we have utilized the family-development framework to serve precisely these purposes. We trust that the blocks of variables we have identified will serve as an "accounting model" to account for most of the variance in our dependent variable. Moreover, I trust that these blocks of variables are ordered in such a way that the associations which are identified between them and the dependent variable, planning effectiveness, will demonstrate more than "construct validity."

It is worth noting that each discussant and participant in the subsequent discussion has suggested additional items to be incorporated in the study: knowledge about the market, individual motives and preferences, reactions to outside events such as inflation, more on savings and on the money value of the asset inventory. The schema has proved to be a useful expository device for involving consultants in the research problem and helping them embrace it imaginatively, thereby increasing the scope of the study and increasing the power of the "accounting model" to *account for* variance in the criterion variable.

MORGAN: Thomas is perfectly correct that much has yet to be done in specifying the way in which motives, incentives, and expectancies combine in affecting behavior. That they work together in something more than an additive fashion seems a useful working assumption stemming from the theory.

He also suggests that the theory might have made more use of group influences of the sort used in small-group and group-dynamics research, where things like group size and cohesiveness affect the actions and interactions of the group, and where there are some evidences that the group may modify individual preferences. There is a problem here of whether these should be pushed into the structure I have already been discussing, or whether still more elaboration and other levels of variables must be added. I should hope that we might bring such group influences to bear within the model without adding complexities. For instance, the group might modify individual preferences through a communication process whereby the individual sees new ways in which a particular action may lead to desired outcomes, or whereby he sees that others in the group whom he values want a particular result, or whereby he is even able to achieve new insights as to relationships which affect choices.

Watts suggests that the diagram might better go from needs through incentives and subjective probabilities to a tendency to prefer that alternative. It is true that there are triplets combining need, incentive, and expectancy for each need (and for each alternative), but in our model the arrows are intended to convey causal direction and it could not be said that motives cause incentive values or probabilities. The three combine in some nonadditive way to produce a propensity to prefer at that instant the alternative they relate to.

It is also true, of course, that there is uncertainty as to the position of others in the family. The dynamics by which people learn enough to act (and they may do this only in the important decisions that are salient and attended to) are important to investigate and understand.

I must say, however, that the attempt to coerce under a single rubric of "utility" such different things as the contribution of a decision to a feeling of affiliation with some group in society, to a sense of exercising power over others in the family, and to satisfying some physical want such as hunger appears to have little more than heuristic usefulness, if that. I did not fragment the utility concept for fun. We would all like to be good disciples of Occam, but sometimes it becomes necessary to look the real complexity of reality in the face (or almost in the face), and then start chopping.

Both the suggestion that we think of decisions in terms of changes in flows rather than discrete choices and the suggestion that decisions are really a sequential process raise the problem of the definition of "decision." While I have been working on a theory to handle major decisions, it appears to solve some logical problems to insist that every moment that passes means an implicit decision between the present course of action and the most promising alternative. (Most of these decisions are resolved negatively, i.e., no change.) If we add to this a characterization of decisions that lumps most of them into the uninteresting category where the choice involves no real problem, no weighing of important issues, no salience to the person involved, that is, no "real" decision, we can then proceed to deal with the cases where there is a real decision between alternatives, where the individual "attends to" the choice and weighs the alternatives. This does not mean that a choice means action; the decision may be a decision to do nothing. It is possible to have a good deal of tension, problem solving, and motive involvement and still do nothing, as when there are compelling reasons not to answer a phone when it is ringing.

III. Decision-Making Regarding Allocation and Spending

An Economist's Approach to the Study of Spending

H. S. HOUTHAKKER

My assignment is to give you a self-conscious account of the methods used by economists in consumption research. In order to be properly self-conscious, I shall make my story highly egocentric and stress that fact by a liberal use of the word "I." This means that much of what I shall say applies only to myself and not to other students of the subject. In a way, therefore, I am shirking my responsibility, but there may be some compensatory advantages. In the first place, practical research workers rarely have time to be self-conscious about their procedures; the assumptions that are common to practitioners in a profession are usually implicit rather than explicit; and consequently it is hard to know when one is expressing a consensus and when a private heresy. In the second place, I am painfully aware that my own approach is less broad-minded and more narrowly economic than that of many of my colleagues who are more closely in touch with current sociology and psychology than I am. Since I am addressing myself mainly to noneconomists, a statement of my own narrow point of view may help to give a clear outline to the issues.

I must start by speaking about theory. In so doing, I do not want to suggest that economic research in consumption is merely a verification of ideas that have been conceived *a priori*. Far from it, for what economic theory has to offer in the way of definite and verifiable ideas is as much the result as the foundation of empirical research. Nevertheless, I consider it important to keep economic theory constantly in mind. It is only the link to theory that keeps scientific research distinct from mere data-gathering.

The relevant theory falls naturally into two parts. The first part is concerned with the individual and the second with the way in which statements about individuals can be applied to aggregates. The first part is the more developed and the more controversial, and perhaps also (for reasons that I shall discuss later) the less important of the two. However this may be, I shall have to devote much of my discussion to it.

The theory of individual choice has a long history, in the course of which much dead wood has been cut out. It is only in recent years that the essentials of the problem have been isolated. It would serve no useful purpose to go through the rubbish heap of discarded notions, but one of those deserves to be mentioned by name. It is the notion of cardinal utility, once so dear to the economist's heart and even now not without its distinguished defenders. In the final decades of the nineteenth century, the buying decisions made by a consumer were explained in terms of the utility that the quantity bought had to him. This utility was thought of as a function of the quantity, whose value could, in principle at least, be measured. In itself, this view was a great advance over earlier opinions, which regarded utility as determined by the nature rather than the quantity of the commodity considered. Once this advance had been made, the conception of consumer's choice as the maximization of utility became generally accepted. All this, it should be noted, was on a purely theoretical level; the empirical work done in those days was quite separate from economic theory. A rationalistic faith in deduction from introspectively given axioms reigned supreme, and even today it has not entirely disappeared from economics.

The development of cardinal utility theory, whatever its defects, had another important consequence. The formulation of consumer's choice as a maximization problem opened the way to the application of differential calculus. In fact, those who made lasting contributions to the subject (particularly Gossen, Edgeworth, Pareto, and Slutsky) all used mathematics freely. The rigor thus imposed, though perhaps stifling in some respects, led in due course to an improved recognition of what is essential. The literary proponents of cardinal utility had felt that they were saying a great deal when they explained consumers' behavior from utility considerations. To their more behavioristic critics, this explanation was little more than a tautology. In fact, it was gradually recognized that the measurability of utility was quite irrelevant to the problems under discussion. The vital assumption that remained—and I am now telescoping a trend in theory that extended over some 50 years—is that the individual can rank the spending alternatives open to him according to his preferences for them.

The dethronement of cardinal utility reinforced the subjectivistic tendency in consumption theory. As long as utility was conceived as a measurable magnitude primarily tied to the quantity of a commodity, it was easy to overlook its relation to the individual. The concept of preference ordering, on the other hand, is so clearly subjective that it is the relation to the properties of commodities that now tends to be forgotten. For the modern theory of consumer's choice, the actual content of preferences, as distinct from their consistency, is a contingent fact about which nothing is said. That people have to eat in order to live, for instance, is of no particular interest to pure theory. Such important and well-established propositions as that the proportion of incomes spent on food declines when income increases are not derivable from the assumption of a preference ordering, although they do have an indirect bearing on the validity of the pure theory.

If not the above, what propositions then *is* the theory interested in deriving? Clearly they will be of a much less concrete character. To understand their significance, it is necessary to consider the primary concerns of economics in general. The subject matter of economics, put briefly but not too inaccurately, is the mutual adjustment of means and ends. On the whole, it is not interested in the nature of means as such or of ends as such; it is the relation between them that matters. Now, the adjustment process just referred to is typically a social one, in the sense that the decisions of any one individual are strongly influenced by the decisions of all other individuals. This is not so primarily because there is direct interaction among individuals, for instance, through consultation, emulation, or differentiation. Such interaction does take place, but for economic theory it is not of central significance.

The social nature of the adjustment process manifests itself in a different way, namely, in a system of prices. If a commodity commands a positive price, this indicates—at least in principle—that the means available for producing it are insufficient to satisfy those for whom the commodity is an end. This applies equally well to com-

modities in the strict sense (goods and services) as to the labor and
other factors of production made available by individuals. The
prices for the factors that an individual supplies determine his income; and his income in turn is a constraint on the consumption
possibilities that the individual can realize. The constraint is,
roughly speaking, that his total expenditures, given the prices of
the goods he wants to buy, should not exceed his income in the long
run. The individual's preferences then determine which of the
possibilities open to him he will actually choose.

This much is elementary—and crude in many respects. I shall discuss some of the many objections to this formulation in a moment.
Let me just emphasize now that, in the context of the adjustment
of means to ends, the most immediate problem is the influence of
changes in prices and incomes on consumption decisions. The relevant theorems, which usually have the form of inequalities, can be
stated and derived in a few pages, but their consequences for general economic theory are far-reaching. Whether or not the economic
system can work at all depends entirely on the quantitative characteristics of the response of individuals to changes in prices and income. Moreover, economic planning—whether by the government
or by others—has to take the magnitude of those responses into account at all times. From the economist's point of view, therefore,
their estimation is of primary importance. More particularly, it is
necessary to have as precise an idea as possible of price and income
elasticities, which are convenient measures for the responses just
mentioned. The estimation of elasticities is one of the tasks of econometrics, of which more later.

Before going into the theoretical and practical problems of econometrics I should go back for a moment to the pure theory of consumer's choice. I have already alluded to one possible objection to
this approach; namely, it is too abstract and pays no attention to
such common-sense determinants of consumption as the necessity
to eat in order to live, or the fact that the way in which one chooses
to heat one's home is not entirely a question of arbitrary preference,
but also of such hard facts as calories and climate (prices, of course,
are taken into account). This contrasts with the approach taken
by nutritionists, for whom food consumption is mainly a matter of
proteins, carbohydrates, and what have you. In recent years, economists have become more aware of the possible advantages of incorporating these technological features into consumption theory,

although this is by no means as easy as it sounds. There is also a danger that consumption economics may become not more but less realistic by looking at those seemingly practical considerations. Thus it has been found that the cost of a nutritionally adequate diet is only a small fraction of what people in the more developed countries actually spend on food, and it would be naïve to conclude from this that most of the money spent on food is wasted. Nevertheless, this area deserves to be studied further.

More serious, perhaps, is a frequently heard objection to the effect that the classical theory pays insufficient attention to uncertainty. With much justice, it is pointed out that consumers are often in the dark about the properties of the commodities they buy and that they may not even be very sure about the prices they pay or about the income they have. The idea of a fixed scale of preferences for all combinations of commodities is attacked for the same reason and also because it is hard to imagine that people's minds should be equipped with anything so elaborate as an all-embracing scale of preferences. Perhaps it is best to keep those two objections separate. Attempts to meet the difficulty about uncertainty have usually taken the form of a probabilistic theory, an endeavor to which great mathematical ingenuity is now being devoted. I do not think that a solution along those lines is as yet in sight. Apart from the fact that this approach has not yet been pursued to a level where it could be helpful to the study of spending decisions, a basic weakness, in my opinion, is that it introduces a whole class of variables—the subjective or the objective probabilities—of which individuals are just as uncertain as about the utilities themselves. Moreover, I am not sure that all of the proponents of the probabilistic approach have a very clear idea as to the phenomena which they hope to explain.

The skeptical reductionism that has already had so healthy an influence on classical utility theory has yet to complete its impact on that approach. The recently revived interest in utility measurement is a case in point. I am not convinced that so many economists are wrong in regarding utility measurement as a waste of time. There are many things in economics that need to be measured, but utility is not high on my list.

The other difficulty, which refers to the impossibility of simultaneously keeping all alternatives in mind, has a more immediate bearing on empirical research. It is closely linked to another weakness of classical consumption theory, namely, its neglect of the time factor. Consumers do not decide on their spending patterns once and for all, nor do they carry out all their plans simultaneously. This does not mean, of course, that consumption can usefully be viewed as a sequence of unrelated events in time; about such a sequence nothing very interesting could be said. What it does mean is that consumption theory should pay considerable attention to the time pattern of spending.

There are two principal ways in which time enters into consumption decisions. The first is through habit formation, and the other through the existence of inventories. Habit formation means that the effect of changes in prices and income, which are the determining factors of consumption, is not immediate but subject to a time lag. Lags have been recognized by economists for many years, and they are a basic element of many dynamic economic models. It is only very recently, however, that appropriate statistical methods of dealing with them have been developed. In the extreme case, lags may be of infinite duration, thus giving rise to so-called irreversibility of demand functions. When this phenomenon is present, a change in the determinants of consumption, whatever its nature, will have a permanent effect on consumption patterns. There is as yet no unanimity among economists as regards the importance of irreversibility, a problem which is intimately connected with that of the validity of certain statistical procedures such as the taking of first differences. An example of the operation of irreversibility may perhaps be seen in the existence of so-called national dishes in various countries, which are probably no more than a reflection of price and income conditions of long ago.

The second manifestation of the time element in consumption, namely, the existence of inventories, brings us close to one of the traditional concerns of economic theory. That capital (either in the form of inventories in the narrow sense, such as stocks of raw materials and work in process, or in the form of fixed equipment) is necessary in production has never been overlooked, but that capital is also important in the area of consumption has not always been sufficiently emphasized. The classical theory of consumer's choice, in fact, has customarily treated all commodities as if they are all currently consumed. This does not necessarily mean that durable commodities are excluded from the analysis; the distinction between durable and nondurable commodities depends on the time period considered; and if that period is long enough, very few, if any, commodities are durable. Thus, it is reasonable to regard a car as a durable good if one is concerned with a time period of a year or less, but if the time period were 10 or 20 years, cars should be regarded as currently consumed just like clothing, which is not usually counted among durable commodities. So the question is really what period of observation is most useful.

With this, we return for a moment to a question raised earlier, namely, the capacity of the human mind to formulate and carry out plans. Generally speaking, it is clear that the shorter the period, the more likely it is that an individual can be meaningfully said to be carrying out a preconceived plan. But when we admit this, we are also forced to assign a prominent place to inventories of all kinds in the theory of choice. Whether we describe the commodities of which inventories are held as durable or not is merely a matter of terminology.

It may be interesting to consider briefly the reasons for which inventories are held. In the case of the more spectacular items, such as houses and cars, we have of course been told *ad nauseam* that people buy these primarily to impress their neighbors as "status symbols," to use an "okay" word. There are also more subtle, and perhaps more important, reasons. Consider for instance the case of bread, inventories of which are presumably less affected by suburban rivalry. Bread is bought by the loaf rather than by the slice because it is cheaper to do so. More particularly, it is often cheaper to buy in larger quantities, not only because the price per unit is smaller, but also because the time and trouble required for purchasing increases less than proportionately with the size of the purchase. Much the same applies to inventories of durable goods. Thus, one good reason—though certainly not the only one—for owning a car is that driving oneself is less expensive or troublesome than relying on taxicabs.

The above explanation of the holding of durables relies on what economists call "economies of scale," which exist whenever the cost of large quantities is less than proportionate to the cost of small quantities. Usually economies of scale hold only in a limited range; for instance, a loaf of bread is proportionately cheaper than a slice of bread, if one could be bought, but three loaves are not proportionately cheaper than one loaf. Even where economies of scale exist over a wide range, there may be obstacles to their complete realization. Financial resources (including the availability of credit) are one of the obstacles; another is the risk that large inventories may turn out to be unwanted by the time they are available for consumption.

Unfortunately choice problems of this kind, although perfectly well defined, are not very accessible to marginal analysis, the traditional method of economic theory. The theory of consumer inventories is, therefore, still in its infancy. Some interesting work has been done in the last few years, most of which involves the notion of a "desired" or "preferred" inventory. The latter is interpreted either as the level around which actual inventories fluctuate under the influence of depreciation and replacement, or as the level to which actual inventories would converge if the time span were long enough and other circumstances remained unchanged. A comparison between these two interpretations remains to be made.

I have spent much time on the theory of choice for the individual consumer, and I dare not tax your patience further by an equally lengthy discussion of the case, which is evidently of greater empirical interest, of a group of consumers. Its interest is greater because some of the difficulties discussed earlier are less serious when we go beyond the single individual, with his sometimes random behavior. Even if I had the time, however, I would find much less to say on this subject. The main issue is one that is well known to social scientists in other fields, namely, whether a group is to be regarded merely as the sum of its components. Because no one would seriously deny the existence of interaction altogether, the issue is more precisely whether interaction needs to be taken into account explicitly, or whether it can be included in what the communication engineers appropriately call "noise." Casual observation is not a reliable guide on this question as just reformulated; what little empirical evidence there is provides no clear-cut answer either. My own inclination, therefore, is against dealing with interaction explicitly, if only because it would complicate any statistical analysis considerably if taken into account rigorously. In fact, to my knowledge, no one has attempted an analysis with explicit interaction, but the general idea of interaction has been used to explain certain anomalies found in the behavior of savings over time and among people with different incomes. The so-called relative income hypothesis sees consumption as determined not by a household's absolute income, but by its income status relative to the community where it is located. There is some evidence for this hypothesis, but much needs to be done before it can be definitely accepted.

It is the task of empirical research to submit the implications of pure theory to the test of confrontation with observations, to give numerical precision to parameters introduced in the theory, and to suggest phenomena which the theory should take into account. As I mentioned before, this formulation does not imply that empirical research is subordinate to theory. Even though I probably attach greater importance to theory than most investigators of consumption economics, I do not want to suggest that theory provides more than a basic framework together with some theorems whose premises may or may not have empirical relevance. I have already pointed out a number of defects, some of considerable empirical importance, to which existing theory is subject.

Of the tasks for empirical research just enumerated, the first and second, namely, the testing of hypotheses and the estimation of parameters, are very close to each other. This is so because in the present state of the subject the most immediate test of the relevance of pure theory is the empirical constancy or stability of the parameters that it introduces. Because the economic theory of consumption puts such great stress on prices and incomes as determining factors, the requirement of constancy applies in particular to price and income elasticities, parameters whose dimensionless nature makes them particularly suitable for purposes of comparison. Even though the theory might be logically valid without such constancy, it clearly can have no predictive or explanatory value unless the parameters possess some degree of stability over time or between persons and communities.

Actually, the words "constancy" and "stability" are not quite accurate. It is theoretically impossible that price and income elasticities should remain exactly constant when prices and income change, although the variations in elasticity called for by the theory are normally quite small. What is required, more precisely, is a pattern of elasticities that is consistent with theoretical preconceptions. In practice, moreover, we can hardly hope to find exact constancy, for the data are never quite accurate and there are all sorts of more or less random disturbances. The best we can hope for is that the parameters applicable to various time periods and communities are not too different from each other.

The data from which elasticities can be estimated are primarily of two types: cross-section surveys and time series. The most important species of cross-section data are provided by household-budget surveys, which consist of observations of the expenditures, and sometimes the incomes, of a fairly large number of households during a fixed period of time. Such surveys have been undertaken for more than a hundred years and are now available for a large number of countries. Despite the many technical difficulties associated with them, they have contributed immeasurably to our knowledge of consumption economics, even though that was not usually the purpose for which they were made. Because price changes during the period of observation, which rarely exceeds one year, are normally small, budget surveys provide most information concerning the influence of income on expenditures, or of the composition of urban expenditures in relation to rural expenditures.

Very early in the history of these surveys, some general tendencies were observed, and these generalizations have been confirmed by virtually every survey up to the present day. Thus, it has been invariably found that the proportion of total expenditure devoted to food is a declining function of total expenditure; that the same applies to housing, although the rate of decline is usually less than for food; that the proportion spent for clothing is a constant or slightly increasing function of total expenditure; and that the proportion spent on all other items is consequently an increasing function of total expenditure. In terms of the relevant elasticities, this means that they are confined to a range from about .4 to about .8 for food, from about .5 to about .9 for housing, from about 1 to about 1.4 for clothing, and from 1 to 1.7 for other items for expenditure. These ranges are narrow enough to be of some use for forecasting purposes; moreover, there are good prospects that the differences within those ranges can be further reduced by taking account of the prices prevailing in the periods or countries to which the surveys refer. It is especially interesting—and certainly more than we had ever bargained for—that the differences in elasticities between countries are relatively small, at least if we confine ourselves to the larger items of expenditure (such as food) and do not look into their components. The influence of cultural and climatic conditions on consumers' preferences may be less than even economists had suspected, and economists are inclined to minimize the influence particularly of cultural differences in any case. If this apparent invariance of preferences can be convincingly demonstrated, quantitative research in the fields of economic development and international trade will be greatly simplified.

Household-budget surveys, which tend to cover the whole range of consumers' expenditures, are not the only type of cross-section data. Another type, of which the survey of consumer finances carried out by the University of Michigan is the best-known representative, is concerned less with what people actually do than with what they intend to do. Surveys of this kind do not attempt to cover the whole range, but concentrate on a number of items of particular interest for the appraisal and forecasting of current economic conditions. Questions about attitudes and expectations have been prominent in these surveys. Although short-term forecasting has been the primary purpose, much of scientific interest is also contained in the voluminous information now available, though a comprehensive analysis of it remains to be made. Intentions to buy homes and durable goods have always been conspicuous items in the survey questionnaire. It has been found, however, that people's intentions to buy do not have a very close correlation with their actual purchasing decisions, and it would be interesting to find out whether better forecasts are obtained from people's stated intentions or from a knowledge of the objective determinants of consumption, such as income, liquid assets, and previously held inventories.

An advantage of the partial surveys, like the one just mentioned, over the complete budget surveys is that the former are considerably less costly and can therefore be made more frequently. The ideal would be a budget survey extending over a period of years, although this raises rather formidable problems of statistical inference, the difficulty being that households who are prepared to co-operate over long periods are not representative of the population as a whole. There have been attempts at continuous budget surveys in a number of countries, but not much has come out so far. Partial surveys extending over a period of years are becoming rather more common; they are often known as panel surveys. Such surveys are particularly useful in the case of durable consumer goods, because they provide a moving picture of the course of inventories over time. Incidental surveys do not always provide satisfactory information on purchases of such infrequently bought goods as durables, because in the course of a single year, for instance, most households do not record any purchases at all; moreover, aggregate expenditures on durables are so volatile that data for a single year may not be too meaningful.

I do not propose to go more deeply into the technical problems raised by the analysis of cross-section data, but there is one point which deserves to be mentioned in a conference of this kind. Economists working with cross-section data soon find that narrowly economic variables, particularly income, account for only a small part of the observed variance of expenditures between households. To some extent, this difficulty can be overcome by suitable grouping of the households; as I mentioned before, in economics we are rarely interested in the individual household but only in averages or aggregates of households. This, however, does not always solve the problem, because the noneconomic variables may be closely correlated with income and then lead to biased estimates of income elasticities. The only correct solution, therefore, is to take the noneconomic variables explicitly into account.

The most important of those noneconomic variables is probably family size, or more generally, family composition. It is widely believed that household size is a declining function of income, but in cross-section surveys the opposite is usually found to be the case: the households with the larger incomes also have the larger size. The reason for this positive correlation is primarily that households with more than one earner also have larger household income; it does not contradict the sociological belief just mentioned. Because the influence of household size on consumption is fairly complicated, the methods of analysis used are rather elaborate. Of course, there may be some arguments about the economic or noneconomic nature of family size; some students of the subject do not hesitate to speak of demand for children. It remains to be seen whether this is a helpful way of looking at the problem of household size.

Another such variable, which I would also regard as noneconomic, is the stage in the life cycle that a household has reached. The term "life cycle" has not always been clearly defined; perhaps it can best be measured by the duration of marriage in conjunction with the age of the head. There is evidence that the life cycle has much influence on such expenditure items as furniture, appliances, and education, and on the interrelations among income, liquid assets, and savings. The social class of the household, usually indicated by the occupation of the head, also appears to have an independent influence on expenditure patterns.

The second main type of data used in consumption research is time series. They typically give the annual average consumption of a commodity or group of commodities for a country as a whole. Since year-to-year changes in consumption are as much the result of price changes as of income changes, time series are particularly suitable for the estimation of price elasticities. The statistical problems raised by economic time series usually boil down to the fact that there are too few observations; this is not usually a problem with cross-section data. Another difficulty that has had much attention in recent years is that time series of consumption should, strictly speaking, be viewed as part of a larger system of equations, other parts of which may be unknown. Although in theory it is clear how one should deal with this kind of interdependence, which is typical of much of econometrics, many practitioners still prefer theoretically less adequate methods that appear to give more sensible results. On the whole, however, economists have become more aware of the limitations of short-time series as far as estimations of parameters and predictions are concerned, and I sometimes fear that the early enthusiasm has given way to an equally unwarranted negative attitude. The shortness of time series, which I just characterized as the source of most difficulties in their analysis, is of course less and less a problem as time goes by. Under the influence of national accounting, the coverage and especially the quality of economic time series have much improved in recent years.

Because cross-section data provide information mostly on income elasticities, and because time series are the only source of information on price elasticities, there are obvious advantages in combining these two sources. Those who first attempted to do so were often content to take income elasticities from cross-section data and regard them as given for use in time-series analysis. This procedure has been criticized, however, because it is felt that the elasticities from cross-section data and from time series are conceptually different. A consensus concerning these problems has not yet been achieved, and I will merely state some of the ideas that have been put forward. One conceptual difference that is often stressed is that between short-term and long-term elasticities. More particularly, it is sometimes felt that time series display primarily the short-term effects of price and income changes, while cross-section data are also determined by long-term adjustments. If this is true, the combination of the two sources has to be done with considerable circumspection, and it is even doubtful whether this combination would still be valid. Recently, moreover, the interpretation of cross-section data has been put into a new light by the so-called permanent-income hypothesis, which has as one of its principal aims the reconciliation of the conflicting evidence from time-series and cross-section data concerning the behavior of total consumers' expenditure in relation to income. Unfortunately, this hypothesis cannot be easily explained in non-technical language, and as its evaluation has only just begun, I will confine myself to mentioning it.

Another factor relevant to the problem of combining the two sources is the introduction of new commodities over time, which does not show up in cross-section data. Thus, if a new commodity such as television is introduced, this will have a depressing effect on food expenditure, but generally speaking this effect will show up only in time series and not in cross-section surveys taken at a single period of time. The development of panel surveys, which have some of the characteristics of both time-series and cross-section data, may be of considerable help in resolving these difficulties.

I must now return to the main theme of my discussion of empirical research, which was the estimation of parameters with a view to evaluating their invariance in different sets of data. I mentioned that cross-section surveys show a considerable amount of stability in income elasticities; the estimates of price elasticities obtained from time series, on the other hand, still tend to have too large standard errors to enable a definite judgment to be expressed. In general, the available evidence does not contradict the assumption of invariance, even between different countries. New developments in economic theory and in statistical methods may soon make it possible to give more definite answers to this important problem of invariance.

Although, as I mentioned before, the testing of the theory coincides to a considerable extent with the estimation of parameters, this is not the whole story. The pure theory also has certain implications that are independent of the numerical values of parameters. First and foremost among those is the so-called law of demand, which says that the demand for a commodity falls as its price goes up, subject to certain qualifications. The majority of demand studies certainly support this generalization. In the few cases where a price elasticity of the wrong sign is obtained, it is perhaps more natural to question the data than the validity of the law of demand, time series being what they are. Much less can be said about a more sophisticated implication of pure theory, which has to do with the effect of a change in the price of one commodity on the demand for another commodity. This implication is of particular interest because it is a test of the consistency of preferences. Unfortunately, estimates of cross-elasticities which measure the effect just mentioned are too few and too subject to error to allow a definite test. A few attempts have been made to investigate the consistency of preferences by questioning individuals directly, rather than observing their market behavior. These tests have led to positive results, in the sense that very few inconsistencies were detected, but the choice situations investigated were so simple that the bearing on the validity of consumption theory as a whole is rather remote.

As far as the third task of empirical research is concerned, namely the indication of subjects for theoretical investigation, I think I have covered this largely in the course of the preceding discussion. In addition, I should perhaps mention my conviction that consumption theory should become more specific and try to work out more specialized assumptions than has been the case so far. Generality has been the keynote of the theory of consumers' choice: the emphasis has been on implications that are valid no matter what shape a consumer's preferences have. Now that we are beginning to know more about the actual shape of preferences, it is also important to deduce its implications. This means that the theory should not confine itself to preference indicators of arbitrary mathematical form, but should work out the properties of particular preference indicators as well. The results might in turn be very stimulating to empirical research. It is primarily by this continued interaction between theory and observation that a science can hope to make progresss.

Family Interaction in Decision-Making on Spending

WILLIAM F. KENKEL

The presence at this conference of individuals from several disciplines, and individuals who, within each discipline, have different bents and persuasions and interests, should attest to the varied approaches to household decision-making. Even within the delimited area of "spending decisions," there are various dimensions of the more general problem that can be investigated. Focus can be directed to what was decided, to who did the deciding, or to how the decision was reached. As part of the third approach, attention could be restricted to the stages of the decision-making process and deal with such variables as the recognition that a decision had to be reached, the investigation and weighing of alternatives, and the choosing among them. It would seem, therefore, that our first task is to spell out as clearly as possible the dimension of household decision-making with which we shall be concerned.

As sociologists, we deal with the behavior of man in his relations with other men and the social consequences of this behavior. As family sociologists, we deal with the relations of family members, within and outside the family group, and the consequences of all that behavior on the family and its members. As family sociologists focusing on decision-making, we are concerned with a particular type of interaction within families. The key to our approach is the common factor "interaction." Our focus is on the behavior of family members, what they actually do, when two or more of them jointly attempt to reach a decision.

Somewhat more formally stated, the purpose of this paper is this: *To set forth and describe a provisional guide for an apposite and originative analysis of family decision-making interaction.* Such a model should contain the minimum set of concepts necessary for understanding (a) the interaction itself, (b) the antecedents of the interaction, and (c) the consequences of the interaction. The organization of this paper follows the tripartite division of the model. We shall first investigate more thoroughly the dimension of decision-making behavior with which we are concerned. We shall then attempt to delineate the important conditions that influence the nature of husband-wife interaction. Finally, we shall turn our attention to the consequences of interaction patterns in decision-making. The antecedents and consequences of interaction patterns are logically derived from pertinent theory. At times, existing research will partially serve to test the supportive links in the scheme: at other times, it will expose gaps in the model of uncomfortable magnitude, and at still other times we shall see that we do not have the kind of research to serve either function.

Components of Interaction

Earlier, we stated that our focus is on what family members actually do when two or more of them jointly attempt to work out a decision. When formulating our studies of spending decisions at Iowa State, we rejected the use of secondary information, that is, the reports of spouses concerning how they usually behave in decision-making sessions, or even their recall of how they behaved the last time a spending decision was made. We wanted to observe what they did. Accordingly, we went to the homes of married couples and asked each to assume that as a couple they had received a gift of $300.00 with the stipulation that the money could not be saved in any form nor could it be spent for anything they had already decided to purchase. We then asked them to discuss between themselves how the gift money should be spent and ultimately to reach a decision on the expenditure of all of it. A field worker observed the decision-making session, and a tape recording of it was made. A brief description of the system we used in recording and analyzing the observed decision-making behavior will perhaps be the simplest way of describing the kind of behavior with which we are concerned.

We selected Bales's system of Interaction Process Analysis to give us an objective account of what went on in the decision-making session and to serve as a theoretical rationale for analyzing the behavior. (See 3.) Very briefly, Bales's system consists of a set of 12 categories into which can be placed all types of verbal and nonverbal overt behavior to which the observer can assign meaning. The basic division of the categories is along two lines: (1) task behavior and (2) social-emotional behavior. In the task area are six categories for behavior that relate in a direct manner to getting the job done, solving the problem, or reaching the decision that lies before the group. Three of the categories in the task area can be characterized as categories for questions: asking for orientation or information, asking for an opinion or analysis, and asking for a suggestion. The remainder can be thought of as categories for attempted answers as giving a suggestion, giving an opinion, and giving orientation. All behavior that falls within any of the three question or three answer areas can be considered task-oriented behavior. The remaining six categories have to do with behavior relating to the integration and emotional tone of the group. Three categories contain positive actions: showing solidarity, tension release, and agreement, while three are designated as negative actions: showing antagonism, tension, and disagreement.

It should be noted that Bales's categories refer to the nature of the interaction rather than to its topical content (3, p. 34). In our studies, for example, at this phase we did not record whether a person suggested buying a bicycle or bourbon, but merely the fact that he made a suggestion. The next action, more than likely, would be the spouse's reaction to the suggestion, and this was recorded in the appropriate category. The topical content can, of course, be gleaned from the tape recording of the session. Bales's system of Interaction Process Analysis allows an objective description of the parts a husband and wife play in a joint decision-making session. We have an empiric basis for determining, for example, which spouse talked more, which disagreed more, which gave more suggestions, and so on.

Although we have taken a long time in arriving, we are now at the crux of our approach to household decision-making. We contend that an important dimension of decision-making behavior is that which has to do with how the task-oriented and expressive actions are performed by the deciding pair. We know that the role division differs among married couples; in some cases, for instance, husbands and wives perform about the same number of task-oriented actions, while in others one or the other spouse clearly performs more of the actions that are so labeled. Later we shall attempt to indicate why it is, or can be, crucial to understand the roles husbands and wives play while jointly engaged in making a spending decision. Granted for the moment that it is important to know the nature of husband-wife interaction, it is therefore also important to know what it is that exerts an influence on the roles that spouses take in decision-making. Our next task, accordingly, is to investigate the broad areas of potential influences on spousal roles in decision-making.

Research, theory, and general writing on small groups have been extensive. Strodtbeck and Hare's "Bibliography of Small Group Research," published in 1954, contained 1,400 items (29). Only the later works contained in this bibliography are part of the great upsurge in small-group research. From this extensive literature, much of it in recent years theoretically and methodologically sophisticated, one might expect an emergence of a body of "principles of human interaction." As a matter of fact, something approaching this is beginning now to occur. We will turn our attention to two such principles that have particular relevance for examining the roles assumed by husbands and wives in family decision-making.

The behavior of individuals acting in small discussion or problem-solving groups can be described by use of a relatively small number of behavior dimensions or categories. Carter has reported on factor analyses of the behavior variables used in a number of studies (6). Despite the fact that the groups differed in size, nature of the group task, and leadership structure, there consistently emerged three behavior dimensions. These three dimensions were described as: (1) Individual Prominence, or behaviors related to the person's attempt to stand out from the group and receive individual recognition; (2) Group Goal Facilitation, or behaviors with the common element of aiding the group in the achievement of its task; and (3) Sociability, or behaviors related to the individual's attempt to bring about and maintain satisfying relations with other group members. Those acquainted with the research utilizing Bales's system of Interaction Process Analysis are aware of the repeated discovery of behavior bifurcation into task-oriented or instrumental actions, on the one hand, and, on the other, expressive or social-emotional actions. (See, e.g., 28.) This dichotomization parallels

Carter's, referred to above, if we omit from Carter's the dimension that includes behavior leading to self-aggrandizement, individual recognition, and individual prominence. For many purposes it may be desirable to describe group behavior more minutely than a two- or three-factor system allows. It seems, nevertheless, that much of what people do and say when interacting in small problem-solving groups can be very generally classified as (1) task or goal-related behavior and (2) social-emotional or expressive behavior.

In addition to the fundamental bifurcation of the *action* that takes place in small decision-making groups, there is a strong tendency for group members to specialize, as it were, in one or the other type of behavior. Even though it is necessary, in other words, for both the task and expressive actions to be performed, it would seem to be possible for one person in the group to perform both types of behavior. Actually, of course, group members do exhibit a variety of behavior, but there is a strong tendency for two specialists to emerge from the group, the one leading and excelling in task-oriented behavior, the other outperforming other group members in expressive behavior. Only rarely, it is reported, does one superleader excel in both of these areas. Slater makes the point that there is a basic incompatibility between the roles of task leader and expressive leader, which, coupled with possible psychological differences in the role incumbents, makes it unlikely that a given person can successfully fill both roles (26). This decided tendency toward role specialization in small groups can be viewed as our second working principle.

Let us now apply these two principles to the family decision-making group. In view of the facts that (1) two broad sorts of behavior need to be performed and (2) there generally emerge specialists in each of the behavior types, we should expect that there would be a tendency toward dichotomization of roles in husband-wife decision-making. Note that it is not the difference in sex, or age, or position in the family that suggests this bifurcation, but that it stems from factors associated with the very nature of social interaction. Although we would expect role differentiation in couple decision-making, the nature of the requisite interaction does not allow us to predict which sex will play which role. The tendency toward role specialization can be viewed as a fairly strong social-psychological force, inherent in social interaction, that helps to determine how spouses behave in joint decision-making undertakings.

ANTECEDENTS OF INTERACTION

Culture has been defined as "the way of life" of a group. It is more than a play on words to point out that culture includes the prescriptions of the way life should be lived. It begins by assigning individuals to different positions in society and by instructing them in what they can and cannot do, and even how they should and should not think, when they are filling a certain position or status in the group. A universally found reference point for the assignment of individuals to different statuses is that of sex. All societies, everywhere, have established one set of rights and duties for men and another for women. While the reasons for this division are not as germane to our discussion as the possible effect it has on their respective roles in decision-making, the role division by sex nevertheless bears a little investigation.

Earlier studies stressed constitutional reasons for the differentiation of the roles of the sexes. It has been pointed out, for example, that the universal tendency toward the superiority of the male in size, strength, and motor ability has led to his assignment to roles in society that call for energy, aggression, and dominance, while contrasting roles have been assigned to the female (31). Noted too has been the nature of the female's role in the reproduction of the species (21, p. 7). The demands of pregnancy and nursing would seem to make it advisable to prepare women for roles that require less physical vigor and, particularly, that do not take them far from home and family. It has been suggested, too, that these explanations are but society's attempts to explain away the division of labor by sex that somehow in the dim past of their history was determined for reasons not primarily physical or physiological (17). A cataloging of what constitutes "woman's work" in some societies lends definite support to this hypothesis (ibid., pp. 116–17). Tasmanian women, for example, were the seal-hunters, swimming out to the rocks, stalking the large animals, and clubbing them to death. It is reported that Arapesh women are expected to carry heavier loads than men because women, by nature, have so much harder heads. The list could certainly be continued. Perhaps the crucial lesson is that, for whatever reason or reasons, all societies have come up with different role specifications for males and females. What is more, preparation for one's sex role begins early in life and is continued with a vigor not found with respect to any other aspects of social conditioning (18). It is no wonder that psychological differences between adults of different sexes exist and that they appear to the society to be basic and unquestionable.

We also need to take a closer look at the family as a specific unit of society in which differentiation of the roles of the sexes occurs. The nuclear family, consisting of the married pair and their immature offspring, is a small group. As such, we should expect to find the division of functions common to all small groups. We would expect, that is, the emergence of an instrumental leader and an expressive leader. When we restrict our discussion to the married pair and to our own society, the next question is this: Which member of the pair should we expect to find in the instrumental specialist role and which in the expressive role? Traditionally our society has assigned the instrumental role in the family to the male and the expressive role to the female. It is the husband who is expected daily to leave the home and so to manipulate the external environment as to provide for the physical needs of the family. To the wife-mother is assigned the task of remaining at home and ministering to the needs of the family members, particularly the children. The fact that the woman's duties traditionally centered about the home is not insignificant. Indeed, the concepts "home" and "mother" interpenetrate one another to such an extent that it is sometimes difficult clearly to separate them. Both are used in our society to personify the very essence of psychological comfort, the source of help, and the focus of security and warmth.

So far we have noted that males and females are conditioned from infancy for life in a society with differentiated sex roles. Frequently, as in our own society, the differentiation is in the direction of assigning the instrumental roles to men and the expressive roles to women. Within the family, the differentiation along these lines is particularly marked. Both sexes thus have been thoroughly trained to expect sex differences in behavior and to look upon role differentiation as only right and natural. Traditionally in American society women have been expected to be more expressive of emotions, more aesthetically sensitive, and more sympathetic than men (13). In short, women have been expected to possess those very traits that would prove desirable in the taking of the expressive role. Men, in turn, are thought to be more self-assertive, more aggressive, and more dominant. Much has been done, and is still being done, to make these expectations come true; from early childhood, males are trained so that they will, if at all possible, possess those traits thought to be desirable in the male, while similar effort is expended to make women, in the psychological sense, out of little girls. We are sug- gesting, therefore, that the cultural prescriptions with respect to the roles of the sexes, both within and outside the family, operate better to prepare the male for the instrumental role in decision-making and the female for the expressive role.

Scarcely anyone needs to be reminded that ours is a complex, heterogeneous, and rapidly changing society. Because of these char- acteristics, which are no less true because they are oft-repeated, it is a gross oversimplification to speak of *the* cultural prescriptions of the society. American society contains two major races, many ethnic groups, scores of religious groups, and all these groups are enveloped in a system of differential social status. It might well be expected that there would be some essential differences in marital roles within these diverse segments of society.

Class and Status Variations

All known societies have a system of differential social status. To a greater or lesser degree, rewards, power, privilege, and prestige are distributed unequally, with the result that each member of society has a certain determinable rank relative to other members in his society. In the United States alone, hundreds of studies have demon- strated that a person's position in the status hierarchy is related to scores of important social and personal characteristics. (See 8 and bibliographies cited therein.) There are several lines of evidence that would lead us to suspect that among these important differences we would include different attitudes toward the roles of husband and wife. It has been discovered, for example, that lower-status males, as opposed to middle-status ones, more readily accept the notion that "women's place is in the home" (*ibid.*, p. 249). While many lower- status married women are employed, in their reasons for working they stress the financial reward, whereas middle- and upper-status employed wives are more likely to stress other rewards. The lower- status wife, in other words, like her husband, seems more committed to the idea that her primary role is homemaking and childrearing, even though she may for many years find it necessary to supplement the family income. The middle- and upper-status wife, by contrast, is more likely to be truly pursuing a dual career. This is but one line of evidence that seems to suggest a greater separation between men's and women's roles in the lower-status groups. (See also 20.)

It is not farfetched, we submit, to take cognizance of the differences in sexual behavior discovered among people at different status levels. Kinsey's studies of marital sexual practices seem to indicate that middle- and upper-status males are more willing to accept practices that depart from the male's traditional superior role. We have, finally, the many studies of childrearing practices among people of different statuses. Although there is still more confusion than consensus in this area of inquiry, it is possible to conclude that lower-status parents tend to train their children more rigidly to fill specific age-sex roles, whereas parents at higher-status levels are more likely to take into account individual differences, aspirations, and capabilities, even though they must perforce prepare their children to operate within the general sex-role framework of their society (24).

Ethnic Variations

To the extent that a group of foreign-born individuals or recent descendants of the foreign-born constitute an ethnic group, they share a common culture derived largely from the society of their birth. The ethnic influence on marital roles would, therefore, demand an investigation of the culture of the many ethnic groups that are found in the United States. In each ethnic group are found different prescriptions for the roles of husbands and wives. Thus, each ethnic group departs to a different degree and perhaps in a different direction from the family pattern in the United States. It is true that in many ethnic groups found in our society today, such as the Polish, Italian, Puerto Rican, and German, the ideals are a strong father-figure and a rigid distinction between the roles of the sexes. But these ethnic groups have changed and continue to change. It is frequently misleading to consider all groups of the same national origin culturally similar. Contrast, for example, two groups of German-Americans: one has been living in an ideological and geographical enclave in rural Iowa for over one hundred years, the other has more or less recently arrived in Chicago. We should expect to find sharp differences in the marital roles prescribed by these two groups in keeping with their differences in economic ideologies and activities, the religious bases of the groups, their physical and social isolation, and their degree of acculturation. As a general proposition, we would expect that socialization in many ethnic groups found in

the United States today strongly conditions men to play the instrumental or task role in family decision-making and women to play
the expressive role (35). To the extent that research bears out this
posited relationship, knowledge of ethnic origins would allow us
better to predict the roles spouses would take in family decision-
making.

The Changing American Family

Earlier, we made reference to the changing nature of our society.
The family pattern in general and the roles of marriage partners
in specific are part of the relatively rapid cultural change that characterizes our society. Pertinent to our discussion, Foote sees these
changes as including more sharing of authority in the family, less
division of labor, and greater companionship of husband and wife
(9). He sees these characteristics as part of an emerging prototype
toward which all classes, races, and religious and other groups are
moving at varying rates. He concludes, however, that "women of the
educated and mostly salaried upper middle class are leaders, models
and mentors in moving the public toward the prototype hypothesized" (ibid., p. 254). This supports the notion of class and other
differences in marital roles at the present time and points up the
necessity for remaining alert to changes in these respects.

The Family of Orientation

Although we have talked of cultural and subcultural prescriptions
regarding marital roles, it should be clear that a person does not
come into contact with culture. He comes into contact with people.
The behavior of these people toward him and toward one another
only imperfectly embodies the culture of the group of which they
are part. To understand further the marital roles of adults, we must
consider also the family—the family of orientation. Before the general cultural prescriptions of marital roles and the specific subcultural variations of them could affect the child, they were filtered
through the interpreting agents of socialization, the family of orientation. Within a class or a race or an ethnic group, therefore, we
should expect to find a certain family-to-family difference in the nature and intensity of influence brought to bear on the later roles of
their children in marriage.

Several studies immediately come to mind that can be used to
document the importance of the family of orientation on later mari-

tal roles. Lu, for example, discovered that conflict with mother, re-action to home discipline, and a number of other unique experiences in the family of orientation allowed her to predict whether a mar-riage would be characterized as husband-dominant, wife-dominant, or egalitarian (36). While the predictive value of these factors was not extremely great, it is nevertheless suggestive of the importance of experience in the family of orientation for later roles in marriage. Ingersoll's studies led her to the conclusion that in general the au-thority roles learned by the individual in his family of orientation tend to be projected into the authority interaction between himself and his spouse (10, p. 36). The re-enactment of roles witnessed in the parental family tends to be most pronounced when both spouses bring to marriage similar and complementary roles, as when, for example, both husband and wife lived out their formative years in a patriarchal family. Brim, to take a final example, has discovered that the presence of a cross-sex sibling, as opposed to a sibling of the same sex, had a definite relationship with the content of sex-role learning, in the direction of cross-sex siblings tending to assimilate traits of the opposite sex (5). It would seem that we could conclude, therefore, that predictability of spousal roles in decision-making would be enhanced by a knowledge of the structure and relationships in the husband's and wife's families of orientation.

Peer-Group Influence

Very likely the peer group should be examined as a potential in-fluence on the marital roles of the sexes. In periods of rapid social change, we might well imagine that a given generation of age mates would have conceptions of the proper, normal, or expected roles of the sexes in marriage different from their parents. There is some evidence that this is exactly the situation in contemporary American society. Neiman's study seemed to indicate this and also that the peer group may be more important than the family in shaping cer-tain attitudes toward the feminine role (22). He discovered further that peer-group influence begins to be manifest at a relatively young age. Although Neiman's study was restricted to single persons, there is good reason to believe that after marriage the actions and attitudes of one's associates or one's "crowd" can to some extent affect the conceptions of marital roles he brought with him to marriage. We cannot begin to go into the various factors that would be related to the relative influence of the peer group as opposed to the family of orientation. However great may be the influence of one's group of associates, both before and after marriage, it is probably of sufficient importance so that it should not be ignored in any attempt to understand the roles husbands and wives play in family decision-making.

The third broad set of potential influences on spousal roles in decision-making has to do with those characteristics of the family group that may serve to alter, to counteract, or to reinforce the prior cultural and subcultural influences on marital decision-making roles.

In accordance with our theoretical statement on the reasons for role differentiation in family decision-making, a crucial feature of the family would be the presence or absence of children. Regardless of the role conceptions brought with her to marriage, a whole series of expressive tasks are thrust upon the wife who becomes a mother (37). Comforting an infant when he cries, soothing the feelings of a child, listening to his troubles, and ministering to him when he is sick are but a few of the duties assumed by most mothers, whether or not they feel comfortable in the role. Although some expressive duties are inherent in the role of wife, it would seem that motherhood normally carries with it far more demands for expressive behavior. What is more, the mere addition of another person to the family would seem to be potentially weakening to an egalitarian, partnership, little differentiated relationship that may have been developed by husband and wife. As Simmel has pointed out, at times the third party may unite, at times separate, the original dyad, but always the original dyadic relationship is altered (33). Parenthood implies the development of new role relationships of each parent with the child and the parents with one another. We are suggesting that at this stage of the family life cycle, with the intrusion on the previously existing dyadic relationship, there may also be a reorganization and redefinition of the roles of the original pair as husband and wife.[1] We suggest, too, that such a redefinition of marital roles would be in the direction of more clear-cut distinctions between husband's and wife's role, usually along the traditional lines. In families with a child or children, we would hypothesize that wives would be more likely to play the expressive role in family decision-making and husbands the instrumental role, as compared with childless married couples. The age of the children in the family, finally,

[1] For other effects of the number of people involved in interaction, see 27 and 19.

should not be ignored. Wolgast discovered that wives with children of preschool age had considerably less independence in economic decisions than other wives (34, p. 9). Perhaps as the need for expressive, nurturant mothering diminishes, women take on or resume a more instrumental role in family affairs.

Labor-force status of the wife would seem to be a characteristic of theoretic importance with regard to her more general marital role. In general, we would posit that wives regularly in the labor force would be less likely to play the expressive role in family decision-making. There are several refinements concerning the wife's employment that would seem necessary. Family life cycle is one variable which should be controlled. At the early stage of marriage, before there are children, over half of all married women are employed outside the home. We might well imagine that the less than half who are not employed at this stage of the family life cycle are in some important respects different from those who are. At the early childrearing stage, relatively few mothers are in the labor force. Mothers who have preschool-aged children and who are also working outside the home are thus statistically rare and may well be distinctive in other ways related to their roles in decision-making. Taking account of the number of years the wife has worked, or expects to work, would seem to be desirable. The nature of the wife's usual job, particularly the extent to which it is usually thought to constitute a career, may very well prove important. There should be some way, finally, of getting at the married woman's motives for out-of-the-home employment. Although there is little direct evidence that either supports or refutes our proposition, we are suggesting that knowing the labor-force status of the wife, with at least the aforementioned variables controlled, would allow us better to predict which women would usually take a primarily expressive role in family decision-making.

So far we have dealt chiefly with the woman's role in the family. Referring now to the husband, we would want to determine the extent to which he is performing the role of family provider. Various studies during the Depression discovered that, concomitant with his inability to support the family, the male experienced a changed status in the family (14).[2] The unemployed man frequently suffered a loss of self-worth and developed a feeling of being less a male. The

---

[2] Difficulties other than unemployment can serve to alter family roles. (See 15.)

inability of the man to provide financially for his family, to fulfill his legal obligation, apparently strikes close to the core of his masculinity. This being the case, what type of role relationship would we expect to find in those families where the role of provider is shared by husband and wife? Note that we are not now dealing with all families in which the woman is employed. Some such families maintain a fiction of the male being the sole provider, while the wife is merely "helping out" until there is enough money to pay for the last baby, the present car, or the next television set. Sometimes the wife's income is spent only on "extras," is saved, or is "put into the house." Contrast these cases with couples who have accepted a two-income marriage as a more or less stable way of life, allocating the total family income in ways that disregard its husband-wife components. In this and in similar cases where the spouses admit to themselves and others that both are playing the role of family provider, it would seem unlikely that the male would hold exclusive control over the instrumental role in decision-making. Reciprocally, because of her function in the family, we would not expect the wife to see her role in decision-making chiefly as an expressive, integrative one. While the proportion of the total family income contributed by each spouse may be important, we would suggest that the more crucial variable would be the extent to which husband and wife defined the role of each as a partner in the provision of family income.

The last family characteristic we want to consider as a potential influence on spousal roles in decision-making is the stability of the particular family as a social system. Probably most of what we are getting at here could be measured simply by the number of years the marriage has endured. Pertinent theory on the process of role learning allows us to predict the direction of influence of number of years married. (Cf. 7.) Phrased in terms of marital partners, we would state the theory as follows: Through interaction with one another, husband and wife come to crystallize the conceptions that they have brought with them to marriage concerning what is appropriate behavior for them by virtue of their status in the family. At the same time, husband-wife interaction allows each to develop expectations regarding the role behavior of the other. Knowledge of the role of the other comes about principally by attempting to take that role, usually by imagining how the other person would act. Taking the role of the other thus results in the learning of new responses, which are then available to the actor to use in future interaction. Repeated interaction between husband and wife, therefore, should lead to a certain amount of assimilation of the two roles, each incorporating into his own role some behavior originally part of the role of the other. Thus, over the years, we would expect increasingly less differentiation in spousal roles in decision-making. The convergence of roles of the spouses would be aided, of course, if each was rewarded for attempts in this direction and, conversely, would be arrested if each was punished for his attempts to incorporate elements of the other's role into his own. In other words, although repeated interaction should normally lead to role assimilation, there are conditions that would slow down the process or prevent its development.

The search for empirical evidence relevant to the assimilation of marital roles in decision-making was not fruitful. Wolgast discovered that younger couples showed a considerably higher frequency of joint decision-making than older couples, among whom, in turn, husbands and wives were more likely to decide issues alone (34, p. 8). In part, this may reflect intergenerational differences in our society, the younger couples exhibiting the newer role patterns. If we interpret the findings, as Wolgast apparently did, to mean that in a given group of marriages joint decision-making declines as the married pairs move on through life, then we have indirect support for our thesis of role assimilation through interaction. The longer a couple is married, in other words, the closer they would come to a hypothetical state of perfect assimilation in which each would respond identically to a given situation and each spouse would know that this is the case.[3] Each partner would thus feel capable of taking the role of the other, and each would recognize the other's ability to take his role. In these circumstances, joint decision-making would scarcely be necessary, and sheer efficiency would dictate its abandonment. We need, of course, a more direct test of husband-wife role assimilation, particularly one which would yield information on the extent of role differentiation in those areas where joint decision-making is retained. For the present, we can merely suggest that controlling on the number of years married would enhance the predictability of role differentiation in family decision-making.

[3] Slater, working with experimental groups, discovered that role specialization increased with the frequency of group meetings. Because the groups were one-sex and met a total of only four times, they were manifestly different from families. This possible exception to the theoretical relationship between time and role assimilation should nevertheless be noted. (See 26.)

It has probably already become apparent that the various forces that impinge on marital roles in decision-making may not always operate with the same intensity. We can posit a number of situational factors that would serve to modify, and in extreme cases to counteract, the usual role arrangement of the couple. Among these situational influences we would most certainly want to include the type of decision that had to be made, the physical location of the decision-making, and the persons witnessing or taking part in the decision-making.

Quite a number of studies have been made that attempted to determine whether spousal roles in decision-making were related to the kind of issue that had to be decided. Although their methods varied, almost all these studies have relied on the recall of the respondents concerning past issues resolved or past purchases made. Respondents were simply asked who made the decision or who had the most influence in such matters as the last time they purchased a car or went out for an evening of entertainment. Thus, in Sharp and Mott's sample of 727 wives, 70% reported that the husband had more influence in deciding what car to get, whereas, conversely, 54% stated that the wife had more influence in determining the family's weekly food budget (25). For a number of other types of decisions, the predominant pattern was reported as joint discussion and consultation rather than decision by one or the other spouse.

While much previous research, of which Sharp and Mott's is but an example, seems to indicate that the type of decision has a bearing on spousal roles and influence, it should be made clear that these researches are not tapping the same dimension of spousal roles with which we are here concerned. We must also question the ability of husbands and wives to recall accurately all aspects of their past decision-making behavior. In our own study, for example, we discovered that most couples were unable to answer accurately, immediately following a decision-making session, which spouse talked the most, which had the most influence, which contributed the most ideas, or which did the most to keep the session running smoothly (12). Perhaps it is easier to recall who did, or usually does, execute a certain decision than it is to describe the roles played by the parties to the decision. We would suggest, at any rate, that the implicit assumptions of much decision-making research that spouses are able to recognize the roles they play in decision-making and that more are further able at some later date to recall their roles bear more thorough investigation. Taking the findings of this type of decision-making study at face value, we would conclude that verbal responses about roles played by husband and wife in past decision-making indicate the importance of the type of issue upon which a decision was reached. Although this is suggestive of relationship, we need more direct tests of the relationship between role differentiation in family decision-making and the nature of decision-making issues.

Often overlooked in research is the fact that family decision-making has a location in space. This variable may be quite influential with respect to the roles taken by husband and wife. We might imagine, for example, that either or both would behave differently in the privacy of their home than they would in a retail store or in some other public place. Closely related to the location of decision-making would be the personnel involved in or witnessing the process. The same couple might behave differently when talking about the problem of buying an automobile at their weekly card party, at home and alone, and in the dealer's showroom. The extent to which their "at-home selves" are abandoned and the direction of any change in their roles could be predicted if we knew how each thought the outsiders expected them to behave and how these expectations related to their at-home roles.

In our own decision-making studies, we have made a partial test of the effect of an observer on the roles played by husbands and wives. Couples in the first sample were interviewed by a male who also observed their actions during the decision-making session, whereas a female interviewer-observer was used for couples in the second sample. Preliminary tests indicate that in the second study, the one in which the female observer was used, the wives had more influence and more of them performed highly in the area of giving ideas and suggestions. In short, we have some evidence that the sex of an observer of family decision-making does make a difference and, by inference, that any outside party witnessing the couple's decision-making may serve to alter their behavior.

We have so far discussed a number of cultural and social forces that, acting singly or in some combination, affect the roles that husbands and wives play in family decision-making. The psychological characteristics of the parties to decision-making may also have an influence on the parts they take. Although the conceptions one has of marital roles and the expectations he has developed concerning situational and other influences on marital roles are all part of his personality, we are now referring to a deeper dimension. Deep-seated personality needs can impel one individual into behavior at variance with custom, convention, and even the law; they can paralyze another individual into inactivity when activity carries even the threat of negative sanction. Deep psychological forces compel one man to take a mate with whom he is destined to a life of unhappiness, another man never to take a mate. There is some indication that all of us are guided in our marital choices by unconscious personality needs (32). It is reasonable to expect, therefore, that the behavior of *some* people in decision-making tasks is more in response to personality needs than other forces. More than this, we should expect that in the role behavior of *most* people personality needs would have some influence.

It would be a formidable task to delineate the various personality needs that could have a relationship to spousal decision-making roles. We will use but one personality constellation as an example of the extent to which the existing body of theory allows us to hypothesize the effect of personality patterns. Probably most are acquainted with the work of Adorno and his colleagues on the authoritarian personality (1). From this study, Levinson and Huffman later developed a scale called Traditional Family Ideology for assessing an individual's position on a continuum with polar types labeled "democratic" and "autocratic" (16). The autocratic extreme stresses a hierarchal conception of familial roles, it emphasizes discipline in childrearing, and it indicates a sharp differentiation of sex roles. The democratic polar type emphasizes decentralization of family authority, equality in both husband-wife and parent-child relationships, and individual development within the family. Scores on Traditional Family Ideology, incidentally, correlate plus .65 with the E (Ethnocentrism) scale and plus .73 with the F (Authoritarianism) scale of *The Authoritarian Personality*. Factor analyses of Authoritarianism, Ethnocentrism, Religious Conservatism, and Traditional Family Ideology scales indicate that the four patterns are part of a more general personality syndrome (23). It is suggested, however, that Traditional Family Ideology, one dimension of the general syndrome, may be thought of as an organized pattern or ideological orientation regarding the family.

It would be immediately supposed that the personality pattern here in question would be predicted to have a relationship with how an individual acts in a decision-making session with his spouse. We would suppose that a male falling close to the autocratic extreme not only would strongly prefer to play the task role but would find it difficult to do otherwise, even when, objectively, his wife was better prepared to handle this role. To play the expressive role himself and to "allow" his wife to play the instrumental role would be defined as weakness by a man with a personality syndrome including concepts of supermasculinity, rigid sex-role dichotomization, and stress on hierarchical arrangements. It is unfortunate that little research has been directed at the relationship between Traditional Ideology and behavior in various social situations. Sutcliffe found that personality factors of this general sort influenced verbal responses on how conflicts would be resolved (30). Allen found that authoritarianism was related to what he terms antifemininity attitudes in men, a pattern involving intolerance for anything smacking of femininity in men and admiration for the rough, strong-willed kind of exaggerated masculinity (2). In this latter study, of course, one way of thinking is related to another way of thinking. It does not detract from the real importance of such studies to reiterate that we need also many studies of the relationship between ways of thinking and ways of acting.[4]

CONSEQUENCES OF INTERACTION

In the foregoing section, we have looked at several different orders of cultural, social, and psychological characteristics that, according to pertinent theory, should have a bearing on how the task and expressive functions of family decision-making are divided. As the state of our knowledge increases—and a start in this direction would be the empiric testing of the various hypothesized relationships, followed by revision of the model as necessary—we should be able better and better to predict spousal roles in decision-making. We need now to give some attention to the consequences of decision-making roles. What difference does it make, in other words, whether or not couples rigidly dichotomize their decision-making tasks or whether, for that matter, they make their decisions by reciting frenzied incantations while dancing around a fir tree in the nude? We

[4] In our current decision-making studies, we are determining the effects of various personality characteristics on spousal roles. Although the data have been collected, they have not been analyzed.

propose that for several important reasons it is valuable to know the roles spouses play when engaged in joint decision-making.

Rather frequently in family decision-making research, an attempt is made to measure how influence is distributed within the pair. Influence, it seems, is often viewed as a sort of open-sesame that will throw open the door to a vast unknown complex and allow the researcher to comprehend all kinds of decision-making problems. Unfortunately, partly because of the way influence has been conceived and measured, these results have not been forthcoming. Most frequently, as we indicated earlier, the procedure for measuring influence involves asking a person whether he or his spouse had the most influence when this or that purchase was made, or by asking who decided to make the purchase. This assumes, of course, that individuals know the relative amount of influence they have, that they are willing to admit it to themselves and others, and that they are able to recall with accuracy how influence was distributed in some past decision-making session. It is hardly necessary to point out that each of these assumptions is fraught with difficulties.

In our studies at Iowa State, to take but one example, we asked each spouse, before engaging the couple in a decision-making problem, how he thought influence would be distributed, giving him a five-response choice ranging from "I will have the most influence" to "Spouse will have the most influence." Immediately following the session, we asked husbands and wives who *did* have the most influence. The inability of the Iowa State couples to predict influence distribution, even knowing the type of decision problem they had to solve, and the inability of couples to recognize their own and their mate's relative influence in a decision they had just reached was indeed remarkable. Only 18% of the respondents predicted the influence distribution accurately, and only 22% identified their influence pattern accurately after the decision-making session. Of the remainder, about half, both in the pre- and post-session tests, were classified as "very inaccurate." This designation was used when the respondent either wrongly stated which spouse had more or most influence, or when he stated that he and his spouse would have similar influence when in actuality one of them had decidedly more influence, as opposed to somewhat more.

It could be argued, of course, that the respondents and the observers were not defining influence similarly. This interpretation, which assumes that influence is a nebulous concept, subject to many definitions, casts serious doubts on the wisdom of simply asking people about their influence or, rather, of interpreting unequivocally what they say. A competing interpretation of our findings would be that the concept of influence is understood with a certain clarity, but that people in general are not aware of how or how much they and others exercise influence in social interaction.

Before turning to the measurement of influence, let us raise another theoretical issue. It is our contention that most spending decisions involve several levels of decision-making and that for meaningful results we should investigate the influence pattern at each level. There are, for example, the decisions that are made at the level of allocation of family resources to broad budgetary categories like food, housing, or recreation. Obviously if these allocations are adhered to at all, they affect more direct spending decisions. Let us posit another level of decision-making. In view of, and indeed because of, the over-all allocation of income, a family may find that it has resources sufficient to purchase a new large appliance. Who determines whether they will use the money for this purpose and, if used in this way, who determines which of several appliances will be bought? Once the decision to purchase, let us say, an air conditioner has been made, we have still another level of decision-making and thus another point in the sequence for influence to be considered. This is the actual selection of one type or brand. With other spending issues, there may be even more levels involved. We are suggesting that it is probably well to isolate these various levels and to investigate the influence pattern separately for each level. We might imagine the hypothetical case: the husband had the greater influence, however we define it, at the level of determining whether or not there were resources for a major appliance; the husband and wife had a similar amount of influence when it came to determining what type of appliance should be purchased; and finally, the wife alone decided the style she wanted and made her selection among brands. Who, then, had the most influence? It depends, of course, to which level or stage of decision-making we are referring.

In our studies of influence in family decision-making, we considered influence to be *the degree to which a person is able to have his own wishes reflected in the decision of the group* (11). In the decision problem in which the couples jointly determined how to spend a hypothetical gift of $300.00, the operational definition of influence became the proportion of the final list of items adopted by the couple that was suggested by each spouse. The one who first suggested an item that eventually was accepted was the one considered to have had his way, or to have had influence, in the family decision. Undoubtedly there are difficulties with this conception of influence and, what is more, not everyone will agree just what the difficulties are. We should add that the coefficient of correlation between the proportion of the total items that was suggested by each spouse and the amount of money spent by each spouse on items he suggested was found to be plus .73. In other words, suggesting items that turn out to be acceptable correlates well with control over the group's financial resources.

Having defined influence in terms of the proportion of the accepted items suggested by each spouse, we next developed operational definitions of "high," "medium," and "low" influence. We then related degree of influence to the roles husband and wife played in the decision-making process. The results of this analysis were provocative. Generally speaking, influence was linked to the performance of traditional marital roles. For example, all high-influence wives, 86% of those with medium influence, but only 43% of those with low influence, contributed most of the social-emotional actions during the decision-making session. Eighty-six per cent of the high-influence husbands, 64% of the medium-influence ones, and 25% of those with low influence outperformed their wives in the task area of giving ideas and suggestions. Our sample was much too small to allow neat generalizations, but the findings strongly suggest that the role a person plays in group decision-making is related to the degree of influence he will have. If our findings could be generalized, we could put our conclusion like this: "Tell us how a couple divides up the task and expressive behavior in joint decision-making, and we will predict with some accuracy who originates more of the acceptable ideas."

In addition to the matter of influence, there are other reasons why it would be important and useful to know, for a given type of spending decision, which spouse would play the instrumental role. Let us assume that in family decision-making there are elements of "rationality," with a discussion of spending choices, an investigation of alternatives, a weighing of pros and cons, and the like. Could we also assume that this way of proceeding is related to the decision outcome? If so, advertisers would immediately come to mind as a group that would be interested in knowing which spouse was the "idea man" of the pair, leading the discussion, bringing out the informational points on the suggested items, and evidencing knowledge of alternatives. Suppose we could pinpoint the matter more precisely and say, for example, that in the group that constitutes the best potential customers for clothes dryers, husbands and wives share equally the task decision-making functions related to styles and types of this item. Would not this make a difference in advertising, in the sense of the kind of information that is directed at which sex? Knowing this would seem to be more important than knowing, for example, which spouse made the actual purchase or even than knowing that the decision was made jointly without further specification regarding *how* the joint decision was reached. It would seem, finally, that those concerned with product innovations or new-product development would also be able to benefit from knowing how their products are discussed and evaluated, in the sense of which family member takes the lead in these respects.

A challenging consequence of role arrangements in spending decisions is that seen in the possible relationship between spousal roles and the types of products purchased. In our studies, we classified the items that the couples would buy with their $300.00 according to the ultimate user of the item, as "husband," "wife," "children," or "joint family." [5] The proportion of the gift money devoted to each type of item will next be related to the way in which the couple divided up the instrumental and expressive behaviors and also to the amount of influence each spouse had. While the analyses have just barely been initiated, it appears that some role relationships will have predictive value, although probably it will be low. It is a fascinating thought that, without knowing what families already possess and without knowing anything about their immediate or long-range plans, we may be better able to predict how they will spend their money merely by knowing the roles they play in decision-making.

We must freely admit, in conclusion, that we have the least and the weakest evidence on the consequences of spousal roles in decision-making. There are only hints of its importance. If it proves to be as important a dimension of decision-making on spending as

---

[5] Other classifications of the items might also be made. See Van Bortel and Gross's attempt to get at family values like comfort, knowledge, and health through the way in which families would spend gift money (4).

we think, then work in the area of identifying the antecedents of spousal roles should be accelerated and refined. The opportunity for prediction and control is exciting. Let us hope it is also real.

REFERENCES

1. Adorno, T. W., *et al. The Authoritarian Personality*. New York: Harper, 1950.
2. Allen, Dean A. "Antifemininity in Men," *Am. Sociological Rev. 19* (Oct., 1954), 591–93.
3. Bales, Robert F. *Interaction Process Analysis*. Cambridge, Massachusetts: Addison-Wesley, 1951. Pp. 30–84.
4. Bortel, Dorothy G. van, and Irma H. Gross. *A Comparison of Home Management in Two Socio-economic Groups*. Technical Bull. 240. East Lansing, Michigan: State Agricultural Experiment Station, 1954.
5. Brim, Orville G., Jr. "Family Structure and Sex Role Learning by Children," *Sociometry, 21* (March, 1958), 1–6.
6. Carter, Launor F. "Evaluating the Performance of Individuals as Members of Small Groups," *Personnel Psychology, 7* (Winter, 1954), 477–84.
7. Cottrell, Leonard S., Jr. "The Analysis of Situational Fields in Social Psychology," *Am. Sociological Rev., 7* (June, 1942), 370–82.
8. Cuber, John F., and William F. Kenkel. *Social Stratification in the United States.* New York: Appleton-Century-Crofts, 1954.
9. Foote, Nelson N. "Changes in American Marriage Patterns," *Eugenics Q., 1* (Dec., 1954), 254–60.
10. Ingersoll, Hazel L. "Transmission of Authority Patterns in the Family," *Marriage and Family Living, 10* (Spring, 1948).
11. Kenkel, William F. "Influence Differentiation in Family Decision Making," *Sociology and Social Research, 42* (Sept.–Oct., 1957), 18–25.
12. ——— and Dean K. Hoffman. "Real and Conceived Roles in Family Decision Making," *Marriage and Family Living, 18* (Nov., 1956), 211–16.
13. Komarovsky, Mirra. "Cultural Contradictions and Sex Roles," *Am. J. Sociology, 52* (Nov., 1946), 184–89.
14. ———. *The Unemployed Man and His Family*. New York: Dryden, 1940.
15. Koos, Earl L. *Families in Trouble*. New York: King's Crown, 1946. Pp. 91–111.
16. Levinson, Daniel J., and Phyllis E. Huffman. "Traditional Family Ideology and Its Relation to Personality," *J. Personality, 23* (March, 1955), 251–73.
17. Linton, Ralph. *The Study of Man*. New York: Appleton-Century-Crofts, 1936.
18. Mead, Margaret. *Male and Female*. New York: Morrow, 1949.
19. Mills, Theodore M. "Power Relations in Three-Person Groups," *Am. Sociological Rev., 18* (Aug., 1953), 351–57.
20. Motz, Annabelle B. "Conception of Marital Roles by Status Groups," *Marriage and Family Living, 12* (Feb., 1950), 136 ff.
21. Murdock, George P. *Social Structure*. New York: Macmillan, 1949.
22. Neiman, Lionel J. "The Influence of Peer Groups upon Attitudes Toward the Feminine Role," *Social Problems, 2* (Oct., 1954), 104–11.
23. O'Neil, W. M., and D. J. Levinson. "A Factorial Exploration of Authoritarianism and Some of Its Ideological Concomitants," *J. Personality, 22* (June, 1954), 449–63.
24. Rabban, Meyer. "Sex-Role Identification in Young Children in Two Diverse Social Groups," *Genetic Psychology Monographs*, Aug., 1950.

25. SHARP, HARRY, and PAUL MOTT. "Consumer Decisions in the Metropolitan Family," *J. Marketing, 21* (Oct., 1956), 149–56.
26. SLATER, PHILIP E. "Role Differentiation in Small Groups," *Am. Sociological Rev., 20* (June, 1955), 300–10.
27. STRODTBECK, FRED L. "The Family as a Three Person Group," *Am. Sociological Rev., 19* (Feb., 1954), 23–29.
28. ———. "Sex Role Differentiation in Jury Deliberation," *Sociometry, 19* (March, 1956), 3–11.
29. ——— and A. PAUL HARE. "A Bibliography of Small Group Research," *Sociometry, 17* (May, 1954), 107–78.
30. SUTCLIFFE, J. P., and M. HABERMAN. "Factors Influencing Choice in Role Conflict Situations," *Am. Sociological Rev., 21* (Dec., 1956), 695–703.
31. TERMAN, LEWIS M., and CATHARINE C. MILES. *Sex and Personality.* New York: McGraw-Hill, 1936.
32. WINCH, ROBERT F. *Mate-Selection: A Study of Complementary Needs.* New York: Harper, 1958.
33. WOLFF, KURT H. *The Sociology of George Simmel.* Glencoe, Illinois: Free Press, 1950. Pp. 128–32, 135–36.
34. WOLGAST, ELIZABETH H. *Economic Decisions in the Family.* Ann Arbor, Michigan: Survey Research Center, 1957. (Mimeograph)
35. WOODS, SISTER FRANCES JEROME. *Cultural Values of American Ethnic Groups.* New York: Harper, 1956. Chapters 11 and 12.
36. YI-CHUANG LU. "Predicting Roles in Marriage," *Am. J. Sociology, 58* (July, 1952), 51–55.
37. ZELDITCH, MORRIS, JR. "Role Differentiation in the Nuclear Family," in *Family, Socialization and Interaction Process,* ed. Talcott Parsons and Robert F. Bales. Glencoe, Illinois: Free Press, 1955. Pp. 312 ff.

Discussion

F. THOMAS JUSTER

Houthakker has prepared a tightly knit and comprehensive treatment of the theory of consumer behavior as viewed by many economists. I agree with much of what he says, although I find it a little hard to believe that an important reason why people buy cars, especially new ones, is that they are cheaper than taxicabs. There may be some status content that he omits, e.g., Cadillac versus Volkswagen.

The main question that I would raise is about the lack of explicit attention given to the impact of forward-looking variables on consumer behavior. Houthakker does discuss the influence of uncertainty and inventories on spending decisions. But my reading of his paper is that prices, income, assets, and demographic variables are viewed as the only important determinants of consumption expenditures, with appropriate lags and bearing the expectational burden. Yet it seems to me quite clear that short-term income prospects and subjective estimates by households of long-term financial prospects have significant bearing on purchase decisions, particularly on the timing of replacements or additions to the consumer stock of durables. On occasion, price expectations and expectations about general business conditions would play an equally important role. None of these variables is uniquely related to the recent experience of consumers. Although it is unfortunately true that we know relatively little about the way in which these expectations are formulated, they are significant and must be taken into account. Any model of spending behavior that does not take explicit account of these factors is not going to be very successful in explaining consumer actions in the short run.

Houthakker devotes a substantial amount of space to the problem of combining cross-section with time-series data. The discussion here is excellent for the most part, although I think misleading in one respect and seriously incomplete in another. The author argues that price elasticities cannot be estimated from cross-section data "because price changes are normally small during the period of observation," whereas income elasticities can be obtained from such data. But this surely cannot be because income changes are large. In fact, of course, we can obtain estimates of income elasticities because *income differences between households* at the same point in time are large, not because changes over the period of observation are large.

In this respect, might we not likewise be able to use cross-section data for price-elasticity estimates? What is needed are differences in the price alternatives that are open to different households at the same point in time, with other factors remaining the same. Surely there are substantial regional differences in prices due to transport costs; for example, automobiles in Detroit compared to California, and fruit in Florida compared to New York. If we could obtain cross-section data on representative family budgets in two such areas, I see no good reason why price-elasticity estimates could not be made. Admittedly, there would be problems of controlling other variables, but this problem is also present in time-series data.

In his discussion of intentions surveys, Houthakker suggests that it would be interesting to see whether income, assets, and stocks of durable goods yield better forecasts of purchases than do stated buying intentions. This kind of comparison has been made both on the macro and micro level by a number of researchers, although not all the data that are desirable have usually been available. (Actually, this is one object of the current reinterview study of Consumers Union members' buying plans now being conducted by the National Bureau of Economic Research.) The interesting comparisons here, however, are not those mentioned by Houthakker. We are not really interested in whether intentions, expectations, or attitudes predict better than assets, income, and demographic variables, but rather in the size of the marginal contribution of expectational variables to financial and demographic ones.

Further, and more important, it is by no means clear that a variable is useful for aggregate prediction merely because it has significant net prediction value on a cross-section basis. For example, in a static population with invariant age distribution we would doubtless find that age was a very important variable in determining which households were heavy purchasers of furniture. But simply because age distribution is almost invariant, this variable would be worthless for predicting changes through time in furniture purchases by the population as a whole, and yet the latter is the problem we are mainly interested in.

The objective of research in this area is really to isolate factors that are both importantly related to individual purchase decisions *and* that have an unstable distribution over time in the population as a whole. In effect, we want to isolate variables that tend to affect many households in the same way at the same time and that are significantly related to purchases.

One of the most interesting illustrations of this kind of requirement is the problem of determining the most useful time horizon to use in surveys of buying intentions. If we make the question very confining (definitely plan to buy) and of very short range (tomorrow), we undoubtedly would get very good predictions on a cross-section basis. But it is clear that such data would be useless for predicting changes in the aggregate. On the other hand, if we make the question very loose (what would you like to purchase?) and of very long range (in the next five years), we undoubtedly would get very bad predictions on a cross-section basis. The chances are that we would also get bad predictions on an aggregate basis with the latter question. The best question would be one that combines predictive value on a cross-section basis and variability in distribution among households over time in a way that maximizes aggregate predictive value.

The last point that I wish to raise is concerned with Houthakker's emphasis on the invariance of parameters and the advantages that would accrue to the development and application of theory if invariance could be demonstrated in variables like price and income elasticities. It seems to me that looking for invariance is like searching for the fountain of youth—not likely to be successful and very likely to direct energy into retrospectively useless channels. What is needed, rather, is to direct attention to the factors that influence the magnitude of elasticities in different circumstances. This does not necessarily mean that we must build up a complete model of individual decision-making based on fundamental variables of a social-psychological-physiological nature, and then aggregate. It seems to me that there are short cuts available and that the decision-making process can be usefully intercepted at perhaps a fairly advanced stage rather than at a fundamental level. Thus, for example, the important effects of a recession on the income elasticity of consumption spending might be gleaned from a relatively simple combination of price expectations, the range of prospective income changes regarded as possible by the household, and expectations about business conditions generally.

Kenkel's paper constitutes an attempt to examine some of the factors that are thought to be significant in determining the respective roles of husband and wife in joint decisions. The major emphasis is on relating the roles played by each spouse—classified as either task-oriented or social-emotional—to the amount of influence that each had on the purchase decision (or to the amount each was alleged to have). My comments on Kenkel's paper are necessarily limited by my comparative unfamiliarity with the sociological material that he discusses.

The major conclusions are derived from an experiment carried out by the author and his associates among Iowa couples. The conclusions about the relationships between spousal roles and influence on purchase decisions may be valid, although the evidence presented in the paper does not seem to me very convincing. However, the design of the experiment gives me pause and, in fact, seems to me sufficiently suspect so that even if clear-cut statistical conclusions had been obtained, it might not mean very much.

In the social sciences, we generally test models of behavior by observing how people act when their environment undergoes change or by observing differences in behavior between people in different environments. In both cases, the environments are real, in the sense that the subjects are reporting about (or being observed in) their behavior in a natural environment. But the experiment described in the paper asks the subjects to assume that they had been given a substantial gift of money ($300.00) and that the funds must be spent. In addition, an observer sat in on the decision-making session, and a tape recording of all conversation was made. The author himself points out that spousal roles in the decision-making session varied markedly with the sex of the observer and also that the environment in which decision-making takes place is likely to make a substantial difference in who says what and seems to play which role.

Further, and perhaps most important, the decisions being made are not real ones, and the subjects must surely have been aware that such is the case. Since the couples are not actually going to purchase the items being talked about, the session must have some aspects of a parlor game. Behavior in parlor games is not necessarily the same as behavior in real life.

It is clear to me that data gathered under these conditions must be very carefully handled, if indeed it can be handled at all. If my suspicions are correct, the goods on the approved list at the end of the session were generally items that the couple would enjoy having but which they would not have bought if they actually got the money. Also, I would guess that the female partner took a more important role in this session than would be found under more realistic circumstances, women being typically more fascinated by this sort of game than men.

Kenkel discusses a number of social factors that might be significant as a predictor of spousal roles in decision-making. Most of Kenkel's observations here seemed to be both fruitful and interesting. With regard to his analysis of the influence that the number of years married has on role specialization versus role assimilation, however, I find myself in disagreement with his conclusions. He argues that the theory of role learning leads to the conclusion that the longer a couple has been married, the more one would expect that the roles played by husband and wife are interchangeable. To quote: "Knowledge of the role of the other [spouse] comes about principally by attempting to take that role, usually by imagining how the other person would act. . . . Repeated interaction between husband and wife, therefore, should lead to a certain amount of assimilation of the two roles, each incorporating into his own role some behavior originally part of the role of the other. Thus, over the years, we would expect increasingly less differentiation in spousal roles in decision-making."

In empirical support, Kenkel relies on Elizabeth Wolgast, who found that younger couples showed a considerably higher frequency of joint decision-making than older couples, the latter being more likely to make unilateral decisions about most issues. Kenkel interprets this finding to mean that the roles of husband and wife become more perfectly assimilated through experience and interaction, each spouse resonating identically to a given situation and each knowing that this is the case. Hence, he argues, joint decision-making becomes unnecessary and sheer efficiency dictates its abandonment.

I would interpret the data in exactly the opposite manner; that is, suggest that role *specialization* and differentiation become increasingly important through time for a married couple. In the beginning years of marriage, a couple must feel its way, since the process of joint decision-making is a new experience. Gradually each finds areas where the primacy of the other becomes recognized, because, I would suppose, of a mutual recognition that one or the other makes better decisions about some kinds of problems or is more affected by the decision. To suggest, as Kenkel does, that "each would feel more capable of taking the role of the other" is to suppose enough practice in the role to perform it competently. Yet, how many husbands can duplicate the wife's role as mother when the wife goes off with the local theater group? Or how many wives would be able to decide whether to invest the family savings in General Motors or keep it in the savings bank? Taken seriously, the theory in the paper seems to suggest that a husband is as competent as his wife to decide what to serve an important guest for dinner, the more so, the greater number of years they have been married.

One further general point in the section of Kenkel's paper dealing with factors that influence the roles played by spouses: The author discusses a large number of what he calls "cultural and subcultural" forces, including physical structure of male and female, social attitude toward the propriety of different roles, family and ethnic backgrounds of spouses, peer-group influences, the impact of family structure (children present, one versus two income earners). It seems to me quite possible that the apparent influence of some of these factors may be in turn simply a function of the family income level. It might be argued that low-income families typically have fewer aggregate decisions to make, since the range of alternative activities open to the family is sharply limited by their financial situation. Hence, we would expect less dichotomization of roles between husband and wife, other things being the same. On the other hand, as income increases and a growing number of alternatives require decisions, increased specialization would be expected. Thus, differences between the character of roles played by dual-income families in which the wife is a career woman and those played by dual-income families in which the wife is regarded as temporarily helping out may be due mainly to the fact that the first unit would normally have a much higher income than the second, rather than to the social attitudes of the two units. By the same token, the spectacular growth in leisure for both spouses over the past century—due mainly to higher hourly wages—must have had a major influence on the proportions of expressive versus instrumental roles played by each spouse. One interesting aspect of a variable like income is that its influence would be important for analyses of differences over time as well as differences between families at the same point in time. The same may not be true for many of the factors discussed in the paper, since the distribution of cultural or subcultural factors is very stable over time.

The last point I wish to mention is concerned with Kenkel's treatment of influence. Knowledge about which spouse has the most influence clearly has great significance for economists as well as sociologists. If for no other reason, it enables us to address our questions about attitudes, expectations, and intentions to the spouse who has the most impact on purchase decisions. However, defining influence as the author does—the proportion of prospective purchases suggested by A that are eventually agreed upon by both A and B—has serious weaknesses. Suppose family groups specialize in decision-making roles along the following lines: The wife suggests things that might be purchased; the husband analyzes the alternative merits of purchasing now or purchasing later and of purchasing X as opposed to Y; both indicate their preference map with regard to the alternatives posed by the husband; and the husband has the prerogative of vetoing any proposed expenditure if he feels strongly that it cannot be afforded now. In Kenkel's scheme, as I understand it, the wife would receive a 100% score on influence, since she does all the suggesting. Yet the veto power seems to be clearly a more critical variable, if it exists. I would not be surprised to find that the above pattern was rather common.

Discussion

VERNON G. LIPPITT

Preparation for discussion of papers at this session led me to a consideration of the concept of a model and of the desirable properties of a model as related to the purpose for which it is developed. Let me summarize my thoughts on this score as a background for discussion of the two papers.

I would define a model as a representation in symbols of the structural elements and the essential relationships of some real system of behavior, insofar as it is helpful to the problem at hand. By elements of a system I mean the component parts and the forces that lead to change or action of those parts, or to change in the system. The usual purposes for developing a model are: (1) to communicate information economically about the real system, or (2) to provide a logical aid in the comprehension, analysis, and prediction of the structure and actions of the real system. Examples of some real systems and the types of models used to describe them include:

(1) a word description of the solar system or of an organized group of persons, and of the relationships and interactions involved

(2) a blueprint of a machine

(3) an artificial heart made out of plastic vessels and tubing, with pumps and fluid

(4) a circuit diagram of a television set

(5) a system of equations for describing the United States economy

(6) the machine programs and punched cards providing information on the structure and operation of a business organization

The schematic diagram in Chart III.1 illustrates the types of information involved in a model. In the center is a box symbolizing the structural parts of the system itself, including all characteristics of the component parts that are relevant to the action being studied. On the left is an indication of the environmental conditions, the constraints and forces that act upon the system; these may be considered inputs. On the right is indicated the change (activity or behavior) of the system; this is the output involved in the study. The nature and detail of the desired outputs govern the nature and the amount of detailed information required to specify the system and the appropriate inputs adequately for the problem at hand.

CHART III.1

GENERAL MODEL

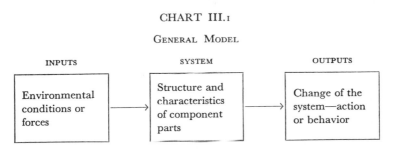

This conference is considering models of household decision-making in several areas. We wish to understand or to predict the content of decisions that households will make in these areas, given adequate information about the structure and characteristics of the household and about the environmental forces operating upon it. The properties desired in the model which we formulate will depend greatly on the purpose which we have in mind in developing the model and on the degree of detail desired in the output decisions. In my own work, I am interested primarily in predicting the content of the spending decisions of households, by major categories of goods. From this point of view, the following characteristics would be desirable in the household model developed:

1. *Operational character.* The component parts and the forces involved in the model must be capable of definition, observation, and (usually) measurement. Only so can hypotheses regarding the structure and the relations within the model be capable of verification or refutation through observation or experiment.

2. *Causal relevance.* The concepts (the component parts and forces) involved in the model must have explanatory and predictive

power with regard to the output behavior which it is desired to specify. The model developed should refer to the specific content of spending decisions, i.e., types of products purchased and amounts spent, as well as to the nature of the decision-making process itself.

3. *Completeness.* The degree of detail in specifying the parts and the relationships within the system must be complete enough to explain and predict buying behavior at whatever level of aggregation (by consumer units or by products) is needed for the problem at hand. Thus a much more detailed knowledge of households and the forces acting on them would be needed to predict refrigerator purchases by individual households than to predict aggregate expenditures for all goods and services by all households.

4. *Dynamic properties.* In prediction, what we are concerned with is essentially the understanding and forecasting of *changes* in the system from its current status. Consequently the specification of the system should permit determination of the reaction of the system to varying external forces, and it should also allow for determination of changes in the structure and relations within the system over a period of time.

With this preface, I shall now discuss Houthakker's paper, "An Economist's Approach to the Study of Spending." Houthakker describes his assignment as providing us with "a self-conscious account of methods used by economists in consumption research." In fulfilling that assignment, he has elaborated an economist's model of household spending behavior. His purpose is apparently to set up a model that will be useful for empirical research in its tasks of testing hypotheses, evaluating parameters of the system, and suggesting new causal factors for investigation. Probably he would not quarrel with the suggestion that the model should also be useful for predicting consumer spending.

As I see it, Houthakker is considering two types of systems: (1) a single consumer unit, and (2) consumers in the aggregate. The elements are comparable for the two systems, interaction being neglected in summing over all individuals. The structure of the system (placed in the center box of Chart III.2) is specified basically by the utility map, tastes or pattern of wants of individual consumer units, as reflected in their preferences among alternative allocations of their incomes. Preference patterns root back in climatic, biological, and social factors and also in such characteristics of the household itself as family composition, stage in the family life cycle, occupation of

CHART III.2

HOUTHAKKER MODEL

INPUTS	SYSTEM	OUTPUTS
Environmental conditions and forces relating to spending	Consumer units (individual or aggregate)	Spending decisions and buying behavior

the head, habits, and attitudes and expectations. Preference patterns manifest themselves primarily in the price and income elasticities, which are simply ratios between the per cent change in physical quantities purchased of specific goods (outputs) and the per cent change in price or income (inputs).

Although income and price are considered the dominant elements among the environmental conditions and forces acting on the consumer, other factors are granted some influence on buying behavior, for example, actual and desired inventories, financial reserves and credit opportunities, and new commodities. These inputs (in the left-hand box) act upon the consumer system and lead to buying decisions that eventuate in the output behavior indicated in the right-hand box.

Houthakker and I apparently think pretty much alike; hence, I have no major criticism of his model. It possesses most of the desirable properties of a model as specified above.

1. *Operational character.* With the possible exceptions of utility and uncertainty, the elements of the model seem to be definable, observable, and measurable.

2. *Causal relevance.* The elements in the model would seem to be relevant in a causal sense to consumer spending decisions.

3. *Completeness.* Some additional factors might make the model more complete. For example, place of residence and home tenure are household characteristics that may affect buying of some goods, and advertising and sales efforts by producers may well influence spending, as may also considerations of social status. The discussion of problems involved in aggregating over-all consumer units also seems inadequate.

4. *Dynamic properties.* Time, according to Houthakker, enters into consumer decisions primarily through habit formation and through the existence of inventories. The first introduces time lags

in consumer responses, and the second presumably alters preference patterns. (Variation in income, prices, and other environmental conditions will also affect consumer spending directly, but this is not a change in the consumer system itself.)

Houthakker maintains, however, that the relevance of pure theory and the usefulness of the model for predictive or explanatory purposes hinge on the constancy or stability of the income and price elasticities and of other parameters. This seems to be too restrictive a viewpoint. If one could determine how the parameters describing the response of the system varied through time, then the system would become truly dynamic and still be useful for prediction and explanatory purposes. His model contains the factors whose change might account for changes in the parameters, for example, stage in the family life cycle, social factors, or attitudes and expectations.

On the whole then, it seems to me that Houthakker has presented us with a respectable model in the area of consumer spending. Our friends among the psychologists and sociologists may point out that the model is superficial. Objective characteristics of consumer units have been related to consumer spending behavior, but there has been no real causal analysis of the underlying psychological and social forces at work, no true model of the decision-making process developed. The economist might answer that use of objective characteristics of consumer units as explanatory factors may prove sufficient for his purposes of explaining and predicting consumer behavior and also that the evaluation of parameters in this simplified model will absorb all the research resources which he can muster. Also it may well be that use of the objective characteristics as explanatory factors may be more helpful for forecasting and aggregating the spending behavior of all consumer units. Nevertheless, any additional insights and information that can be gained from psychological and sociological investigations of consumer decision-making will be gratefully received and incorporated into the economist's model as quickly as feasible.

Kenkel brings just such psychological and sociological factors into the picture in his paper on "Family Interaction in Decision-Making on Spending." It seems to me, however, that his paper deals with a model of spousal roles in family decision-making rather than a model of household decision-making regarding allocation and spending. Kenkel states: "Our focus is on the behavior of family members, what they actually do, when two or more of them jointly attempt to reach a decision." Again he states: "The purpose of this paper is this: *To set forth and describe a provisional guide for an apposite and originative analysis of family decision-making interaction.*" I judge that the interaction phases of household decision-making are of intrinsic interest to the author and that this is why he has developed a model of spousal roles rather than a model of household spending behavior. Prediction is mentioned in several places, but it usually refers to prediction of spousal roles or of the nature of the interaction process. The author is not primarily concerned in this paper with the content of the spending decisions or with the buying behavior which results.

Chart III.3 illustrates what seems to me the nature of the model that has been developed. In the center block is an indication that

CHART III.3

KENKEL MODEL

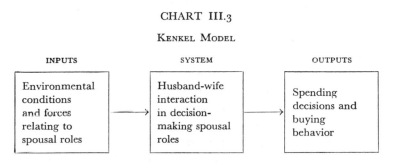

INPUTS	SYSTEM	OUTPUTS
Environmental conditions and forces relating to spousal roles	Husband-wife interaction in decision-making spousal roles	Spending decisions and buying behavior

husband-wife interaction in decision-making is the basic system on which Kenkel focuses his attention. In particular, the task- (or goal-) oriented behavior and the expressive (or social-emotional) behavior of husband and wife are under scrutiny. The paper gives considerable attention to the "antecedents of interaction," or conditions that influence the nature of husband-wife interaction. These may be considered the inputs or external forces acting on this system, as shown in the left-hand block. Little consideration is given to the "consequences of interaction" or outputs from the system, which are placed in the right-hand block. However, as mentioned before, the primary contribution of this paper lies in its analysis of the interaction process, and particularly the spousal roles in this process, rather than in the specific content of the decisions reached. The author is focusing intensively on a subassembly, a component part of the structure of the over-all model set forth by Houthakker.

A discussion of the model developed by Kenkel grows logically out of considering how it meets the desirable characteristics of a model, which have been specified previously. It must be borne in mind, however, that his purpose and the scope of his model differ greatly from that described by Houthakker for predicting the spending decisions of households by major categories of goods.

1. *Operational character.* The experiment devised by Kenkel and his associates suggests that the concepts of role, influence, cultural and subcultural factors, situational forces, and psychological characteristics of husband and wife may be satisfactorily defined, observed, and measured. I suspect that this paper and the experiment described make an appreciable contribution along these lines.

2. *Causal relevance.* Given the purpose of the author to understand and predict the spousal roles in husband-wife interaction, it would seem that he has developed an excellent model of the cultural, situational, and psychological factors that enter into the determination of spousal roles. I was a little surprised by the lack of emphasis on needs and goals in influencing the interaction process and would suggest that the specific content of the decision to be made probably affects the decision-making process considerably. For example, the process may well be quite different for decisions to buy food, or clothing items, or a car.

As for the broader problem of predicting household spending behavior, the author suggests "possible relationship between spousal roles and the types of products purchased," but admits that "we have the least and the weakest evidence on the consequences of spousal roles in decision-making." I strongly suspect that an ability to predict spousal roles would not contribute greatly to one's ability to predict the way in which the family income is allocated. As Kenkel and his associates go further toward analyzing the relation between spousal roles and the content of specific spending decisions, I urge upon them the necessity of multivariate analysis to estimate the influence of spousal roles simultaneously with other variables that may have as good a claim to consideration as basic causal factors.

3. *Completeness.* Not being a psychologist or sociologist—for example, I had never heard of Bales's system of Interaction Process Analysis—I am not competent to criticize the completeness of the model as far as predicting spousal roles is concerned. I did have a vague feeling that the task- or goal-oriented content of the housewife's role was underestimated. It seems to me that in addition to the expressive element in comforting an injured child, there is also the task of doctoring the child. Also, what about the goal-oriented

decisions and production-line scheduling involved in assembling, preparing, and serving a nutritious, tasty, and hot meal at the proper time for a hungry family? I wondered also about the possibility that a nondirective approach by the wife in the decision-making interaction might permit her to lead the husband into directions that she desired. Perhaps the effects I am thinking of will come out of the analysis of Kenkel's experimental data, because I note that wives can have a high degree of influence on the spending decisions even when their major role is in the expressive area in the interaction process.

For predicting the content of spending decisions, the model is clearly far from complete. Many factors other than spousal roles or the nature of the interaction process influence spending decisions— the traditional economic factors such as income level, present possessions, social aspirations, attitudes and expectations, prices, new products, and advertising. The author is excited by the "fascinating thought that, without knowing what families already possess and without knowing anything about their immediate or long-range plans, we may be . . . able to predict how they will spend their money merely by knowing the roles they play in decision-making." Having been disillusioned by the explanatory power of variates regarded by economists as more important than spousal roles, I must confess to little excitement on this score. For one thing, it should be noted that a large share of consumer units are not headed by married couples. It should be pointed out also that even the establishment of a strong causal relation between spousal roles and spending decisions would contribute little to the prediction and control of consumer behavior unless changes in the number of families exhibiting various types of spousal interaction could be predicted in the months and years ahead. The prediction of changes in spousal roles might well prove as difficult as predicting consumer behavior directly from other variables. Houthakker's paper has indicated the nature of these other explanatory variables, and many of them would seem to influence spending directly rather than mediately through their influence on spousal roles in husband-wife interaction.

4. *Dynamic nature.* Although it would be a mammoth undertaking to quantify the various influences affecting spousal roles in order to predict those roles from knowledge of a family's background and environment, the model is potentially capable of doing so. It also contains the social and psychological elements whose change through

time might enable one to predict over-all long-term shifts in spousal roles in our culture. I would wonder whether short-term shifts could also be predicted and aggregated.

On the other hand, if a model of household spending decisions is desired, the dynamic aspects of the additional causal factors cited above would need to be brought into the picture.

In summary, the two papers that we have heard this morning point out well the model that economists use in their research into consumer spending behavior and the opportunities for psychologists and sociologists to deepen our understanding of the underlying decision-making process. I trust that we may increasingly find ourselves to be companions in ignorance as we attempt to understand consumer behavior.

Discussion

KOMAROVSKY: I should like to emphasize a point suggested by both Kenkel and Juster on the schema. I mean something here more limited than the model. Consider brand choices. We got further by breaking up the problem—for example, What feature attracted? Where did you learn about it?—when we learned the art of asking why in more specific ways.

The process model of decision-making that we have been using is probably too simple. We appear to be thinking of two wills in conflict and a victory of one over the other. As was suggested, one may originate proposals and the other may have veto power. The result may be not a victory for one but a compromise. The question of who first made the proposal refers only to one step, and we need to consider all steps.

The answers our respondents give to the question, "Who makes the decision?", may not be comparable precisely because they have different stages or features of the process in mind. Our own disagreements are probably due to lack of articulation of the steps involved in the decision. Imitation, compromise, and learning more about the matter all deserve inclusion.

Another distinction must be made, between the authority structure of the marriage and the control of particular activities. There is discontinuity between authority and economic decision-making; one cannot be assumed from the other. From the point of view of the advertiser, it may be important that the wife makes the decision about certain purchases. But if her husband ordered her to take responsibility for these purchases, against her own desire, this may mean a defeat in her marriage.

KENKEL: Confusion arises from mixing decision with execution. Influence may well be different at different stages of decision-making. Initiation may be more important, not who contributed the most ideas or who did the buying, which may be another party.

JOHN: Referring to both today's and yesterday's papers, decision-making has been considered in regard to purchasing, not deciding not to purchase. Much decision-making activity, much of it quite aggressive, consists of rejection of proposals. If the result for the family differs, the process may, and so rejection needs to be included to make our theory complete.

MEYERS (to HOUTHAKKER): You have discussed prediction of behavior based on different and changing income levels, using the device of studying elasticities of demand. You have used data from both cross-section (one-time) and panel studies, seemingly with equal confidence.

Yet in empirical research, there have been a number of presumably comparable studies in which there were sizable differences in the estimates of aggregate purchases, using the two different collection-of-data techniques. In general, there seems to be an upward bias in the one-time studies of nondurable goods; the consumer reports a much higher level of purchases than his actual, as found through a panel.

Does not this question about the source of your data suggest that you put certain limitations on the conclusions you draw?

DANIERE: When aggregating at the national level, and checking survey purchase data against other data on income and sales, we found this bias not too important and not all in the same direction. The worst bias occurred in personal services. Toiletries are also much overreported. But tobacco and alcohol are notoriously underreported. However, panel study does tend to reduce such biases.

ORCUTT: Houthakker is mainly interested in the relationships among spending categories, not in estimating aggregates. A different problem is involved. A graph showing income elasticities for various products may not be useful for aggregates, but each curve demonstrates a relationship.

FOOTE (to JUSTER): Referring to your criticism of Kenkel's technique of acting out purchase decisions, you should not dismiss it. In your own work, you are depending on questionnaires, yet the personal interview is always superior in validity and reliability to the filling out of questionnaires, and the playing of a scene in turn is a better simulation of real behavior than interviews. In the work Stanton and I and others did at Chicago, we got our best predictions through role-playing. Borgatta has done an experiment demonstrating that the closer the simulation of the behavior to be predicted, the better the prediction.

STANTON: It is real. In a Puerto Rican field survey using a similar technique, people really behaved during the "interview." They accepted the artificial conditions set and acted as they would if these conditions occurred.

KENKEL: Although our technique may seem strange to economists, it was no parlor game to the couples, who considered the decision seriously. We chose the exact amount of money carefully for authenticity. Sometimes there was a heated argument. Some would say, "Now that we have the money. . . ." We felt they were very close to reality.

MILLER (to HOUTHAKKER): Just to add a comment on Trienah Meyers' question: We tried to compare the findings of LIFE's Consumer Expenditure Study with actual national aggregates. We were close on most, but low on liquor and high on a few others. But in seeking current figures on aggregates, some sources we approached told us they had new aggregates based on our study.

On income elasticities, Irwin Friend at the Wharton School is fitting demand functions to our date on some 30 or more product groups and comparing them with the 1950 data. For some categories, there is no change, for some, remarkable change. He is also analyzing elasticity of demand by a large number of demographic characteristics.

HALBERT (to JUSTER and KENKEL): To support Kenkel's position, I should like to refer to a study I was engaged in a few years ago at Alderson Associates. We developed a shopping game, which was played as a game by the women involved. Yet in spite of the "parlor-game" atmosphere, the women reacted with high ego involvement. They shopped in a series of mock stores and selected a "best buy." At the end of each session, one out of ten participants actually received the item she had selected. From behavior in this game, we were able to predict actual shopping behavior in terms of stores selected. Moreover, we were able to predict the average price of the free gift selected by participants at the end of the experiment. The interesting fact here is that, because the gift was free, it was expected that the women might all select items near the top of the price range. The women all knew the prices of the items. But our predictor (a statistical procedure), which made no allowance for the parlor-game effect, estimated that the average price of items selected would be about equal to the average price of items available. It was. There was no feeling of "It's free, so let's get all we can." The laboratory had simulated the real-life situation.

ALDERSON: I should like to second what Halbert has said about the value of experiments in consumer behavior, using the simulation or game approach. In the research project in which we collaborated, we attained remarkably close results on certain parameters, such as the probability estimates in the minds of consumers, by the three standard research methods of recording observed behavior, asking for judgments from the respondents, and inferences from the results of shopping games.

Each of the methods of observation, question-asking, and experiment has, however, its own special shortcomings and hazards. The simulation of real-life situations confronts us with risks in interpretation and inference. I certainly believe that experiments such as that undertaken by Kenkel should be encouraged. On the other hand, he faced serious problems in interpreting the data. Negotiation as to how to spend $300.00 is obviously instrumental behavior from the standpoint of both parties. If either party appears to engage in such expressive behavior as smiling or weeping, this may simply be his preferred negotiating technique. If one appears to be trying to prolong the conversation, that could also be explained as a negotiating stance or tactic. In real life, one side may try to force concessions by pretending not to care whether a deal is made or not. The other side may press for reaching an agreement on the assumption that the occasion is favorable and the opportunity may pass.

With respect to Houthakker's paper, Juster pointed to the lack of reference to advertising and promotion in his picture of consumer behavior. To me this is part of the broader defect of omitting all reference to market development. In a dynamic, consumer-goods economy such as ours, many major products emerged in the twentieth century, and quite a few were unheard of as recently as ten years ago. To understand the market for such a product, we must recognize that it has a history. The product is introduced and struggles for a foothold. If successful in this first stage, it may go through a period of rapid expansion by adding new uses. Growth levels off as the sponsors of the new product run out of new prospects. If they manufacture a durable good, they must now look primarily to replacement purchases for their business, as with automobiles today. The pattern of consumer response differs in these three stages, depending on the degree of interest in or need for the particular type of product. There are corresponding differences in the actions taken by the seller in market development. To gain a foothold, he must concentrate on getting basic performance to meet minimum standards of satisfaction. To gain new users rapidly before competition catches up with him, he is likely to make increasing use of price appeal. When he reaches the stage of being dependent on replacement buyers, he may turn to obsolescence of style, improvement of service, and innovation of secondary features. Some of these features may be important enough to start a new cycle of growth.

Advertising and selling play a role throughout, but it is a changing role. The market for advertised products cannot be understood merely in terms of lags in response to price and income changes. A market in our economy has a beginning, a middle, and an end. A market develops and passes through clearly marked historical stages, which are an essential part of a dynamic picture of consumer behavior.

BILKEY (to KENKEL): Isn't a mother's work in the household as instrumental as it is expressive? Isn't it artificial to press all roles into one or the other?

KENKEL: Although she may also play an instrumental role, she is better prepared throughout her life to play the expressive role within the family. The husband is not expected to play the expressive role in decision-making.

KATONA: Both surveys and experiments are needed to study the underlying factors of consumer behavior. In principle, there is no difference between the use of direct and projective questions in surveys and the simulation of real conditions in experimental setups. But does this mean that anything goes? Or are there some limits on the researcher in his attempt to clarify basic causal factors?

Studies conducted over many years by the Survey Research Center reveal at least two considerations which restrict the researcher. First, we should abstain from asking "iffy" questions or setting up "iffy" experiments. If a consideration has never occurred to a person, if it is foreign to his way of thinking, then one does not gain anything—and may be misled—by ascertaining his reactions to that consideration.

Let me illustrate: Answers to a question inquiring about future behavior if savings banks were to pay 10% interest on deposits would be meaningless in predicting behavior. Or: In an inflationary period when nobody expects price reductions, it is worse than useless to inquire about probable reactions to substantial price reductions.

Secondly, one should not imply, either in survey questions or experiments, that future circumstances and reactions are certain. One should not exclude the possibility of uncertainty—of "it depends on" answers—and should not insist on definite commitments. By insisting that a respondent, though unwilling, make up his mind and choose between alternatives which the researcher presents, one may falsify findings. Some people are too accommodating: they say, or do in experiments, what they think the researcher wants them to say or do.

Whether these considerations apply to the experiment reported here, I am unable to say.

JUSTER: I do not ridicule Kenkel's procedure, but the Alderson experiment does seem to me more realistic. The rules were effective, and the game was played out to where some people acquired goods. Kenkel's was not. I myself would not act the same way before an observer and a tape recorder that I would otherwise, and I base my doubts on that. There are limits beyond which we cannot go if we want to create a situation in which people can act as if it were real.

We must set up some criteria. I have used five different questionnaires, and in this respect some were definitely better than others.

SCHLAIFER: In Von Neumann's work with an investing game and with bets, the utilities were not the same as for real situations, but the more striking observation was that they were not too different in the hypothetical games. "Gusher," a game played by oil drillers, becomes very real for them. But you cannot go too far outside the range of experience; outside this range, the utilities get "noisy." Systematically false answers can be used and are useful, but "noisy" ones cannot.

I am puzzled, however, by the use of Bales's scheme of categories for observing problem-solving. His model does not provide for conflict. It is all right for tinker-toy building, but I do not see how it fits into this bargaining situation.

KENKEL: This use fits Bales's requirements; the same elements are present. There must be the possibility of disagreement. He thinks it fits many other situations.

STRAUS: This discussion of the "artificiality" of small-group experiments seems to imply that when experimental research is undertaken, the stimulus variable must always be some kind of game or hypothetical situation. This, of course, is not necessarily the case. As in survey research, it is possible to utilize actual events and problems. For example, the couple could be asked to prepare their budget for the next three or six months, and their roles and interactions while doing so be observed by Bales's or some other appropriate technique.

I should also like to add a qualification to the "model of a model" which Lippitt presented. He lists as one of the requirements of a good model that it be "complete." One must be very careful about the way this requirement is interpreted. If taken literally, it represents an almost unattainable, perhaps self-defeating, criterion. This is because the number of possible elements influencing a system of behavior is usually almost infinite. To aim to include *all* these elements in a model is to invite being smothered in an avalanche of detail. Even if the model-maker emerges still breathing, his model will probably prove unusable. Rather than completeness in this sense, the criterion should be inclusion only of variables necessary and sufficient to account for operation of the system.

Also, Kenkel noted that studies based on *recall* of participation in decision-making show typical areas of predominance of husband and wife, and he also indicated why such recall may be inaccurate. Have your experimental studies shown anything about predominance in different areas of decision-making?

KENKEL: Our respondents could not accurately report their real roles either before or after the decision-making session. What they conceive and recall their roles to be conforms with traditional roles for husband and wife, but not with their behavior. We have not been able yet to repeat the experiment for different areas of decision-making, however.

HOUTHAKKER: The critics have been kind to my paper and there are only a few remarks that need a reply.

Lippitt and Juster both question my position on invariance, which is indeed an extreme one. Nevertheless I will stick to it until proved wrong. It seems to me that without such a goal there is a great risk of not seeing the wood for the trees. Thus, the kind of social relativism that is now popular would logically lead us to estimating the income elasticity of the demand for Palmolive Soap among middle-income nonwhite undertakers with two children and a cat in the suburbs of Hallelujah Junction, California. I do not contest the possible importance of demographic variables, but we should not lose sight of more general phenomena.

Juster thinks I put too little emphasis on expectations. On this point I am prepared to be convinced by empirical evidence, but I do not think this evidence is available yet. The test, contrary to Juster's opinion, is predictive ability. Experience with the Michigan survey suggests that people's statements about their expectations and intentions do not have a very close correlation with their actual behavior.

While Juster's formulation of the factors that need to be isolated for short-term forecasting is interesting, it is not a reliable guide for empirical research. Thus the factor of age should not be ignored when analyzing expenditures on furniture on the ground that the age distribution is stable; omitting this factor might bias the estimates of factors of other variables. There have already been studies of price elasticities based on the cross-section data, as Juster proposes, notably for electric power and gasoline.

Whether Alderson is right in emphasizing "market development" depends mainly on one's purpose in consumption research. The market for the Edsel had a beginning, a middle, and an end, but the market for food as a whole has not. I would also suspect that the similarity in consumption patterns among different countries casts doubt on the importance of advertising and of sociological factors in general.

KENKEL: There are only a few points I would like to make in response to the comments of Juster and Lippitt. I believe that Lippitt has done a good job of describing what a model is and that he correctly described the phenomenon, spousal interaction, around which the model here presented is built.

I feel it unfortunate that Juster devoted so much of his time to a discussion of the research findings and methods of my studies at Iowa State. I cannot agree with him that the major conclusions of my report are derived from my own studies. What I have attempted to do is create a theoretical model of spousal interaction in decision-making, and have used the findings of my own and approximately two dozen other studies partially to test the relationships posited in the model.

The point raised by Juster on the effect the number of years married has on spousal roles in decision-making seems to require a little clarification. Perhaps I did not make it plain in my paper that I was not referring to all the roles of the spouses, or even to their total marital roles, but only to their interaction with one another in discussions and decision-making. Accordingly, the husband would not necessarily be better able to prepare and serve a meal to company after many years of marriage than after only a few years. Let us imagine, using a similar example, that over the years a husband and wife had often discussed whether to give a formal or informal dinner. I would conclude from the theory on role learning that each spouse should be better able to take the role of the other in discussion, anticipating the reasons, arguments, and counterarguments consistent with the view of the other. Morgan makes the same point in his paper.

I feel that a serious void in my discussion of role learning and role assimilation is the failure to have stressed the effects of countervailing forces on role assimilation. In other words, although role-learning theory suggests that spousal roles in decision-making could converge over time, and thus that there would be less differentiation in decision-making roles, certain forces could prevent this from happening and could even be strong enough in themselves to produce the opposite effect of greater specialization. Juster seems to think that this is usually the case, and there is certainly merit in his point of view. Whatever research eventually demonstrates, the present model is incomplete to the extent that it has failed to incorporate the diverse effects of repeated interaction on spousal roles.

Juster has raised some other good points with regard to spousal influence in decision-making. In part, it is a matter of terminology, but it is more than this. To me, the originator of ideas has an important function in group decision-making. Quite obviously, an idea can neither be discussed nor adopted nor vetoed unless it is first brought before the deciding group. Whether we call the function of originating ideas "influence" or something else, I do not think that we can deny its importance. Juster rightly points out that there are other important functions, such as the "veto power." I would not like to see influence defined solely in terms of veto power any more than Juster likes to see it refer solely to the origination of ideas. I am sure that many of us would like to see a thorough reworking of the important concept of influence and an eventual operationalization of its salient features.

IV. Decision-Making Regarding Buying, Including Brand Choices

The Automobile Buying Decision
within the Family

GEORGE H. BROWN

A number of studies have been conducted on the household decision process with respect to the purchase of an automobile. Of these studies, two have been selected for discussion in this paper to illustrate both the potentialities and limitations of such research as a contribution to the construction of a model of household decision-making.

The first of these studies was conducted in 1957 by Daniel Starch and Staff for *True* magazine (2). The research consisted of semi-structured "depth" interviews conducted separately with husbands and wives in 107 households in which a new car had been purchased 90 days or less prior to the interviews. The sample was restricted to urban areas and to intact families (both husband and wife present). Within these limits, a probability sample design was followed.

Two findings of significance can be drawn from this study. First of all, there was substantial agreement between the husband and wife when interviewed separately on the details of the purchase transaction. In 85 to 90% of the cases, both husband and wife were in agreement about the role played by each member of the household in the purchase decision. The fact that only 4% disagreed on the question of who drove when both were in the car, whereas 15% disagreed on the person responsible for choosing the color of car bought, suggests that memory failure or the unimportance of the event rather than ego-bias is the source of the differences reported.

(It would be interesting to re-examine the discrepancies to determine if any ego-bias did occur.)

The second finding concerns the role of the husband as the person who initiates the decision to purchase and selects the make to be purchased. The exact data are as follows:

TABLE IV.1

	Purchase Discussion Initiated	Model Make Decision
Husband	67	59
Wife	10	1
Mutually	11	33
Special Circumstances	6	3
Conflicting Reports	13	11
Total Cases	107	107

The "special circumstances" affecting the decision to buy are such things as accidental damage to the car or failure of a major mechanical item. In the case of the decision about make, the special circumstances were such things as employment with an automobile dealer. Eliminating the conflicting reports and special circumstances and assuming that the "mutual" decision category would, on further probing, reveal the same pattern of influence as the pure cases, it appears that the husband initiates the decision to buy in 85% of the cases and is responsible for the make bought in almost 100% of the purchase decisions.

The Starch organization reports that the verbatim comments suggest that the role of the female head is to resist the purchase of a new car. The resistance appears to stem from a difference between husband and wife in the hierarchy of values rather than opposition to a new car per se. Furnishing the home, saving money, providing for the children are goals that are valued somewhat more highly by the female head of the household than by the husband. The difference in values reflects in the concept of the budget. The male head of the household believes the family can afford a new car, whereas the female head of the family does not know where the money for a new car will come from. The conflict between husband and wife tends to take the form of the impact of the car purchase on the limited budget of the household.

The existence of a difference between husband and wife in the way commodities are valued is indicated in a study conducted by the Research Department of the Curtis Publishing Company. One hundred and three husbands and 97 wives in separate families were asked when they expected to buy a new car. They were then asked to indicate on a check list of 24 "big ticket" items (a new refrigerator, color TV set, money for college tuition, and similar expenditures) which they would buy before getting the new car. In the case of the husbands interviewed, 25% said the car came first and only 26% named more than one item to be purchased prior to the car. Among wives, however, only 1% mentioned the car as the first item to be purchased while 50% mentioned two or more items to be purchased prior to the car. Perhaps the study was biased in covering items of more interest to women, such as household equipment. It is possible that another list of items could reverse the percentages. However, the points of interest are the facts that different valuations are placed upon specific items by husband and wife and that the automobile tends to be valued higher by the husband than by the wife.

General confirmation of the Starch-*True* study is also contained in a research study conducted through the national consumer panel maintained and operated by the J. Walter Thompson Company for its clients. This panel is composed of 6,000 families, stratified to provide good representation of United States families with respect to geographic distribution, city size, income and other social-economic characteristics. Although this panel has been in operation for a number of years, the relevant research is confined to the calendar years 1955 and 1956.

As part of the panel operation, each member of the household 15 years of age and older was asked to report each month the make of car preferred and the family's buying intentions with respect to a car—i.e., whether they intended to buy the car new or used, and when they planned to make the purchase. In addition to providing this data, each family reported monthly whether an automobile had been purchased and, if so, what make and model year and whether the car was purchased new or used. During the period studied, a total of 703 families who had both a male and female head reported new car purchases. By comparing the actual car purchased with the makes preferred as expressed by individual members of the family, it was possible to draw some conclusions with respect to the person in the family most influential in determining purchase. The findings of this tabulation were as follows:

TABLE IV.2

Make Purchased Was Preferred by	Number	Per cent
Both Husband and Wife	296	42.1
Neither Husband nor Wife	246	35.0
Husband Only	99	14.1
Wife Only	62	8.8
Total	703	100.0

That is, in 77% of cases there was no conflict between husband and wife. As can be seen from this table, the largest category concerned those cases in which both husband and wife had expressed the same make preference. No detailed analysis was made to determine the process whereby the make preference had come to be agreed upon. This process can be inferred only from other data indicating that 60–70% of automobile-buying families tend to repeat the make purchased primarily as a result of their inability to predict with certainty the outcome of a decision to purchase any other given make car. This "brand loyalty" factor is quite uniformly stable for all but the smallest makes. In the absence of such ability to make firm predictions, buyers tend to stay with the make known to them by previous experience, supported in a minority of cases by such special circumstances as unusual confidence in a particular dealer or a friend or relative engaged in the manufacture or distribution of a particular make.

Some analysis was made of that group in which the preference of neither the husband nor the wife was satisfied. The analysis was confined primarily to observing that the make purchased was lower in price than the make preferred in the great majority of these cases. We inferred from this that the reason for purchasing a make other than the one preferred was the discovery that the actual price was higher than the expected price. Our experience in conducting automotive research makes clear that the purchase price of a new car for most people is the "cost-to-trade" or the cash difference between the dealer's price on a new car and the price offered for the car traded in. Because consumers do not have clear concepts of either new-car prices or trade-in values, it is not unlikely that the expected price for the preferred make could be several hundred dollars lower than the actual market price. Also, we have the phenomenon of "trading up."

Turning now to the cases where a different preference for make was expressed by husband and wife, and where one of these two makes was actually purchased, we find that in two-thirds of the cases, the preference of the male head of the household prevailed. In view of the smallness of this segment of the sample, no further analysis was made of the data and we have no insights concerning the direction of preference of the frustrated husband or wife. It is possible that the "success" of the wife as reported in the panel data may be due to her preference for a lower-priced car than was preferred by the husband. In this situation, the cost to trade into the higher-priced make might force the purchase into the lower-priced make, confirming the wife's preference. We reviewed the data to see if wives preferred lower-priced makes but this was not clear, except when wife was victor; there the evidence was clear that wives preferred the lower-priced make.

Panel data give confirmation to survey data. In addition to the two studies already reported, there is a great deal of supplementary data confirming the importance of the male head of the household in determining the purchase of a new car. For example, readership ratings for automobile advertisements run almost twice as high among men readers of a magazine as among women readers of the same magazine. Similarly, the recall of television commercials for automobiles is over twice as high among men as among women exposed to the same program, even with commercials beamed at women. Still further confirmation is contained in occasional surveys in which a question about the relative influence of men and women on the purchase of a car is included (e.g., 1).

It is worth noting that the influence of teen-age children in the household on the make of car purchased appears to be "unimportant." This is shown both in the Starch-*True* magazine survey and in the J. Walter Thompson consumer panel analysis. Teen-age children were not credited with influence on make by either of the parents interviewed in the Starch study, and there was no evidence of a significant influence of the teen-age preference when neither wife nor husband predicted the make of car purchased in the Thompson study. From what little data are available, it appears that the preference of the parents has a strong influence on the make preference of their children. When they differed, children seemed to prefer the higher-priced make. Data on the influence of children on the frequency of purchase of a new car are not contained in the Thompson panel study. The Starch study indicates, again, that the influence of children is not great, a fact confirmed by the small difference in new-car-purchase rates by families with and without teenage children. There is some evidence that when a car is needed for the teen-ager, he seems to become influential.

Research by business organizations on the household decision with respect to the purchase of a new car has been directed primarily to identifying the role of each person in the household. Such an orientation is to be expected because the information secured is used to direct advertising effort toward the most influential family member, both through the content of the advertisement and the medium employed. It is very hard to find a medium with higher male readership than female. As a consequence, very little automobile advertising is placed in women's magazines and no daytime television is employed by automobile companies in spite of the fact that a large female audience can be delivered at a very low cost. At the same time, automobile manufacturers do not overlook that segment of the market where the influence of the wife or female head of the house is dominant. This is reflected in the use of media such as newspapers, nighttime television, and outdoor bulletins, which tend to reach men and women equally.

For the future, research on decision-making with respect to automobile purchasing should be directed toward the decision process rather than toward the outcome of the process. For example, it would be helpful to know the nature of the expectations of each family member concerning the costs of owning the old car and the costs of owning a new car. In addition, the status goals of each member of the household and the expected contribution of the new car to those goals would contribute to an understanding of the household decision process. Some parts of the car are for women—interior trim—some are for men—horsepower—but where a choice must be made in design, men are favored at present.

The purchase or nonpurchase of a new car appears to be a fruitful area for basic research into the household decision-making process. First, the purchase decision is one that involves all the adult members of the household. Second, there is evidence of conflicts in those goals of husband and wife which are served by the purchase of a car. Third, there is very little precise knowledge about the costs and benefits of acquiring a new car over keeping an older car, making room for the full play of nonlogical factors in the decision process. Finally, consumers appear to be relatively uninhibited about discussing the car purchase, making it possible to secure insights that cannot be obtained in other purchase decisions. Automobile interviewing is impressively uninhibited. The substantial progress made to date in understanding the household decision-making process through the analysis of car buying is evidence of the potential productivity to be obtained from continued research on the family decision-making process.

References

1. FERBER, ROBERT. "On the Reliability of Purchase Influence Studies," *J. Marketing*, *19* (Jan., 1955).
2. *Male vs. Female: Influence on the Purchase of Selected Products as Revealed by an Exploratory Depth Interview Study with Husbands and Wives*. New York: True: The Man's Magazine, 1958.

Family Composition, Motivation, and Buying Decisions

C. JOSEPH CLAWSON

No one who has worked closely with demographic data showing demand for various products and brands can help being struck by the wide variations in purchases by families of different compositions. One notes, for instance, that the average family with children spends about 40% more on food, 84% more on refrigerators, 160% more on washing machines, 13% more on automobiles, and 37% more on motion pictures than does the average family without children. However, the average family with children spends 20% *less* money on laundry sent out to be washed and 16% less money on interurban transportation than does the average family without children (according to the Survey of Food Consumption, 1948, Department of Agriculture, and the Survey of Consumer Expenditures, 1948, Department of Labor).

It will be noted that these differences in consumption rates vary rather widely both in sign and magnitude and tend to raise a question whether any of the figures can be dismissed as either obvious or trivial. Why, we are led to ask, does demand vary with families in different stages of the life cycle? What is the process by which families of different makeups arrive at their buying decisions? How can a firm with something to sell to consumers do so more effectively by a better understanding of family composition?

If we can some day construct an adequate family decision-making model, it should certainly help to answer these questions, among many others. My purpose in this paper is to invite greater attention to a limited but highly interesting segment of the complex decision-making model that will some day be constructed, perhaps by this group or others like it. This segment of a model concerns the dimensions of a motive. To appreciate the importance as well as the limitations of such dimensions, it is desirable first to look at the problem in its larger perspective.

SOME DEFINITIONS

The *family* will be discussed here as including those people related by blood or marriage, pooling their incomes, and having their permanent addresses in the same dwelling unit except for such temporary absences as attending school, traveling, and working out of town. Although decisions are made by and for many different kinds of organized groups in our society, the family is no doubt the most vital decision-making unit among ultimate consumers. We can say this even while recognizing that the family is not a perfectly integrated unit and that it is not isolated from external influences on the part of people in larger or overlapping decision-making units.

By *family composition,* we will refer to different combinations of numbers, ages, and sexes.

The *buying decisions* which need to be explained will include those choices which are generic in nature as well as those choices which are selective in nature. Product choice and brand choice, of course, are only two of the multitudinous choices which families make as consumers. There are choices to be made among stores, delivery methods, price ranges, terms of payment, places and methods of storage, alternative uses, alternative methods of disposing of left-overs, and so on.[1] Although the road of consumer choice forks at many points, we are focusing on only two of these forks—product choice and brand choice.

BROAD OUTLINES OF A DECISION MODEL

Even such specialized decisions as product choice and brand choice are highly complex and affected by a variety of variables. An adequate decision model for these choices, as for other types of choices,

[1] See further discussion of these choices in my article entitled, "Problem-Solving Functions in the Behavior of Households," *Cost and Profit Outlook* (Sept., 1957).

will of course recognize that demographic characteristics such as family composition do not directly determine family choices. (I am pleased with the term "proxy variables" that has been used for these in this conference.) They do so only through intermediate factors. The broad causal sequence runs in somewhat the following fashion:

1. A *stimulus* is brought to bear. This may be an advertising jingle, it may be a past action that serves as the stimulus for future actions, or it may be any of a large number of observable marketing activities by various firms.

2. *Intermediate factors,* or intervening variables, are often altered by these stimuli. These are almost all of a subjective nature, including the motives of different members of the family, their knowledge, expectations and perceptions, and their roles in the structure of action.

3. The *behavior* that results from the shifting of intervening variables may involve choosing one type of product or a particular brand rather than some other. It is this type of behavior in which we are interested in this discussion.

The demographic characteristics of number, ages, and sexes making up a particular family are simply signals or clues pointing to the intermediate factors. A marketing executive is interested in family composition characteristics not so much because he loves statistics, but because he feels these characteristics provide clues to certain motives, knowledge, perceptions, and expectations that tend to predispose that family toward accepting or rejecting the product or brand he offers. His task is to select those segments of the total family population which are reasonably predisposed to buy what he has to sell, to control the marketing situation with which they are presented, and to persuade the families in the market in an effective, profitable way.

The causal sequence is thus anchored in observable stimuli on one side and observable responses and behavior on the other side. The marketing theorist's task is to construct a model that will show how and why the stimuli affect the intervening variables and, through them, the behavioral responses, in the way that they do. The marketing researcher's task is to take a conceptual model and translate it into measurable dimensions, so that theories about these connections can be tested, and above all so that marketing programs can be developed to fit the particular markets, products, and brands.

NARROWING DOWN TO THE CRUX

It is hardly necessary in this gathering to emphasize how important such factors as stimuli, perceptions, knowledge, expectations, roles, and responses are in the theory of behavior. Nor should it be necessary to apologize for setting aside a thorough discussion of all these areas so that we may concentrate better on one area which seems particularly interesting. This is the area of motivation.

We shall emphasize here, then, the relationships between family composition and motivation on the one side and product choices and brand choices on the other side. In the process, we shall note how marketing firms can develop programs for effectively influencing demand through proper *selection, control,* and *persuasion* (to be explained below), thereby affecting the motivational variables about which we shall speak.

In discussing the motivation of families of different compositions, we shall ask you to grant, for the time being at least, some rather heroic assumptions, perhaps the most important of which is that consumers engage in maximization behavior. That is, households attempt to maximize their expected net satisfactions by selecting the alternative product or brand which promises to give them, when the whole process is complete, the greatest excess of benefits over sacrifices, of advantages over disadvantages. This maximization includes the expected satisfactions or dissatisfactions of the motives of all members of the family that may be taken into account by the decision-maker and likewise includes any motives which are subconscious as well as conscious, concealed as well as revealed.

It is further assumed that usually there are several motives considered in any one decision by a particular person. The motives considered are assumed to be of unequal saliencies and intensities, some favorable and some unfavorable to a particular choice. Each of the motives is also regarded as capable of wide variations in intensity through time and among different individuals in a family and among different families.

Finally, it is assumed that differences in total net attractiveness of alternative products or brands can be explained by first determining the positive or negative weight of *each* motive going into the decision. The task today, therefore, will be to draw up a model attempting to explain why a motive has the amount of favorable or unfavorable influence that it does have on the attractiveness of any particular choice.

DIMENSIONS OF A MOTIVE

I would like to suggest that the influence, either positive or negative, of any individual motive on a choice is determined by the quantitative interplay of certain levels and dimensions that are common to all motives, no matter how dissimilar in nature these motives may be. The motives may range all the way from a desire to be considered a good housekeeper or to be attractive to the opposite sex to a desire to be economical or to save space in the refrigerator.

It is suggested that there are two primary dimensions, and several levels on each of these dimensions, that need to be taken into account conceptually and if possible measured. On the horizontal axis (see Figure IV.1), we show the status dimension, while on the vertical axis we show the intensity dimension.

On the *status dimension,* there are two key levels that must be considered in the analysis of motivation—the achievement level and the expectation level. The *achievement level* is defined as the future

FIGURE IV.1

MODEL FOR THE ANALYSIS OF MOTIVATION LEVELS

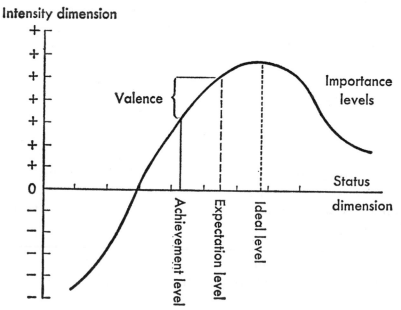

status, supply, or achievement that a person expects he will have if he does *not* act on any of the alternative programs of behavior that he is considering. It is a sort of achievement level in default of action. It could in some cases be the same as the present achievement level, but more often than not it could lie above or below that point. For instance, it might represent the poor level of health expected to occur if medicine is *not* taken, or it could be the cash expected to be left on hand if a certain purchase is *not* made.

The *expectation level* is the status that the person expects he might achieve with respect to the motive if he *does* choose a particular course of action among the various alternatives, such as buying a particular type of product or a special brand. Consequently, there will be a different expectation level for each alternative he considers. For instance, a girl may expect different degrees of improvement in her complexion from using different brands of facial cream, and each brand will have its corresponding expectation level in her mind.

On the *intensity dimension,* we are interested in the *importance levels* corresponding to each and every possible status along the horizontal dimension. This can be shown as a continuous curve or as separate bars connecting the possible positions. It may run from extremely negative up to a maximum and then down to a negative again for excessive positions beyond the ideal, or it may take a great variety of other shapes, which would have to be determined in specific cases. The various importance levels are independent of the present achievement level, the expectation level, or any of the alternative courses of action that might be considered.

When one or more of the three types of motivation levels is varied, the resulting changes in the intensity and direction with which that motive affects the demand for the product or brand being considered can be read off the vertical axis. (To do this, it is not necessary to know where the *ideal or aspiration level* is located, but it is interesting to note the position of this level, which lies just below wherever the importance curve reaches its highest point.)

In order to determine the valence or strength of influence which a given motive will have on the desirability of a particular product or brand, we note the effect of moving one or more of these motivation levels. Take the achievement level. If this level moves to the left, it means the person's need for satisfaction of this motive increases, as there is a greater distance between the achievement and ideal levels. Even if the expected gain from using a particular product or brand is the same as before, its attractiveness or valence will be greater because we have moved onto a steeper portion of the curve, at least in the segment shown here.

On the other hand, if the expected gain from using a brand or product is increased, with the achievement level and importance levels remaining the same as before, the attractiveness of the purchase again increases.

Changes in the importance curve also have strong effects. If this curve tilts more sharply upward to the right (regardless of its height), the motive will exercise a stronger favorable influence because of the greater difference in importance between the achievement and expectation levels. A flat or falling curve between these two points would cause a negative influence of this motive on the demand for whatever is being considered.

Closely allied to changes in the importance levels are changes in the ideal or aspiration level. If a person sets a higher standard of satisfaction, other things remaining the same, this may simply reflect a shift of the entire importance curve. The resulting valence would increase or decrease depending on the slope of the curve in the area between the achievement and expectation levels.

There are many other changes or combinations of changes in these levels, the effects of which can be easily read off this figure. In some cases, also, the achievement level, the expectation level, or both may get over onto the right side of the ideal level, where overachievement is involved or expected. The effects of these changes could be discussed at length.

Self-Other Dimensions of a Motive

If we were to abandon the discussion of the dimensions of motivation at this point, one might be left with the impression that we are concerned only with the self-centered wishes and fears of a decision-maker who disregards the motives of others in the family and is not influenced by them in any way.

Most motives, from our observations and experience with various marketing and motivation research studies, have a number of *self-other dimensions* or frames of reference. Each one of these variations may affect the decision of the particular person we are seeking to understand, and each one of these variations has an achievement level, an expectation level, and one, two, or even three importance curves.

To understand this idea better, we must recall that every decision-maker—indeed, every motivated person—sees his own behavior and satisfactions, as well as the behavior and satisfactions of others, through his own eyes and also (as well as he can) through the eyes of the other people. All these points of view which he considers motivate his behavior to some extent.

To express this, we may draw up a two-way table (see Figure IV.2)

FIGURE IV.2

SELF-OTHER FRAMES OF REFERENCE INFLUENCING A DECISION-MAKER

Views Refer to the Behavior and Satisfaction of These People	Decision-Maker Considers the Views of These People					
	Family Members				Outside Influencers	
	A (Mother)	B (Father)	C (Son)	D (Daughter)	E (Friend)	F (Teacher)
A (Mother)	aAA	aBA	aCA	aDA	aEA	aFA
B (Father)	aAB	aBB	aCB	aDB	aEB	aFB
C (Son)	aAC	aBC	aCC	aDC	aEC	aFC
D (Daughter)	aAD	aBD	aCD	aDD	aED	aFD

First letter in square designates the decision-maker.
Second letter designates the person whose views are considered by the decision-maker.
Third letter designates the person whose behavior and satisfactions are being viewed by some decision-influencer.

in which we write at the head of each column the name of each person whose views and standards are taken into account by the decision-maker. Let us label these view-holders *A, B, C, D, E, F*. The first four of these people may be members of the family, while the last two may be nonfamily acquaintances, friends, or other individuals whose attitudes are taken into account by the decision-maker. Then we may label the rows with the names of all the people in the family whose achievements, status, or behavior are viewed by the individuals listed at the heads of the columns. These may include only *A*, *B*, *C*, and *D*.

In each of these squares we may put some designations. For instance, let us start with a lower case letter *a* to remind us that we are ultimately concerned with the motivations and choices made by the decision-maker, who in this case may be the mother (*A*). The second letter will represent the person whose views and standards are taken into account by the decision-maker. The third letter will represent the people whose behavior, achievements, or status are being viewed by the parties listed at the heads of the columns. For instance, in the upper left-hand square, we have the symbols *aAA*, meaning that the decision-maker (*A*) is, of course, taking into account her own views and standards (*A*) as to her own behavior, achievements, or status (*A*). As another example, in the third row down, second column from the left, we place the letters *aBC*, indicating we are looking at the current decision-maker's (*A*'s) estimates and guesses as to the views and standards set up by another person (the father, *B*) for the behavior or satisfactions of a third person in the family (the son, *C*).

In the latter square, as in any other square, we would draw a separate motivational diagram, showing the various levels. We would indicate in this case where the decision-maker thinks person *B* places the *achievement level* of person *C* on a certain frame of reference. For instance, we may show that the mother recognizes that the father knows his son weighs around 70 pounds.

On this diagram, we would also show the perceived *expectation level,* for instance, the weight which the mother thinks the father would expect his son to achieve if he followed some particular change in diet which might be under consideration.

When we come to the *importance curve,* there are three such curves that have to be considered in order to understand the effect, if any, which the father's preferences regarding his son's weight will have on the mother's behavior. First, of course, the mother may take into consideration the strong objections her *husband* would have to their son's weighing less than 70 pounds, his preference that the boy should weigh about 80 pounds, and his feeling that a weight of 90 pounds or above would be excessive.

A second importance curve in the *aBC* square which may be taken into account by the mother would show how important she thinks the father's standards are to the *son,* that is, how anxious the boy is to please his father.

The third importance curve in this square represents the decision-maker's *own* evaluation of how important it is for the boy to live up to the weight standards set for him by the father. This curve may be influenced, of course, by the previous two.

It is the third curve, showing the importance to the *decision-maker* of another person's attitudes toward a variety of statuses (weights, in this case) which is of greatest immediate interest to us. From this curve we will be able to learn the intensity of the mother's motivation toward buying a specific product to help her son weigh more nearly what her husband thinks he should. We simply find the increase in height of the curve between the achievement and expectation levels. If it is great, the motivation is strong; if it is small, the motivation is weak.

We could go on to fill in and discuss the other squares but again time does not allow. We have at least suggested a pattern which could be elaborated. Not every square must be filled in for every decision, of course. They provide a pigeonhole for classifying, and the motivation levels diagram provides a vehicle for understanding the strength of whatever motivations are strong in a given case. The important point to note here is that the decision-maker is making decisions that will affect the satisfactions, achievements, and statuses of other people in the family as well as her own. In this sense, she is acting as the decision agent for the others, and it may be that she will also make the actual purchase for them, although this is not necessary to our discussion.

Another important factor to consider is that a decision-maker considers the motives of other people inside and outside the family, even though they may not be the immediate beneficiaries or sufferers from the action that is being considered. To the extent that the decision-maker believes any member of the family cares what his status or reputation is with these outside people and thinks that the purchase under consideration will affect his status, these outsiders must be reckoned with as decision-influencers. Their influence on the product or brand choice, of course, may be active or passive, depending upon whether they communicate their views to the decision-maker or the decision-maker simply takes their interests and views into account anyhow on his own initiative.

Implications for Marketing

The potential usefulness of motivation levels analysis, taken in conjunction with self-other dimensions, lies in the fact that it can represent different forces influencing the decision-making process in families of different compositions. It can take account, more specifically, of the fact that families differ in the number of members, the kinds and intensities of motivation of the different members, and the varying degrees and directions of influence of different members upon each other and upon the decision-maker. Allowance is also made for indirect influence on the decision-maker by the standards, views, and judgments of respected individuals outside the family, such as friends of the same or opposite sex, campus leaders, teachers, and doctors.

Marketing executives, it may be inferred from these dimensions and structural relationships, need to learn who the purchasing agent and users of a particular product will be, who the principal influencer (decision-maker) is, who the other decision-influencers are within the family, the strength of their influence, the reasons for their influence, and who the potential influencers are, if any, outside the family, together with the strength of their influence and the reasons why their influence is as strong as it is.

It will then be a challenge to the marketing executive to devise a plan whereby he too can become a successful decision-influencer. He may influence the decision through a wide variety of marketing activities, all of which boil down to three fundamental methods of affecting the motivation levels in the various self-other dimensions. These methods of influencing are by selection, control, and persuasion.

In *selection*, it is the task of the marketing executive to determine which types of families are most favorably predisposed toward accepting his generic product or brand. This will be largely based upon their *need* or desire for certain types of satisfaction which his product can supply and their *ability* to pay for it and perform all the other functions necessary to its complete processing through all stages. He will undoubtedly find, for instance, that families of certain sizes, with or without children, scattered through certain age ranges, with a given sex distribution may be the most likely prospects, with these "demographic characteristics" serving as the best index to the existence of the motives which matter.

In *control,* the executive manipulates the real marketing situation or product in such a way as to increase the family's pre-existing readiness to buy. He may make certain product improvements, develop a different pricing policy, a better package, more appropriate channels of distribution, and improved store layout or counter displays, or offer premiums and other inducements to attract particular members of the family.

Finally, in *persuasion,* he will use advertising, personal selling, and publicity devices that will help to change the motivation levels *via* the psychological aspects of the marketing situation. The marketing executive will select those media which reach the key influencers inside and outside the family and devise promotional messages which will have the greatest appeal to these decision-influencers.

Examples of Interplay

Perhaps the most concrete way to describe the interplay of family composition, buying choices, and marketing action is to discuss some hypothetical although realistic cases. There are three types of choices to be exemplified: (1) generic product choices, involving consideration of major differences in product features; (2) brand choices, involving consideration of certain differences in product features, while the marketing situations remain relatively the same; (3) brand choices, involving consideration of brands that are virtually identical in features and price, but that differ markedly in the conditions and practices under which they are marketed, such as the media which are emphasized, relative availability at the retail level, and appeals to different classes of respondents.

Generic Product Choices

To illustrate the first type of choice, we note that the demand for motion-picture admissions varies widely with the number, ages, and sexes of the people composing a family. For instance, the Survey of Consumer Expenditures, 1948, conducted by the Department of Labor showed that the average family with children spent about 37% more money on motion-picture admissions than did the average family without any children in it. How would this be depicted or measured in our model?

The horizontal axis of the motivation levels diagram would show the total number of theater admissions per year for the whole family, and a curve would be drawn in to show the desirability or undesirability to them of various numbers of admissions ranging from zero up to some fairly large number. There would, no doubt, be a peak in the curve for some particular total number of admissions, probably the sum total of the ideal number of admissions for each member of the family taken separately. As the number of people in the family increases, the peak of the curve would tend to shift to the right, indicating the increasing number of admissions which would be ideal for the family as a unit.

Even among families of given size, there are wide differences in movie attendance, depending on age and sex compositions. These differences in movie demand can be attributed to several factors which can be shown in the model, including different wants, different expectations from a given motion picture, different abilities to purchase tickets, and different degrees of influence by the children on the principal decision-maker.

Teen-agers, for example, are drawn to greater frequency of attendance at movies than are children under ten. This can be shown by separate curves for each child, with different *aspiration levels.*

Younger people are often more optimistic about being able to enjoy a particular movie than they are as they get older. This difference would be shown by a wider spread between the *achievement level* and the *expectation level,* thereby depicting the higher degree of confidence in the claims made for the movie.

Teen-agers probably have considerably more influence on their parents in getting permission to attend motion pictures than do younger children. This would be shown in the model by indicating an *importance curve* for the parents which is relatively close to that for the teen-agers, but would be considerably below that for younger children. Even though the younger children might want to attend many movies, the resistance of the parents is based on not wanting them to be losing sleep so often, eating so much popcorn and candy, or making undesirable acquaintances.

In the case of the teen-agers, however, the parents are more likely to evaluate the desirability of motion-picture attendance somewhat more as do the teen-agers. They recognize the right of the teen-ager to make increasing decisions for himself as to how he spends his time, his smaller need for getting to bed early, greater need for going on dates, and, of course, greater ability to bring counterpressures at home.

The differences in amount of influence on parents exerted by children of different ages may in other cases be traced to the greater confidence that parents have in a teen-ager's ability to select movies he actually will enjoy. This would result in an *expectation level* on the part of the parents, which is approximately equal to that of the teen-agers, but considerably below that of the younger children.

There are further differences in the influence of teen-agers, as compared with youngsters, on their parents which are traceable to the fact that many of them have their own money to spend, either as allowances or as money they have earned. We would show the teen-ager's attitude toward money, for example, as an importance curve, his present supply as an achievement level, and the amount he would have left after seeing the motion picture as an expectation level lying to the left of that. The negative valence, or amount of resistance which he would put up to spending this money for a motion picture, would be read off the vertical axis, just as we have done earlier. The attitude of the parents can be shown on the same diagram by an importance curve which is considerably flatter than the teen-ager's curve. This reflects the fact that it is not the parent's money, although the parent may still have some vicarious resistance to seeing the child spending his own money on the motion picture.

BRAND CHOICES WHEN FEATURES ARE DIFFERENT

In the case of generic product choices, major features differ from each other. Features are also different, but to a lesser degree, as among some brands. How can we show in our model why it is that the demand for two brands with different features varies with family composition?

Let us take a hypothetical choice between a Volkswagen sedan and, shall we say, a Chevrolet sedan. The choices are being made by families of different demographic characteristics. For instance, we may expect that a young married couple with one child would be more attracted to a Volkswagen sedan than would a family with five children. Because of the difference in number of people, the larger family has need for greater passenger capacity, which would be shown by an *importance curve* with a peak or ideal level lying to the right of the curve for a smaller family. If the Volkswagen comfortably seats four people, it has slightly more capacity than required for the smaller family, but they do not consider this a great disadvantage or waste, as other things can be carried inside the car. On the other hand, the Volkswagen would be uncomfortably crowded for the seven-person family, both for seating and for luggage space.

There are also different *kinds* of wants to be reckoned with in families of different composition. Families with very young children might find the Volkswagen quite attractive because of its resemblance to a toy, while families with children in college might prefer a standard size car like the Chevrolet sedan because the children would have more comfort and room on dates and the grownups would have better styling and performance.

Moreover, the larger family may very well have a higher income aspiration, as shown by the *importance curve,* and higher actual income, as shown by the position of the *achievement level.* Although the Volkswagen costs somewhat less than the Chevrolet sedan, the outlay for that car may, therefore, be as much of a financial burden for the small family as the larger outlay is for the larger family.

There is also a different influence pattern to be reckoned with in brand preference determination in families of different characteristics. If a family has a teen-age son, his influence on the parents' decision as to which make of car to buy may be great. First, the parents may feel that since the boy is a probable driver of the car himself, his preferences should be given greater weight than those which would be given in a family consisting of younger children. This would be shown in the model by an *importance curve* for the son that is not materially different from that for the parents.

In the second place, the parents may feel that the son has some particular skill in evaluating the features of one make as against another. If the boy has a flair for automobile mechanics, they may accept his judgment as the the relative roadability of the cars, the probable amount of engine repairs, and so on. This difference would be shown in an *expectation level* for the son that is very close to that for the parents. This shows they have high confidence in his technical judgment, which would not be the case with a younger child or a girl.

Brand Choices When Features and Prices Are Similar

Family composition may also have a strong influence on the demand for one brand as against another brand of the same product, even when the features and the prices are virtually identical. This can happen most clearly when the marketing policies and practices of the companies producing these two brands are sharply different.

For instance, let us take the case of two makes of washing machines. Let us suppose that Brand A distributes to carefully selected franchised dealers who are relatively few in number and concentrated primarily in the larger metropolitan areas. Brand B uses an intensive distribution pattern in which its machines are sold through department stores, hardware stores, appliance stores, discount houses, and many other outlets reaching down into even the smallest cities.

From the consumer's standpoint, the greatest difference is in the distance which he has to travel in order to look at models of the machines. Let us assume this boils down to a difference in time, with the amount of effort required about the same. This would be shown in the model by first sketching in an *importance curve* showing the desirability of having varying amounts of time available for leisure pursuits, a given *achievement level* showing how much time the prospective purchaser would expect to have available that day or week for leisure if she does *not* go shopping for a washing machine, and two *expectation levels*.

The first expectation level, lying slightly to the left of the achievement level, would show that only a small amount of leisure would have to be sacrificed in shopping for Brand B, which is handled by a local store. The other expectation level will lie further to the left, indicating that the housewife realizes it will take her considerably more time to drive 20 miles to and from a larger city in order to examine Brand A. It follows that the negative valence of the time motive for Brand A will cause more resistance to the purchase of that brand than the smaller negative valence of the time factor for Brand B.

However, the whole picture may shift as we turn from one family to another. A young married couple with no children, both holding full-time jobs, would have little free time for shopping, as shown by an *achievement level* that is further to the left than the one shown earlier. On the other hand, in a family where there are two daughters, one age 18 but the other age 20 and commuting to work in the larger city, the mother may simply delegate part of the shopping task to each of the girls. The extra amount of time given up in shopping for Brand A would then not be a material factor, because the older girl would be working nearby.

Some variations among families of different composition in demand for competing brands is attributable to contrasting amounts of influence exerted by other family members on the principal decision-maker. Let us suppose that Brand A washing machine is heavily advertised on television, while Brand B is advertised primarily in national magazines. Families with young children and teenagers who regularly watch television are more likely to see the commercials for Brand A than would be the case in a family with a small baby or no children at all.

This could cause a difference in demand in two ways. In the first place, the children may serve as sources of information about the features and benefits of Brand A and pass this information on to their parents. Even though Brands A and B might be identical in features and price, the parents would be better informed about Brand A and how any particular feature would yield any given benefit. This would be shown in the model by an *expectation level* that is reasonably far to the right of the achievement level and is about the same for the children and the parents. The knowledge obtained from television commercials means that the decision-maker has a fair degree of confidence that Brand A will yield a certain degree of satisfaction of the motive. As the child grows older, the parents may have even greater confidence in the accuracy of his information.

The second way in which greater exposure to television advertising of Brand A may affect family demand is that premiums may be offered to the children to induce their parents to send in inquiry cards, visit dealers, or purchase the brand. Such an offer brings in a totally different motive favoring the purchase of Brand A. This is shown in the model by drawing a separate motivation-levels diagram. If the premium is something that the parents approve the child's receiving, such as a jet pilot mask, a pen and pencil set, or a miniature circus tent and cutouts, the *importance level* for the parent would be almost the same as that for the children who first saw the offer.

Thus we finish discussing how the model might be drawn to illustrate the interplay among marketing actions, family composition, motives, expectations, and mutual influence in affecting family demand.

CONCLUSIONS

In summary, the main drift of this discussion has been to call attention to the fact that there are systematic relationships between family composition on one side and product and brand choices on the other side. However, to present numbers describing the systematic relationships is not the same as explaining them. Demographic characteristics such as size, age, and sex composition of a family do not in themselves cause demand. They merely serve as external clues to the motivations, perceptions, knowledge, expectations, and other causal factors which lie beneath the surface. These clues correlate with the deeper causes in a particular population at a given time, but the correlations shift as time passes.

We have accordingly developed a model revolving around what might be called "motivation levels analysis," in which we look at the achievement level, expectation level, and importance level. We have noted that a decision-maker not only takes into account these levels for his own self-centered benefits, but also considers what others think and expect of him, of themselves, and of each other. The different motivation levels, with their self-other variations, may be regarded as a model of a very simplified sort which can be expanded to include any number of motives and families of varying compositions. Most important is the fact that the model is expressed in quantitative form.

Conceptually, at least, the model appears able to generate the observed demand variations as we examine product and brand choices by families of different compositions under varying conditions. A proper test of the usefulness of this model would, of course, require empirical measurements.

Discussion

WARREN J. BILKEY

Obviously Brown and Clawson have given much thought to the subject matter they are considering. Although their papers are extremely different in approach, they nevertheless prove to be surprisingly complementary.

Brown describes certain very interesting studies, and then concludes that, "for the future, research on decision-making with respect to automobile purchasing should be directed toward the decision process rather than toward the outcome of the process." And this, it turns out, is exactly the task to which Clawson has addressed himself.

Brown's paper is rather difficult to discuss, because his objective seems to have shifted during the course of its development. In his opening paragraph, he stated that the studies to be presented were intended ". . . to illustrate both the potentialities and limitations of such research as a contribution to the construction of a model of household decision-making." In practice, this broad objective shifted to a description of several studies which add up to the proposition that the dominant role in family automobile purchasing is played by the husband. This conclusion, it seems to me, is established rather cleverly by combining the studies described.

There may be some question, however, regarding the *degree* of the husband's dominance in this matter. The tables presented in Brown's paper imply to me a more limited degree of husband dominance in automobile purchase decisions than Brown argues in the text of his paper. I cannot help but wonder whether his conclusions may have been influenced by additional data not presented to us.

My suspicion that the husband's role in this matter may not be quite so dominant as Brown implies is based on an unpublished study with which I was recently connected. Questionnaires were mailed to a nation-wide sample of 1,000 families in May, 1956. As part of the information requested, they were asked to indicate on a "centigrade thermometer" scale the magnitude of their desire to obtain an automobile, and the magnitude of their resistance to incurring the financial cost that such a car would entail. One year later the respondents to that questionnaire were sent another questionnaire, to determine whether or not they had actually purchased a car during the intervening 12 months. In addition they were asked which family member or members had filled out the first questionnaire and which family member or members were responsible for deciding whether or not to purchase a car. Altogether, 695 usable responses from both questionnaires were obtained for analytical purposes. These questionnaire results were then sorted into two groups: those in which the respondent was listed as the maker of the auto purchase decision, and those in which some family member or members other than the respondent was listed as the decision-maker. Very high correlations were obtained between the "thermometer" values from each of these two groups and their actual automobile purchases during the 12-month period following the first questionnaire. But there was no statistically significant difference between the decision-makers and the nondecision-makers. To me this implies that whatever differences regarding an automobile purchase there may have been between the various family members, the differences were sufficiently small on the whole for some degree of empathy to exist among them on this matter.

Although not stated explicitly, Clawson seems to hold the view that an adequate theory of consumer behavior will be, so to speak, a complex edifice that must be constructed from numerous building blocks and that the final theory can be no better than the individual "blocks" from which it is built. The entire concern of his paper, therefore, is to develop a model of only one very limited (albeit important) portion of the over-all consumption process—a motive. This he also regards in turn as a very complex entity. During the course of his paper, he did not have time to explore such vital problems as measurement or the relation of a motive to consumption. It is almost impossible, therefore, to evaluate the importance of what he has accomplished. The pragmatic test of usefulness cannot be applied until his analysis is integrated into an adequate over-all consumption theory. The test of conformity to actuality cannot be applied until measurement has been achieved. In short, Clawson's model is but one portion of a much broader model which has not been constructed yet. It may take consumer analysis ten years to develop to the point at which Clawson's work can be seen in its true perspective. For these reasons I can make only a few comments regarding it, and they are probably of questionable relevance.

First, Clawson has chosen to look at consumer behavior, so to speak, through a microscope. Such intensive focusing of attention on only one small portion of consumer behavior tends to distort its complexity relative to that of other portions of the consumption process. Thus, when the reader considers the amount of data necessary to construct even one of Clawson's "importance curves," then takes cognizance of the complications resulting from all the difficult-to-measure interpersonal relations affecting it, and considers how many motives are involved in the purchase of only one item, he is likely to conclude that consumer behavior as a whole never can be analyzed.

As an antidote to Clawson's (and Morgan's) efforts, other analysts will have to back away, so to speak, from the consumption process and view it through a telescope. We must strive for an over-all perspective of consumer behavior to ascertain how much of the information that Clawson's model calls for is really relevant *in terms of the rest of the consumption data now available*. There is no point in our trying to obtain a lot of complex information regarding a motive if we do not have sufficient data about other aspects of the consumption process to make effective use of such information. This is not a criticism of Clawson's pioneering efforts. I merely argue that *balance* is called for in consumer analysis as well as in other fields. The rest of us cannot follow innovators effectively until we have developed our own analyses to the point where we can incorporate their works into whatever it is that we are doing.

My second comment is that by choosing to concentrate on so narrow a problem as "the dimensions of a motive," Clawson has ended up with a model that is not adequate for casting much light on practical consumption problems. This, of course, is no criticism of his model as such. Rather, it seems to me that Clawson tries too hard in his paper to make a *practical* justification for his endeavors when the real justification is *theoretical*. On the other hand, I do note one practical use that his theory already has served. His "self-other frame of reference," as he calls it, could explain the seeming discrepancy between Brown's conclusions and my own findings referred to above. That is, the husband may tend to be the primary family decision-maker in purchasing an automobile and yet take sufficient cognizance of the other family members' views so that a reasonable consensus on the matter obtains for the entire family. If such an interpretation is correct, Brown may have to distinguish between the *formal* decision-maker and the *informal* decision-maker for some of his future analyses.

My third comment is that Clawson and Morgan might well get together to harmonize their endeavors. Their efforts and objectives as indicated by their papers are so similar that a cross-fertilization of ideas ought to occur.

My fourth comment involves a value judgment. Personally I should be happier had Clawson tried to show that his theory has uses beyond increasing merchandisers' profits. Can it, for example, aid in improving consumer well-being?

In final summary, Clawson's theory is obviously in an early stage of development. His concepts have to be thought through further, related to the decision-making process, and implemented with empirical data. I hope that he continues the good beginning that he has made. Brown, on the other hand, has summarized considerable data for us, but has not integrated it into any broader concept of consumer behavior. To judge from their complementarity to each other, however, both approaches make essential and congenial contributions to a general theory of consumer behavior.

Discussion

ROBERT SCHLAIFER

The purpose of the models discussed in this conference has not been clear. Do you not have to know what a model is to predict in order to obtain the appropriate parameters of the model? I am going to talk about a model that will predict decisions among branded products.

In some of the prior discussions, it has been implied that something is wrong with utilizing intervening variables in a model. Obviously this cannot be true in general, as witness the value of entropy as a component of physical models. In setting up a model, it is a virtue to suppress as much detail as possible, while going ahead to predict what you want to predict. In serving this purpose, intervening variables are a help as they organize all the implicit detail.

Clawson's model seems to try to explain everything. You would have to know the nature of every interaction among the many variables before you could obtain your answer. Clawson attaches importance to Marshall's concept of utility, but he cannot use it as he does: utility is inherently ordinal. Neither can he talk about slope, since you can only know that one utility is greater than another. You have to know the actual preferences: you get out only what you put in. He could obtain the kind of cardinal utility worked out by Von Neumann, but there is no need to do this either. It would not offer any help beyond his intuitions of the data that went into his model. Utilities deal with the indecomposable consequences of action taken.

Is a model such as Clawson suggests needed for marketing? No. Classical multivariate analysis is complex enough. In fact, crude seek-and-try methods will probably do better in guiding marketing policy than knowing all these internal household details.

Brown by contrast does not want to know all these things. He is moving toward common-sense refinements of the current methods available for ascertaining brand preferences. If you simply ask people what brand they prefer, the results are not worth the asking. This is evident in some of the almost random data Brown reports—50% this way, 50% that. You have to quantify these preferences to make inquiry worthwhile.

Now you could get preferences stated in the form of Von Neumann utilities, but it would require training your respondents. So instead you set up some simpler way of getting nonrandom statements of strength of preference. If you can quantify statements of preference in this way, you might then find that wives would prefer any make of car to another for a saving of $10.00. Or a man might prefer one brand of refrigerator to another for a cigar thrown in.

I have played with the idea of doing some experiments with afternoon women's clubs, to see if it is possible to build up preferences by adding small utilities. If this could not be done, it might prove that it is impossible to alter brand preference by advertising.

My point is that although utilities are ordinal, brand preferences —decisions between brands—result from quite minor differences in the appraisal of the utilities involved. Thus, wives and husbands can differ on makes of cars, and yet there may be no conflict between them. A satisfactory model for marketing needs only to summarize— or to conceptualize as an intervening variable, like the wife's realistic tendency to moderate her husband's aspirations—the differences between them that suffice to account for their decisions.

Discussion

CAHALAN: Through the courtesy of our chairman (West), I am privileged to report on a consensus technique of interviewing. It will be evident how this addendum supplements the paper by George Brown.

This whole conference seems to have the implicit theme that we must study the individual in the context of the primary and reference groups of which he is a part, if we want assurance that our findings predict what the individual (and his group) will do in the future. The time-honored survey procedures, however, assume that the individual is a completely autonomous and independent being —because we proceed to sample populations of individuals and question them as individuals, rather than sampling populations of primary groups and questioning them about opinions and behaviors that imply a consensus or group decision. Our research will become more valid as it approaches the realities of people's opinion-forming and decision-making situations. It is, to be sure, more difficult to study populations of groups than populations of individuals. However, recent experiences in several studies of the simplest type of grouping—namely, the married couple—indicate that groups may not be nearly as difficult to survey as supposed.

The study of married couples' process of arriving at decisions is of special relevance in purchasing decisions. The traditional surveys of individuals may find one respondent saying that the family is going to purchase an automobile during the next year—but if the opinions of the wife were taken into account (as they are in real life), the purchase might well be deferred because she would prefer the money to be spent on something else or saved. A whole range of similar contingencies can operate to invalidate the responses of individuals as predictors of behavior. A husband can report in an isolated interview that a car will *not* be purchased, whereas if he were to discuss the matter with his wife, he might find that she wanted a car and so a purchase might result; a woman respondent might say they would *not* purchase a car merely because she wants to live up to her image of what her husband would approve as being the right kind of a response for a "good manager," whereas actually if she were to discuss the purchase of an auto with her husband, the couple might talk each other into the purchase. Many other like situations might result in a difference between surveys of individuals and surveys which obtain the consensus within groups.

The general technique of several of our recent studies involves conducting *first* a brief *personal interview* of husband and wife *together* on certain factual items on which consensus is desired (e.g., size of wardrobe, who went along on specific shopping trips). Second, we have been using lengthy self-administered questionnaires, filled out separately and concurrently by husband and wife under the monitorship of the interviewer to prevent unwanted discussion between husband and wife.

The preliminary joint interview has the advantage that, in establishing matters of fact, a consensus is probably closer to the truth than two separate versions. Thus, one spouse can help the other remember past events as they actually occurred. Also on issues of fact, persons are perhaps less likely to exaggerate in the presence of their spouses.

The concurrent self-administered questionnaire, monitored by the interviewer, appears to have these special advantages in measuring attitudes and perceptions:

It *discerns* differences in opinions or perceptions between spouses. If one interviews the couple openly on matters of opinion, one person—more often the husband—will tend to dominate the conversation. If one has serial interviews of husband and wife separately, the results, unfortunately, will tend to be influenced by communication between spouses during the interval between interviews. I know of no readily practicable way to minimize these undue influences other than to apply self-administered concurrent questionings of husband and wife.

The technique *measures* selective differences in memories or perceptions of facts by one spouse in comparison with the other, when such comparisons are desired.

The technique provides a means of measuring the effects of private attitudes as variables intervening between the individuals' backgrounds and past experiences and their estimates of their probable future behavior. Again, as mentioned earlier, there may be conflict between "individual" as against "consensus" responses of married couples: for example, it may be that both husband and wife might respond that they plan to buy an auto, yet an analysis of the privately expressed attitudes of the wife may reveal that she would rather spend the money on something else or save it. If so, one would make a more conservative estimate of the likelihood of the purchase of an auto than otherwise.

The similarities and differences in husband and wife responses which this technique discloses can be illustrated by one particular study, a probability sample of married couples interviewed throughout the United States last spring on the general topic of women's influence on men's clothing selections. The study was commissioned from W. R. Simmons and Associates Research, Inc. by the Textile Fibers Department of E. I. du Pont de Nemours and Company, to provide necessary information for producers of men's clothing, so that more effective advertising and marketing would ultimately result in increased sales of synthetic fibers. The Du Pont people are glad to permit me to cite certain findings. It would hardly be appropriate for me to present the findings regarding women's influence on men's wear, or attitudes on the relative merits of various kinds of fibers for men's clothing. However, we asked about sufficient non-clothing items to illustrate the usefulness of the "consensus approach" in surveys.

The procedure was as described earlier: First the couple was interviewed together as regards *facts* (concerning the man's wardrobe and their recent purchasing behaviors). Then the husband and wife, in the presence of the interviewer, filled out self-administered questionnaires on opinions. The interviewer took the materials away without permitting any open discussion of the questions until after both had completed the questionnaires. Concurrent interviews were conducted with 728 couples.

Eight nonclothing items were included in order to obtain information on the ways in which families tend to be organized for division of responsibilities between the husband and the wife. In the section of the self-administered questionnaire that was filled out independently by husbands and wives, respondents were reminded that "Different families make decisions in different ways . . ." and were then asked to check whether the wife or the husband was the one who would be more likely to decide whether to buy a new car or a major appliance; who worries most about spending money; who is more active in community affairs; who is more likely to start conversations in social gatherings; who reads newspapers and magazines the most; and who had changed his or her ideas the most since the couple married.

Couples were usually in consensus that the wife was generally more active in community affairs than the husband, in reading magazines, in deciding whether to buy major appliances (like a refrigerator), in starting conversations at social gatherings, or in worrying about spending money, in that order. The usual consensus was that the husband was more active in deciding whether the couple should buy a new car (although separate research studies indicate that the wife has a substantial voice in the details of the car's make, color, and model) and in reading newspapers. There was a relatively low frequency of consensus on whether the wife or the husband had changed the most in ideas and attitudes since they were married, but one was named about as often as the other.

In general, the wives tended to credit the husbands with playing the decisive role in deciding whether to purchase a major appliance and in starting conversations at social gatherings more often than the husbands took credit as being the more active in these matters. Whether the findings reflect the actual behavior patterns is not established. At the very least, however, the results show that within the American culture, in the average household, the husband by common consent is *supposed* to be more active in these areas than the wife.

Husbands in the high-status families were found to be more dominant (at least as indicated by responses to these questionnaire items) than husbands in the low-status families. Consistent with this is the finding that a larger proportion of the husbands in the low-status than of the high-status group said they had changed more than the wife in ideas and attitudes since marriage.

Results by income level closely parallel those for the highly correlated social-positions groupings, with relatively more of the upper-
income husbands reporting themselves as being active on most points
than was the case in lower-income families. However, it was found
that the husbands in the very top income group ($7,000 or more)
were significantly *less* likely than husbands in the $5,000 to $7,000
bracket to report themselves as being more prone than their wives
to start the conversations at social gatherings. Perhaps this provides
a clue that a more detailed analysis of family decision-making patterns within various subgroups of the population in future studies
will find how special kinds of families are organized in their divi-
son of responsibilities. The understanding provided by further information along such lines would be helpful in marketing to special
groups.

Apparently the husbands within households consisting of childless
couples under 45 years of age were recognized relatively more often
as deciding whether to buy major appliances, but those under 45
who had children tended to be in agreement more often than in
other groups that the husband played a larger role in deciding when
to buy a new car and in worrying about spending money.

It also appears that among younger couples the husbands more
often are given credit for playing a larger role in deciding whether
to buy autos and major appliances and in worrying about spending
money. In couples where the husband is 60 or older, it appears that
the wife tends to have a more active role than the husband in most
of the activities covered in these questions. This same tendency appeared as regards the relatively higher consensus on the wives' influence on their husbands' clothing.

We are of the opinion that this combination of personal and self-
administered interviews can be applied in a wide range of situations
—not only in measuring primary group decision-making regarding
major appliances and household goods, but also in assessing the
processes whereby group decisions are made as to when to save rather
than to spend. Obviously, an extension of these approaches can help,
too, in arriving at a better understanding of important nonproduct
decisions, such as where to send the youngsters to school or what the
family's primary goals should be. At a minimum, further experiments along similar lines should contribute much to our understanding of the dynamics of the decision-making process within primary
groups such as the family.

MORGAN (to BROWN): There is a question here of direction of causation. Some social psychologists have studied the influence of advertising media. In a book by Festinger, he reports a study on whether ads get more attention before or after a purchase. How can you be sure that your data apply to attention to ads before rather than after buying?

BROWN: Evidence indicates great post-purchase attention. Starch's "Buy-ometer" showed that recent purchasers read the ads—90% of the people who had just bought read the ads. Of those who had bought within the past year, 10% had read recent ads for the product. This is known in the trade, however; some ads are designed for recent buyers. And you would expect buyers to read more often than readers buy.

MEYERS: The cost of a car is relatively so much higher for low-income families that I wonder about the effect of income. Does the wife participate any more in a major decision such as car purchase as income descends?

BROWN: That was not computed in these studies, but in general the wife's influence seems no greater with lower income.

ALDERSON: Coming to the aid of my colleague, Joe Clawson, I should like to pose the issue of rich models versus lean models. A rich model is directed primarily toward representation and understanding. A lean model may be adequate—and, if available, is to be preferred—for an attack on a specific practical problem. Both have their uses. Clawson is presenting a rich model of one aspect of consumer behavior. His model emphasizes the multiplicity of motives and seeks a method for handling complex motivational situations. In an assignment for a client, he might use a much simpler apparatus after his preliminary explorations.

In his work in motivation research, Clawson stands for a balanced and comprehensive view of motives. He is opposed to simplifying too fast too soon. There are some fantastic examples in the current applications of motivation research to marketing of simplifying too fast too soon. Limited models—short cuts to fit particular cases—should be developed within the framework of a more general theory of consumer behavior and motivation such as Clawson is attempting to construct.

We have been urged to start with simple models. From many years in marketing, I can recall some shocking cases of oversimplification; the lapses have run more to this than to overelaboration. As late as 1925, the native white population county by county was regularly used as an index of market potential for many products. The clear implication was that Negroes and the foreign-born did not buy anything.

I should like to add that price economics pure and simple presents a model of the market that is inadequate for many marketing problems. In fact, marketing men find it misleading for many of the tasks they perform. In the past twenty years, economics has become increasingly useful to marketing, but it has done so by providing newer, enriched models which are more relevant to the actual problems of the marketing organization.

BRIM: I want to speak to the same point, but from the opposite side of the fence. A very simple model may sometimes work for prediction. In a Harvard study of social mobility, which surveyed the plans of ninth graders for attending college and comparing results with actual later attendance, a complex model was finally abandoned in favor of simply using their answers as to whether they intended to attend. This was the best predictor.

Similarly, in predicting purchases from preferences, we might simply ask if the person has the authority to make the purchase. On the other hand, it may be that savings are as complicated as Reuben Hill's model or Westoff's decision on the third child, in which case mere statements of preference would be no good. Clawson's attempt at a more complicated model of brand purchase decisions may be justified because the simpler ones that have been tried have failed to be useful in prediction. But while granting that more complicated problems need more complicated models, should we not start with the simplest model and work toward the more complicated?

CLAWSON: If you are merely arguing for parsimony, I am with you. Let us get only as complicated as we must. But simple models have not worked too well in such matters as buying a car. Bilkey ascertained not only intentions in the ordinal sense, but also the intensity of intentions, and thus got a better prediction. He was complicating his model.

Now on the matters of intervening variables and multivariate analysis, we find that the usual, readily available indices do not work well in forecasting consumer behavior. The relationship is not 1:1

between our input variables and purchases because there are intervening variables. Moreover, as Stanton pointed out earlier, multiple regression works only backward, not forward. So in order better to predict, we have to go beyond proxy variables such as age, income, and the like and seek out the kinds of intervening variables that Kurt Lewin and Katona have pioneered in exploring.

The marketer needs guidance on how much to spend where. It becomes clear in most surveys that a staggering number of motives gets involved in decisions on brand or on spending versus nonspending. Moreover, the marketer must know the strength of these motives and why they are of this strength. How can the advertiser change demand under these conditions? It is not by manipulating proxy variables, but by directing his message toward the group that is ready for it. He selects certain of these motives and focuses his effort specifically on them.

Finally, I am dubious as to the workability of Bilkey's plea for consumer welfare as the yardstick of good marketing. What objective criteria do we have today which can define consumer welfare? While consumer welfare is the most ethical yardstick, actual sales furnish the most scientific yardstick. Representing observable behavior, they provide an objective criterion of the effectiveness of marketing efforts and estimates.

DANIERE: You can understand the dislike of the economist for going into motives. Economists have no data on motives and no way of generating such data. However, I do not myself think that you can predict changes in motives through surveys. The uses of basic, proxy, and intervening variables are not in conflict. Deciding which variables you want to include in your model is a matter of expediency in action. You have to identify and measure them to act on them. But if you cannot know them or act on them, then you want to include those you can. Economists do not think of acting on motives but on proxy variables, through taxes and so forth. If we can act on proxy variables, this will include altering the intervening variables.

ORCUTT: I am disturbed by what Clawson calls a model. His is not a model at all, rich or lean. What does it actually say about the behavior of a family? It brings no data and makes no predictions; it merely says that certain variables need to be taken into account. This is the kind of study economists are leaving behind, not what I hope they are reaching. Clawson just names things; he does not produce measurable and therefore usable material, for example, his reliance on cardinal utility.

CLAWSON: I am familiar with the arguments over cardinal utility. In my doctoral thesis, in fact, I tried to summarize the history of utility theory. The psychologist Fechner started it in the early days and the economists took it up. About 1915, the economists agreed that cardinal utility was not measurable. Why was it not measurable? Because historically that was about when the psychologists became behaviorists. Some economists continued to feel that utility was a useful teaching concept even without measurement, but others shifted to indifference analysis, feeling they were using something that could be measured. No one was happy with indifference curves until Von Neumann and Morgenstern did get a satisfactory measure of indifference. Meanwhile, psychologists and sociologists have learned to measure motives and status satisfactorily. There are many intensity scales now, deriving from Thurstone, Likert and others. There are so many measures now available that we should and can use them to test our model.

ORCUTT: What would you test in this model—one concrete kind of family behavior?

CLAWSON: First, what motives are operating; second, how intensely; and third, I would try to forecast the result . . .

FOOTE: . . . that family composition affects brand choice?

SCHLAIFER: You have variables to replace family composition, but you cannot manipulate family composition. And you cannot build up the utility of the whole from the parts. So your model of motives does not enable you to predict brand decisions from family composition.

FERBER: It might be helpful to point out that the problem of explaining or predicting consumer behavior is a highly complex one, which may well require the more or less simultaneous application of a variety of techniques rather than choosing one technique as better than the others. In some cases, the simplest technique may be the best; for others this will not be true. For example, motivation research and depth probing may be useful for explaining one class of purchases but may be of little use in explaining other purchases of the identical product, which may be made because of necessity or availability, which do not involve psychological or social motives as such. Removing nonpsychological purchases leaves a heterogeneous residue to be explained by expectation or motivation.

When a workable theory of consumer behavior is evolved, it will very likely involve the application of many different techniques, each best suited for explaining, or predicting, certain types of purchases. This serves to emphasize the need for research comparing the effectiveness of alternative techniques as applied to the same problem. Thus, how effective might a psychological probing approach be in explaining purchase behavior relative to an approach utilizing operations research based on statistical decision theory? Research of this type should contribute immeasurably to our knowledge of the potentialities and limitations of different techniques.

HILL (to CLAWSON): I should think you would want to distinguish intentions from desires, as a kind of intensity. Rossi, in studying residential mobility, went from desires to intentions to how sure the family was about making a move. By tapping incipient action so close to actual action, we can predict nicely.

I am not sure, however, if our task is to understand the customer as a moving person, that we get full understanding that way. Will he be pleased after he has made the move? What will please him after he gets there? I cannot get very excited over getting the product to the right place at the right time. In advertising or marketing, you may want to predict the imminent purchase, but in education you may want to act or predict at some other point in the sequence of the family's action. Thus you would want to investigate dissatisfactions with moves in the past or analyze the pulls of the future. Marketing people are no doubt concerned with prediction for practical reasons, but for the sake of understanding consumer behavior, I think more will come from utilizing richer models.

BIVENS: Your first exhibit is not clear. In a purchase decision, galaxies of motives operate, each with a certain intensity. Does not this fact affect the point you identify as ideal? Would not the marginal rates of transformation have to be equated, rather than always attaining the highest point on each curve? Net total satisfactions of one alternative versus another plus probabilities would then equal purchases.

BERNARD: And where is your game model? Don't your subjects ever say, "It depends"? Your "A" model lacks consideration of discussion and uncertainty.

CLAWSON: It is there, in Morgan's model and in mine, in the expectation level, which is altered by the degree of uncertainty. It is also in Bilkey's.

BRIM: Clawson's brief history has been news to me and has oriented me to some of the misunderstandings here. I want to clarify the fact that measurement difficulty no longer exists between the disciplines. It makes no difference—except to decision theorists—whether you use ratio scales or interval scales in measuring preferences: people respond as if to a cardinal scale.

ORCUTT (to CLAWSON): Do you think of the household as a single acting unit? Has the bargaining all taken place before your model takes over?

CLAWSON: It all depends on where you want to go back to in the process. Someday we may want to study how motivation levels change—what it is that changes the achievement level, the expectation level, and the importance curve. But I don't feel prepared to deal with this yet. For now, I would be happy to know more about the way in which changes in motivation levels, however caused, bring about changes in motive intensities, and how shifts in motive intensities affect buying behavior.

MORGAN: My motives—the motives in my model—are not the same as Clawson's. Mine are assumed to be stable over time, aspects of personality, although subject to probability plus power and influence in affecting behavior. I should say that the motives Clawson has been talking about are at a different level of generality, i.e., much more specific, than the basic personality disposition which I called motives or needs. They may serve as specific explanation for specific acts, but they will hardly help us build any theory of family decision-making.

Problems of uncertainty have been raised, as well as problems of power in the family, and I should remind you that the structure I presented attempted to build both of these into a general theory.

I cannot resist the temptation to say a negative word about the utility of game and decision theory here. I'm not convinced that we shall improve our research on how people actually make decisions if we pay too much attention to theories as to how people *ought to* make decisions, particularly since Raiffa and Luce have now made it abundantly clear that these theories are based on different and mutually contradictory criteria as to what the ideal solution should be.

CLAWSON: The basic question that Bilkey has so insightfully raised about the "motivation levels" type of analysis is whether it is wiser to view the world of consumer behavior through a microscope, as I have done, or through a telescope. I am quite sincere when I say I deeply admire the men who can develop workable theories at the macro-economic level, for they are generals dealing in grand strategy. But surely there is a useful role for the buck private in economics, too, the man who can be content, even happy, while wallowing in the Three D's—the dirty daily details.

Quite simply, the copywriter and the salesman have the inglorious task, day after day, of finding the most effective appeals or sales arguments to use with different individuals or classes of customers. It fascinates me to try to help them with concepts and research.

My theorem merely says to them that an appeal will go over well with a particular set of prospects when (a) they have run pretty short on that particular type of satisfaction (low achievement level), or (b) a small amount more of it seems very, very important to them or their families (steep importance curve), or (c) they are convinced in some way that the product will be unusually effective in improving their position in this respect (expectation level is far to the right of the achievement level), or (d) some combination of these factors. It follows that the job of the salesman, copywriter, or market researcher who wants to help them is to determine which appeals are presently or potentially the strongest and find out how to develop this strength to a maximum.

Turning now to Schlaifer's interesting points, I would like to comment on what appears to be his key idea. He says, "In setting up a model, it is a virtue to suppress as much detail as possible, while going ahead to predict what you want to predict. In serving this purpose, intervening variables [I think he meant to say proxy variables, or demographic data] are a help as they organize all the implicit detail."

First, if we only want to predict, we should certainly simplify our model. But if we wish guidance in developing a program of action, we need more information. For instance, you only need to know the speed and direction of an automobile to predict where it will be in a few seconds, and you will be right in most cases. If you want to drive the car yourself or advise someone else on driving, you have to take dozens of factors into account.

Even the forecaster finds that using proxy variables such as age, sex, and occupation organizes all the implicit details only for a little while. The formula decays rapidly, because coefficients shift in magnitude and even in sign, and independent variables move into magnitudes beyond the ranges covered in the original formula.

So we can expect sales-forecasting formulas to slip out of joint over time as women start wearing shirts and slacks, men start using perfumed after-shave lotion, people start getting married younger, and day laborers buy increasing numbers of hi-fi phonograph records. Then we realize we must get away from *descriptive* factors in our forecasting and spend more time developing *explanatory* variables, even at the expense of complicating the model.

V. Decision-Making Regarding Husband-Wife Roles and Careers

The Implications of Research on Occupational Careers for a Model of Household Decision-Making

HOWARD S. BECKER

The sociological study of occupational careers seems a long way from matters usually considered in thinking about consumer behavior, but the two are more closely linked than one might at first suppose. Empirically, we know that the choice of an occupation is always, in effect, the choice of the standard of living associated with being a member of that occupation. Change in occupational status makes possible, and sometimes mandatory, changes in consumption patterns.

But I am interested in a more fundamental link between these two areas of behavior. In taking on an occupational role, people make or plan to make certain investments of time and money. Increasingly, one needs to be educated in order to hold down a job; promotions require a similar investment, as do changes of job. All these things require that decisions be made about the allocation of individual or family resources. In this sense, much occupational behavior can be seen as a kind of large-scale, long-term act of consumption.

This being the case, we can perhaps add something to our general knowledge of consumer behavior by considering the specifics associated with this kind of consumption. Our goal, I take it, is the development of an abstract model of consumer behavior that will enable us to understand, explain, and perhaps predict people's acts of consumption in a great variety of substantive areas. The refinement of an explanatory model, with a view to increasing its power to explain or predict, can occur in two ways. We can progressively restrict the area the model is meant to explain in order to achieve precise delineation of the operation of a small number of variables under conditions where the effects of other variables can be controlled, randomized, or otherwise disposed of. Because in social research, it is exceedingly hard to dispose of other variables in this way, we often have recourse to the opposite method, in which we forego the formal elegance of the first kind of model in order to build in as many of the important variables as possible. In so doing, we increase the range of the model, making it more differentiated and able to account for a wider variety of phenomena.

My effort, in this paper, has been in the second of these directions. Looking at the research that has been done on occupational careers, I have tried to see what variables are suggested that might be incorporated into a general model of consumer behavior and what suggestions we can find as to the sort of model it ought to be.

RESEARCH ON OCCUPATIONAL CAREERS

The body of research from which I shall work thinks of *career* in a very general way as the patterned series of movements a person makes through the "network of institutions, formal organizations, and informal relationships" (16, p. 327) in which the work of the occupation is carried on. The concept is not limited to those occupations that we conventionally think of as providing "careers"—the civil service and other bureaucracies, the worlds of sports and entertainment, academe—but applies as well to the plumber, priest, or taxi-dancer. In these latter instances, the patterns of movement, as indeed the social structures through which movement occurs, are not formally defined or publicly well known, but they are there to be discovered nevertheless.

In studying careers so defined, sociologists pay particular attention to two related phenomena: occupational definitions of success, and the contingencies affecting career movements, including the achievement of success. We tend to think of success as being largely a matter of money or fame, yet in many occupations the most successful workers (in their colleagues' eyes) do not make the most money and are not those the public regards most highly. Members of the occupation develop their own standards of success, based on criteria the

public knows nothing about. These standards rise out of the recur-
ring problems members of the occupation face; the successful man
is one who has achieved a position in which these problems are most
easily solved. The schoolteacher, for example, faces the problem of
keeping children in order and getting them to learn something;
she has achieved success, as her colleagues define it, when she gets
a position in a school whose children are of a kind that makes
these problems easy to solve (2). Sometimes the occupation's chronic
problems are such that a solution to one only makes some other
problem more difficult. Dance-band musicians face the twin problems of keeping themselves supplied with the short-term jobs characteristic of the occupation and maintaining their artistic autonomy
against the efforts of their nonmusician employers and audiences to
tell them what and how to play. But the positions in the informal
structure of the music business that provide a steady flow of jobs
are most likely to interfere with artistic autonomy, and those which
allow the greatest freedom do not keep one in steady work. In such
a situation, there are alternative forms of success, financial and artistic, but one cannot have both. In any case, it is worth noting that
occupational groups tend to agree on the goal or goals that are
worth pursuing and that the sociologist needs to find out what these
are (1, 3).

Success is achieved by moving from one to another of the positions that the social structure of the occupation makes available.
This brings us to the second main focus of research in this area: the
contingencies that affect such movement. The dictionary definition
of contingency—"an event possible, but dependent on another uncertain event"—makes clear what I have in mind. Career movements
are steps (up, down, or sideways) that may or may not be made,
depending on other events which it is the sociologist's job to discover. The crucial contingencies of a career in a given occupation
take their character from the chronic problems that the occupation
faces, just as do occupational definitions of success. A dance musician's movement into the circles providing steady work is contingent on his renouncing some of his claims to artistic autonomy, and
the teacher's movement to a "good" school is contingent on her having requested transfer to a school that really has the proper characteristics and for which the waiting list is not so long that movement
is unlikely. Career movements can be contingent on a variety of

events—shifts in the person's perspective, shifts in the way others view him, the operation of impersonal systems of rules, and so on—and these vary from occupation to occupation and from time to time.

Let me present a more connected picture of this kind of research by briefly summarizing some aspects of Oswald Hall's pioneering study of the medical career in an Eastern city (16, 17). The successful doctor is one who has solved the problem of acquiring and retaining a clientele of the desired type, a clientele consisting of patients who pay their bills promptly and in other ways fit into the doctor's conception of the "right" kind of patient. He does this by becoming a member of the powerful "inner fraternity," a group of established specialists who control hospital appointments and refer patients back and forth among themselves. A man who is accepted into this group finds himself "automatically" moving up in the hospital hierarchy and receiving referrals from its other members; he is a "success." The major contingency of such a career is sponsorship: the recruit is selected by an older member, who guides him through the various steps to the top. The young doctor serves a long period as a recruit, during which he does much of the hospital's charity work and in other ways demonstrates his willingness to accept the system, ultimately being rewarded by full membership in the fraternity. The achievement of this success is contingent on his acceptance by the "inner fraternity."

One more preliminary distinction before I turn to matters most closely related to household decision-making. We can divide career movements into the first step of entrance into the occupation (what ordinarily goes by the name of "occupational choice") and those steps made after the person is launched on a career in a particular field. Decisions are of a somewhat different kind in the two cases, and family members are likely to be involved differently.

The kind of research I have been talking about is relevant to the study of household decision-making, very simply, because career movements of various kinds seem to involve elements of decision on the part of the person whose career is under study and because it appears likely that his family (either the family he is born into or the one he creates by marrying) would be involved in those decisions. In studying the character of these decisions and the nature of the family's involvement in them, we may perhaps get some leads as to what needs to be included in a model of household decision-making in consumer behavior.

Decisions

When we speak of decisions we mean acts by which individuals undertake to perform one activity rather than another. In other words, we refer to a choice between alternative lines of action at some juncture where the choice is not given but appears to the person to be problematic. The opposite of decision is thus an act in which there is no problem faced and no choice between alternatives. The concept of decision generally implies, too, that the person making the choice does so on the basis of some more or less stable hierarchy of *pre-existing* desires or values.

Much work, particularly on the first career step of entering an occupation, has operated with some such conception of the person making a decision in terms of his own stable desires and then following through on this decision. The large literature on "occupational choice" uses essentially such a model. But some recent research findings, recalling to us the facts of everyday experience, make it unlikely that such a model can account for all that needs to be accounted for.

The graduate students in physiology whom James Carper and I studied (4, 5, 6) had not, except in the most formal sense, chosen or decided to become physiologists. Most of them had chosen to become physicians. But the institutions of medicine had not chosen them. Their applications to medical school rejected, they had settled down to mark time for a year before applying again; not wishing to waste the time, they had decided to spend it in study of a basic medical subject which would help them when they did start their medical training. They had no intention of becoming professional physiologists but, when their applications were rejected for a second time, they continued to work in physiology for want of anything better to do. They acquired Master's degrees and a foothold on a doctorate and finally abandoned their medical ambitions as they discovered that they were well on the way to becoming physiologists. They learned to be ambitious in new directions, wanting now to become academic men, famous researchers, or department chairmen. The few who still thought of taking medical training after getting a Ph.D. did so now because they wanted the medical degree that they needed in order to be able to do research on human as well as animal subjects.

We studied two other groups of students. Those in mechanical engineering intended to embark on a career in that field, but it was one they were prepared to abandon readily should an opportunity arise to move into the ranks of industrial management. Philosophy students, too, had chosen their field, but not because it was something they wanted very much; rather, it seemed to them the best of a series of bad possibilities. With an ideal of the Renaissance Man, well versed in all the sciences and humanities, they saw the academic discipline of philosophy as least constraining and least likely to narrow their wide range of interests. As they approach the Ph.D. and the job market, however, they reluctantly begin to view themselves as potential professors of philosophy and to develop the typical ambitions and perspectives of the fresh, young Ph.D. In all three cases, these developing conceptions were supported by the presence of other students whose selves were undergoing similar transformation and faculty members who saw such changes as reasonable and proper.

What do these examples give us that cannot be accounted for with the concept of decision? In the first place, not all career movements result from decisions to make that particular movement. The unwilling way physiologists back into their ultimate occupational niche shows that the notion of "occupational choice" is too narrow to cover the range of phenomena we know to occur. Second, as the engineers demonstrate, "choices" may be neither stable nor lasting; under some circumstances, they are abandoned with little difficulty. Finally, the case of philosophy reminds us that people can discover their desires in the course of their experience and do not necessarily make decisions on the basis of some pre-existing hierarchy of values.

All this suggests that what requires explanation is not the act of decision itself, but what this has typically been taken to stand for in the literature on these topics. The act of decision has, in effect, been seen as irrevocable and the man who makes the decision as likely to continue along the line his choice indicates. In other words, decisions have been made the explanation for a person's carrying on some *consistent line of action:* he chooses an occupation, the argument runs; therefore, he will stick with it, and this consistency is a consequence of the decision. But we have seen that a decision to undertake an activity is not enough to ensure consistent lines of action and that these can be achieved in the absence of such a decision. The most general explanation that we can formulate of such consistency stems from the concept of *commitment:* somehow or other, the person becomes committed to a line of action in such a way that he finds he must continue it because all other alternatives carry penalties and costs he does not wish to incur.

This is not to say that decisions are never an explanation of a commitment to a consistent line of action, but rather to point out that decision is only one of the ways that commitments come into existence. The opposite case might be conceptualized as *default:* the person increasingly ties himself to the occupation almost without knowing it, until some event forces him to recognize his new condition, this constituting the final stage of the commitment process. What happens is that many small steps are taken whose consequences are not foreseen. Each step tends to limit the alternatives available at the next step until the individual suddenly finds himself at a decision point with only one "alternative" to choose from. The physiology students whom I described earlier begin to make investments of time and energy which progressively tie them to physiology, so that to switch to something else, even medicine, would mean such a waste of those investments that they really have no choice. (This is especially true in a society that demands that young men "settle down" to a suitable occupation in a reasonable amount of time.)

If default has this progressive, step-like character, it is possible that decisions do too, and that the only decisions that culminate in consistent lines of action are those which are continually reaffirmed in everyday minor acts creating a commitment. Decisions would then be best conceptualized longitudinally, as a series of points at which commitments to lines of action are strengthened or weakened. It is an empirical question as to the relative frequencies of defaults, decisions, and whatever in-between categories we might wish to create. But we might take from the preceding discussion the directive that consistent behavior ought to be conceptualized as a series of activities leading to commitment, decision being only one of the ways this happens.

We can draw a second moral from the research cited. People do not necessarily make decisions on the basis of a pre-existing hierarchy of desires or values. Frequently they are like the philosophy students, who discover what they want from their careers in the course of pursuing them. The person searches not only for something he wants, but also for something *to* want. Where values are vague or unstable, support is provided for those going through these processes of commitment by others who are or have been in the same boat. These important others provide suggestions for directions of change and worthwhile values and ratify the actions the person takes.

Although I have focused on these processes as they influence entry into an occupation, they are also found at work at later stages of the career. The person faces many problems in his later career about which decisions must be made, finds himself committed to lines of action without quite knowing how it happened, wonders what the proper things to want from his work and career are. In some occupations these processes are possibly more complex and interesting at later stages of the career than at the point of entry. Choosing to go into medicine is, relatively speaking, a cut-and-dried affair. But after one has become a doctor, the question of what kind of doctor to be arises: general practitioner or specialist? What kind of specialist? Big city or small town? Solo practitioner or partner in a group practice? Teacher? Researcher? Medical students, looking forward to a medical career, continually make and remake these decisions in their imaginations, trying out the various medical roles to see what satisfactions they might provide and whether these seem to be really satisfying. Going through this process together, a class of medical students discusses the question of what the real satisfactions of medicine are: Treating patients? Intellectual discovery? Money? Short working hours? They also learn together (and change their minds together) about the way various careers operate to provide or deny one these satisfactions. Eventually, toward the close of school, some of them begin to settle down, having decided what they want, what their talents can reasonably allow them to expect, and what kind of career is likely to give them what they have learned to want.[1] These choices are provisional, subject to many more changes before being translated from fantasy into action.

FAMILIES

Having seen the way sociologists look at the problem of decisions and their relation to consistent lines of action, we can now look at

[1] I draw here on the studies of medical students that I have been engaged in with Blanche Geer, Everett C. Hughes, and Anselm L. Strauss. Some of the material is reported in 7 and 8; a complete report is in preparation.

the influences outside the person that might be involved in this process. This conference takes its theme from the belief that the family or household unit is importantly implicated in the choice process, but I would like to suggest that this is only a first step toward a more realistic and comprehensive model. Once we admit the family into our thinking, we must begin to look for the other social groups which, like the family, enter into a person's decisions. In the area we are dealing with here—occupational behavior—the most important such group is made up of one's occupational colleagues, who represent and enforce an occupational perspective and code. I shall concentrate here on the influences of these two groups—occupational colleagues and family—but we should remember that there are many other groups that may be equally influential. In a paper entitled "The Peer Group Society," which as yet is unpublished, Herbert Gans suggests that the most influential group among men in Boston's Italian section is the group of age-mates with whom they have gone to school and played in the streets. Decisions, including career decisions, need ultimately to be ratified by this group if they are to be followed through. Indeed, Gans says: "I have a feeling that even among Italian intellectuals, there is considerable conflict between intellectual activity and peer-group devotion; and I suspect that this may interfere with their productivity."

Having made this proviso, I would like to consider four matters relating to family influence on career movements. They are: (1) the circumstances in which the family is likely to attempt direct influence over career movements; (2) the ability of the family to exert such direct influence; (3) ways in which the family exerts indirect influence; and (4) the countervailing influence of the occupational colleague group.

(1) Families do not always attempt to influence the career movement of their members. The question of the degree to which other family members are implicated in the formation of a commitment or in its consequences must be answered by research. We can suggest a provisional guide for such research, by saying that *families will probably take an active part in the person's career activities to the degree that those activities affect the relations among family members.* This is a truism, but by investigating its terms we arrive at a more differentiated conception of family influence. Families may be thought of as groups of people united in formal and informal relations embodying expectations as to the proper behavior to be

engaged in by each of the parties to each relationship. A family, that is, consists of a series of such reciprocal relationships as mother-son or brother-brother, as well as the relationships each individual has to the family as a corporate unit. In each of these relationships, each partner is expected to assume certain obligations and duties and at the same time expects to have certain rights and privileges. These range from such rights and obligations as are formally defined at law to those that have arisen informally within the particular family unit. Any individual family member's activities become the object of family concern when they interfere with the fulfillment of his obligations to other family members. To understand how families affect career movements, then, we must know what the specific expectations governing the person's relations to his family are and how a particular career movement is likely to affect them.

The professional dance musician provides an example. We have already noted that one of the crucial contingencies of the musician's career centers around his inability to live up to his artistic standards and at the same time achieve prestige in the community and financial success. If he is to achieve financial success, he must give up some of his artistic autonomy; if he chooses to remain an artist, he renounces financial security, for steady work does not come to those who make that choice. The expectation that a man will have a regular and sufficient income governs most marriages, and a musician's decision to remain an artist would violate that expectation. Consequently, marriage often causes a crisis in which the musician begins to reshape his career toward more "commercial" goals or, alternatively, breaks up the marriage over this issue. Other professional decisions, which do not affect the husband-wife relation, remain uninfluenced by the wife.

Occupational sociologists discover these influences precisely by uncovering sore spots of this kind. Before we can develop a systematic picture of the areas in which families move directly to influence career decisions, we need to have more complete descriptions, in anthropological style, of the relations that go to make up American families of various kinds. Before we can predict the directions in which families and their constituent members will move to further their interests in an individual's career, we need to know what those interests are and what the expectations are that embody them. Some parents may expect their sons to achieve mobility that the parents themselves could not manage; others may hope to temper what they

regard as unrealistic ambitions in order to spare their sons frustrations which would endanger family solidarity. Wives, similarly, may
push their husbands to achieve great things occupationally in order
to satisfy expectations of a standard of living that have become em-
bodied in the marriage relation; or they may attempt to hold down
aspiration in the interests of a peaceful home life (I cite this area of
interest in achievement or the tempering of aspiration merely as an
example; any full-scale treatment would necessarily have to take
account of many other interests which might affect family relations.
Many jobs, for instance, require a man to travel extensively. A wife
who expects her husband to be a somewhat more constant companion
may push him to seek a more sedentary occupation or a more sedentary position in the organization.)

(2) When families or family members do feel moved to intervene
in career movements, they may or may not be able to do so effectively.
A number of factors are involved. In the first place, there is the
question of the distribution of power in the family. This, presumably, is partly a matter of economic power (the family member who
controls the purse strings naturally is able to influence behavior that
requires financial support by the family), but is probably in larger
measure a matter of family consensus about who has a legitimate
right to exercise power with regard to career issues. A son may desire further education which is only available if his parents furnish
financial aid; his father may actually control, in the economic sense,
family finances; yet it may be the mother who is regarded as the
appropriate person to make such decisions. We do not yet know the
patterns of definition of legitimate authority to act in career areas
which typify families of various kinds. What particularly needs to
be known in order to understand later career stages is the balance
of power between parents and mates; such decisions as whether to
move geographically in order to secure a more desired kind of work
may hinge on this balance.

Secondly, the amount of power a family can exert over one of its
members varies with time; power that can be exerted at one stage
of a career loses its potency at another stage. The philosophy students I spoke of earlier are a case in point. Their parents had only
vague ambitions for their sons, and the sons did not settle, while in
college, on any specific occupation. But they did undergo an "intellectual conversion," becoming convinced that a life of the intellect

(presumably poverty-stricken) was what they wanted. Their parents sensed the seriousness of this decision only when they realized that their sons had not begun to climb one of the conventional mobility ladders; at this point the parents discovered that they did not want their boys to be poverty-stricken philosophers. But by this time it was too late for parental influence to be exerted, for part of the "conversion" was a growing conviction that to succumb to parental demands would be hopelessly conventional and middle-class. Again, we need to know more about the stages of life at which people are more or less vulnerable to parental pressures; similarly, we need to know how the influence of a spouse varies over time.

(3) Families, of course, exert influence over the career movements of their members in more indirect ways as well as by direct interference. It is probably true that social controls would not work at all if they needed always to be exercised directly and that direct exercise may be the sign of the breakdown of social control. More typically, social controls work by indirection; matters are simply taken for granted, are the object of consensus, and people are influenced by others in the sense that they accept the conventional understandings common in the group and operate in terms of them without any coercion being required. This kind of influence over individual behavior might be termed the operation of *family culture,* i.e., the influence of the conventional understandings shared by family members. The understandings about career and related matters characterizing any particular family will have certain unique features, but will also probably be drawn very largely from the social class, ethnic, and regional cultures in which that family participates.

This kind of influence is very important in the matter of "occupational choice," for such choices as are made consciously are made within limits set by the perspective from which the person views the work world, and this perspective reflects the culture in which the chooser operates. Let us consider first the question of education. As earlier noted, the educational level a person reaches determines to some degree the range of occupations available to him. Many studies have observed strong class differences in the evaluation of the importance and possibility of getting the kind of higher education necessary for a wide range of occupational choice. It has been argued that class cultures differentiated in this way account for the sizable differences in proportions of persons actually attending college. In short, if one participates in a lower-class culture placing little emphasis upon education, it is less likely that one will attempt to get the education that would open up certain career routes. Similarly, if the culture stresses education, one may get so much of it that he is effectively cut off from occupations for which he would be "overtrained"; people will not hire him for lowlier jobs, feeling that he would be unhappy in them, and subtle processes of commitment will have been at work, constraining his "choices" to those appropriate for one of his education. Class culture in these fields very likely operates most effectively through the family.[2]

The family, too, is most likely to inculcate cultural standards of the proper kind of work for "one of our kind." The understandings current in the family may label some occupations as *infra dig* and others as impossible of attainment, in effect specifying a certain range of occupations as the proper ones from which to choose. This probably varies with social class too, though it is worth noting that there may be wide cultural agreement on some occupations. Families of all kinds feel that the profession of dance musician is improper, partly because it seems to make impossible the establishment of a family by the person choosing it.

Finally, families influence occupational choice through their limited awareness of the complexity of the work world (9, p. 255). Some kinds of families are aware of the existence of a great number of specific kinds of work that one might undertake and can make a child aware of all these possibilities so that he takes them into account in his own plans and dreams. Other families present the child with no such rich assortment of prospective occupations. The young man seeking his place in the work world cannot very well consider what he does not know exists, so that this aspect of family culture might play an important role in the formation of an occupational commitment.

(4) We must note that family influences operate in an environment that also contains the influences emanating from the occupational colleague group. The individual may be subject to direct pressure from other members of the occupation. Further, the conventional understandings about career matters characteristic of the occupation—part of the *occupational culture* (1, 25)—play a part

---

[2] See here the work of Allison Davis and his colleagues.

similar to those which make up the family culture in influencing a person's career activities.

One's fellow workers represent an important source of support for ideas and plans of action that run counter to those favored by one's family; indeed, they may force one to consider such ideas and plans. The musician whose wife objects to his late hours and unsteady work will find many of his fellow musicians counseling him to put his wife in her place or leave her. The physiology students I mentioned earlier give up their ideas of becoming physicians long before their parents abandon this ambition for them and have grave difficulties in justifying their actions to their families. Because they take their families' ideas seriously, they have difficulty in justifying their move to physiology to themselves. Their colleagues play an important role here, by furnishing them with arguments that the move is really a wise one, that physiology is in fact more worthwhile than medicine. The older students learn from their professors, and transmit to their juniors, an ideology that provides arguments of this kind for most issues that are likely to arise vis-à-vis parents.

In general, it may be said that occupational decisions are likely, in the first instance, to be coerced by facts of occupational culture and structure. Families (either parents, mates, or both) are typically outsiders to the occupational group, and their ideas must necessarily appear somewhat uninformed to the family member whom they are trying to influence. They do not understand the contingencies he faces in the way that he does, are not aware of the ramifications of colleague control and the long-range consequences of his decisions, and do not share the cultural premises of action he has acquired along with his membership in the occupation. He is likely, therefore, to discount their ideas and ignore their attempts to influence him, for in all the ways that they appear ignorant, his colleagues, of course, seem wise and knowledgeable. That is, his colleagues share the common culture of those who work at his trade, part of which consists of a perspective on careers and the decisions and contingencies related to careers. Because of their closeness to him and their greater knowledgeability, colleagues will probably frequently be more influential than family members. In short, family influence will operate only so far as the counterbalancing influence of the occupational group allows. What the actual balance of power will be in any instance has to be discovered; the general propositions governing this relationship have not been constructed.

Conclusion

It is clear that the points I have made about occupational behavior have some relevance for the more general problem of consumer behavior. Career activities include sizable investments of time and money and can thus be included in the category of consumption activities. A generalized model of consumer behavior, therefore, ought to be able to explain, among other things, the kinds of phenomena I have been discussing. I do not propose to construct such a generalized model now, but simply to reiterate some things such a model would have to take into account.

First of all, some consumption activities seem to involve (as do career activities) consistent lines of activity carried on over a period of time. One thinks of brand loyalty here and of associated complexes of buying like the network of purchases that people seem to make once they have purchased a suburban home. Where consumption does involve such consistent lines of activity, it requires a model that sees *decisions* as only one of the possible explanations of such behavior. Exploration of the *commitments* associated with acts of consumption might prove fruitful.

Second, and a corollary of the above, it might also prove valuable to conceive of the genesis of acts of consumption in a longitudinal fashion. Thus, we would inquire into the history of any act of consumption and might be able to build up a typology of the kinds of development characteristic of various patterns of consumption.

Third, while recognizing the importance of the family as a major social unit affecting a person's behavior, we should also recognize the importance of other groups, such as peers and occupational colleagues. Somewhat more generally, we might speculate that acts of consumption are typically made in a context that includes persons or groups representing a special interest in consumption of some particular kind. That is, in buying high-fidelity equipment we find ourselves besieged with advice from others we know who are expert or semiexpert about it; auto purchases contain in their background a long history of discussions with others who claim to have special knowledge. These groups might be seen as operating in the same way that colleagues do with regard to career activities, representing a specialized, quasi-professional point of view, which may counter family points of view and be something of a buffer against them.

SELECTED BIBLIOGRAPHY ON CAREERS

1. BECKER, HOWARD S. "The Professional Dance Musician and His Audience," *Am. J. Sociology, 57* (Sept., 1951), 136–44.

2. ———. "The Career of the Chicago Public School Teacher," *ibid., 57* (March, 1952), 470–77.

3. ———. "Some Contingencies of the Professional Dance Musician's Career," *Human Organization, 12* (Spring, 1953), 22–26.

4. ——— and James W. Carper. "The Development of Identification with an Occupation," *Am. J. Sociology, 66* (Jan., 1956), 289–98.

5. ——— and James W. Carper. "Elements of Identification with an Occupation," *Am. Sociological Rev., 21* (June, 1956), 341–48.

6. ——— and JAMES W. CARPER. "Adjustments to Conflicting Expectations in the Development of Identification with an Occupation," *Social Forces, 36* (Oct., 1957), 51–56.

7. ——— and BLANCHE GEER. "The Fate of Idealism in Medical School," *Am. Sociological Rev., 23* (Feb., 1958), 50–56.

8. ——— and BLANCHE GEER. "Student Culture in Medical School," *Harvard Educational Rev., 28* (Winter, 1958), 70–80.

9. ——— and Anselm L. Strauss. "Careers, Personality, and Adult Socialization," *Am. J. Sociology, 62* (Nov., 1956), 253–63.

10. BOGDANOFF, EARL, and ARNOLD GLASS. "The Sociology of the Public Case Worker in an Urban Area." Unpublished Master's thesis, University of Chicago, 1954.

11. CRESSEY, PAUL G. *The Taxi-Dance Hall.* Chicago: University of Chicago Press, 1932. Pp. 84–106.

12. FLORO, GEORGE. "Continuity in City-Manager Careers," *Am. J. Sociology, 61* (Nov., 1955), 240–46.

13. GOFFMAN, ERVING. "The Moral Career of the Mental Patient," *Psychiatry* (forthcoming).

14. GOLD, RAY. "Janitors Versus Tenants: A Status-Income Dilemma," *Am. J. Sociology, 57* (March, 1952), 486–93.

15. GUSFIELD, JOSEPH. "General Education as a Career: A Sociological Analysis," *J. General Education* (January, 1957), 37–48.

16. HALL, OSWALD. "The Stages in a Medical Career," *Am. J. Sociology, 53* (March, 1948), 327–37.

17. ———. "Types of Medical Careers," *ibid., 55* (Nov., 1949), 243–53.

18. HUGHES, EVERETT C. "Institutional Office and the Person," *ibid., 43* (Nov., 1937), 404–14.

19. ———. "Dilemmas and Contradictions of Status," *ibid., 50* (1945), 353–59.

20. ———. "Professional and Career Problems of Sociology," in *Transactions of the Second World Congress of Sociology, I,* pp. 178–85, 1956.

21. ——— and HELEN M. HUGHES. *Where Peoples Meet.* Glencoe, Illinois: Free Press, 1952. Pp. 83–99.

22. MARTIN, NORMAN, and ANSELM L. STRAUSS. "Patterns of Mobility within Industrial Organizations," *J. Business, 29* (April, 1956), 101–10.

23. SMITH, HARVEY L. "Psychiatry in Medicine: Intra- or Interprofessional Relationships," *Am. J. Sociology, 63* (Nov., 1957), 285–89.

24. SOLOMON, DAVID N. "Civilian to Soldier: Three Sociological Studies of Infantry Recruit Training," *Canadian J. Psychology, 8* (1954), 87–94.

25. WEINBERG, S. KIRSON, and HENRY AROND. "The Occupational Culture of the Boxer," *Am. J. Sociology, 57* (March, 1952), 460–69.

Class Differences in Family
Decision-Making on Expenditures

MIRRA KOMAROVSKY

The husband-wife relationship forms a subsystem within the larger social system of the family. From the point of view of household decision-making, it is a crucial subsystem. This paper deals with the extent of husband-wife communication; in its bearing upon the central problem of the conference, it should throw light on the extent of *joint* (though not necessarily egalitarian) involvement in economic decisions. Under what conditions will each spouse control—more or less autonomously—some spheres of expenditures and, conversely, when are decisions a joint activity of the couple?

Obviously, some husband-wife communication on economic matters is universal, but even within the same family type, i.e., the present-day nuclear family of the Western industrial societies, interspousal communication varies a great deal. Contrast the following extremes described in recent family studies.

At one pole stands a working-class family residing in a long-settled neighborhood in London as studied by Townsend.

> Married people revealed the true state of their financial affairs . . . only when they could be questioned separately. Few wives knew what their husbands earned; many did not think they had a right to know. . . . The wife regularly received a round sum as housekeeping money. . . . To this she added any earnings of her own, or borrowed money from her children. She regarded the housekeeping allowance as her money. . . . There were many references to "his money," "her money," and "what a wife does with her money is her affair."

This division of the wage into two parts and the personal, rather than joint, claim over each part allowed man and wife to spend their money separately, with relatively little consultation about day-to-day expenditures. The wife paid the rent, insurance, and fuel bills and bought all the food and household sundries for the home. She also set aside regular amounts for clothing, loan payments, and Christmas Clubs. Husbands for their part often did not know how housekeeping money was spent. This was evident from the number of married men interviewed who had to turn to their wives for information about rent, insurance, and sums spent on coal. One wife, for example, said, "If you asked him how much he was insured for, he would not be able to tell you."

The wife's ignorance of the husband's wage was often equalled by his ignorance of what her children gave her. When one man was asked how much his two daughters paid in board money, he said, "They give it to Mom. I don't even know how much they give her." Women talk of financial arrangements between themselves and their children as though the husband was not a party to them at all.

Separate management of money was paralleled by segregation in the roles of the spouses with regard to all household tasks. It was greatly influenced by the proximity of female relatives.

> Because she shared so much of daily life with children and grandchildren, the grandmother did fewer things jointly with her husband. . . . Man and wife often went their own separate ways in their leisure time. Men spoke of going to pubs, sports grounds or clubs with brothers or work-mates; women, of going on holidays, to the pictures and to clubs with daughters or sisters. "We don't go out much at all together. He likes a drink, but it doesn't appeal to me, and then he has his work (21)."

In contrast to this stands what has become known as a "companionship" marriage. Some professional couples described by Bott (2) are of this type. They are familiar enough to require only a brief statement. In such families, the division of labor between the spouses is more flexible; there is less division and more direct co-operation instead. There is more consultation on instrumental and leisure-time decision and more communication of personal feelings.

The first part of this paper will set forth some hypotheses to account for variation in the extent of husband-wife communication. It does not aim at anything as ambitious as a model. On the other hand, the hypotheses, though not exhaustive, are to be of sufficient generality to serve in interpreting diverse empirical cases. The particular case to be considered in the second part of the paper is the class differential in the mode of decision-making on expenditures.[1]

The variables included in the following hypotheses affect the extent of communication by creating a need for it, by providing alternative channels or by presenting a barrier. These variables fall into several categories. Some are social norms embraced by the family, either norms of marriage or general social values having some consequence for marriage interaction. Other variables are social-structural: recurrent patterns of interaction which arise in response to norms and to situational pressures; finally, there are the psycho-social variables. These are psychological characteristics shared by a social group by virtue of similar experiences.

Theoretical Expectations

Hypothesis 1: The more future-oriented the couple is in the sense of having aspirations for self and children, the more communication. In contrast, a couple that has no long range goals or is fatalistic will lack the need to weigh alternative choices inevitable in planning. The values we are contrasting are fatalism versus mastery and maintenance of status quo versus mobility for self and children.

Hypothesis 2: The more rigid the institutionalization of marriage roles, the less communication. Conversely, the need for interchange should be greater if behavior is not rigidly defined and especially if some confusion of roles exists.

This hypothesis is indirectly suggested by an experimental study of Steiner and Dodge, "Interpersonal Perception and Role Structure as Determinants of Group and Individual Efficiency" (20). The study revealed that when role structure was highly organized, perceptual inaccuracies on the part of the participants did not affect group and individual efficiency, as was the case in a less structured situation.

---

[1] We are here concerned with communication in instrumental areas of life and, even more particularly, with economic decisions. Self-disclosure of personal feelings—communication in leisure spheres—is another matter. The extent of intercorrelation between these areas of communication remains to be discovered. If Homans' generalization about external and internal systems is valid, considerable interaction in instrumental areas may coexist with little intimate interchange. This will be the case if instrumental activities are carried on in an authoritarian marriage relation. With a more egalitarian relation, high interaction in instrumental areas will tend to be associated with close interaction in other areas as well (8).

Possibly more accurate knowledge is required of participants in an unstructured situation. Although the study did not measure directly the extent of communication in the two settings, it did suggest that if the same results are to be achieved, the less defined situation would require more interchange.

Hypothesis 3: The more prevalent the view of marriage as personal companionship fulfilling the personality needs of the spouses (in contrast to the emphasis on institutional functions of the family), the greater the demand for joint participation and communication.

Hypothesis 4: The more egalitarian the authority pattern, the more communication. Decisions that are not commands of one of the partners are harder to reach. If one spouse has the authority, he may or may not direct the activity of the other or communicate his decision, but there will be less discussion than if both share in the authority.

Hypothesis 5: The less rigid the differentiation in task allocations, the more communication. If husband and wife both market, or take turns at other such tasks, they must discuss sheer organization of activities as well as basic decisions. It is true that in time many decisions become routinized. But if roles are specialized, there is bound to develop a greater degree of autonomy in the respective spheres. Strong sex role differentiation may also mean that spouses develop special areas of competence, as a result of which each decides autonomously in his own area. Of the various combinations of authority and task specialization, the type of family most conducive to joint decision-making should be one with least role specialization and the greatest degree of equality of influence.

Hypothesis 6: The stronger the consanguine ties to parents and siblings involving the individual in a separate network of obligations and rights, the greater the likelihood that some decisions are made in consultation with relatives which would otherwise be shared with the spouse. Studies by Townsend (21) and Young and Willmott (25) in England and Vogel (22) in the United States support this generalization.

Hypothesis 7: The more frequently couples continue to live in neighborhood or small town of their birth so that primary group contacts with like-sex peer groups as well as relatives remain strong, the weaker the interspousal communication. Conversely, migration away from such stable primary groups throws the spouses upon each other. Social mobility may be expected to have a similar effect.

Strong support for this proposition is afforded by Young and Willmott (25), Bott (2), and Mogey (14, p. 62). Young and Willmott followed families from a long-settled working-class neighborhood of East London into a housing development some distance away. The contacts with relatives decreased (p. 106). "The family is more self-contained . . ." (p. 119). Husbands help more with household tasks. "The 'home' and marriage become the focus of a man's life as of his wife's far more completely than in the East End" (p. 119).

Bott (2) classified families in terms of role segregation: separation of the spouses in activities of the household and in social life. The factor that she found to be most consistently related to the degree of segregation was the degree of connectedness in the social networks of the spouses—the extent to which their associates constituted a primary group with everybody knowing everybody else. A closely knit network, she suggests, means a consensus on norms and therefore a controlling social group. Thus, the buddies of the husband may be able to impose obligations and to offer help. In any case, these associates draw the spouse into a network of relations competing with the relation to husband or wife.

Hypothesis 8: If sex-role training is such as to produce mistrust between the sexes, communication may be impaired. Stycos and Hill (7) have exemplified this process in their descriptions of the Puerto Rican family.

Hypothesis 9: The hypotheses listed thus far involve some characteristic of the family, but the nature of the decision itself will also affect the outcome. *Other things being equal, the more a given decision involves a significant economic choice ruling out some alternative for the family, the more frequently will there be consultation.* Routine expenditures for items viewed as necessities by a given couple are, conversely, more likely to fall into the autonomous spheres of one or the other spouse.

EMPIRICAL STUDIES

The foregoing theoretical expectations are now to be applied to a particular case: class differences in the mode of decision-making on expenditures. We are specifically concerned with the contrast between joint involvement and autonomy. Given our hypotheses and the relevant characteristics of socioeconomic classes insofar as these are known, what can we expect?

First of all, we cannot expect that every expenditure will present the same pattern of class differences. If in the lower-income families the purchase of a car is a joint decision, while the upper-class husband makes it autonomously, it does not follow that this is also the case with other expenditures. What is a crucial economic choice on one income level is a routine necessity on another. If it is possible to generalize for a socioeconomic class as a whole, we propose the following master hypothesis: *There is greater autonomy with regard to expenditures at the bottom and at the top of the socioeconomic hierarchy than among the middle classes.*

This curvilinear hypothesis as to class differences is derived from the theoretical expectations listed in the preceding section. At the bottom of the scale, there is less opportunity to debate alternative allocations because most of the available income is spent on routine necessities; at the top, there is less debate than in the middle classes because there is economic leeway (Hypothesis 8). But this is not all. The greater the specialized knowledge required for a decision when such knowledge is sex-linked, the less consultation (Hypothesis 5). At the top of the socioeconomic hierarchy, the husband's role in investments, insurance, and savings, the wife's role in elaboration of standards of consumption, each call for such sex-linked expertise. There is evidence that the lower classes have more traditional views as to masculine and feminine roles than have the higher classes. Bott found more role specialization among her working-class couples in comparison with professional couples. Among the middle classes, one would expect a greater flexibility in role definitions as well as a greater acceptance of the ideal of companionship in marriage (Hypothesis 3). Another factor should promote joint involvement of the middle classes: their mobility aspirations (Hypothesis 1).

A subsidiary hypothesis suggests itself bearing upon the relative influence of the sexes. Because the bulk of the expenditures in lower-income families are for routine household purposes, the role of the wife should be greater than in the upper economic classes. Several studies have found a positive correlation between the status of the husband's occupation and his dominance. In a somewhat simplified manner one may describe the lower-class families as relatively more matriarchal, the middle classes as egalitarian, and the upper classes as more patriarchal.

Another variable apart from class affecting communication (and to be held constant if class differences are to be ascertained) is the age of the couple. The young should exhibit more joint involvement. They are in a stage in which planning for the future does call for choices among alternatives. The sexes have not had enough time to acquire areas of specialized competence. The norms of consultation and equality, being the more modern norms, are more likely to be embraced by the young.

Let us now turn to some empirical studies to test these expectations. Certain methodological obstacles will limit the usefulness of these studies for our purposes. Most of the studies of purchase influence use the questionnaire or short interview method with direct questions as to influence. These methods are of questionable reliability, and it is only in the absence of better data on purchases that we must use them. (See Ferber [3], and Kenkel [11].) Moreover, the income classifications vary from study to study and so do the particular economic decisions. The studies, therefore, are not always comparable.

(1) Wilkening (23) studied (1953) the extent of joint involvement of 614 Wisconsin farm operators and their wives in five economic areas: "what crops to plant, when and where," "buying machinery," "changes to be made in the home."

In general, there is low joint involvement for the low-income group, high for the middle-income group and again low for the high-income group. This nonlinear relationship is consistent with our hypothesis. With gross farm income of under $6,000, only 39.3% of the couples indicated joint involvement. The percentage increased to 50 for those with incomes of $6,000 to $8,999. It fell to 38.2 for those with incomes of $9,000 and over. Wilkening found also that "The greater the degree of commercialization of the farm enterprise, the less joint involvement of husband and wife in major farm and home decisions" (23, p. 183). Wilkening suggests that with higher income hired labor replaces wife labor on the farm, and her role is increasingly specialized in the home or in social spheres (Hypothesis 5).[2]

(2) Olsen (16) studied in 1956–57 the distribution of responsibility within the family with regard to 100 household tasks and decisions in five different socioeconomic classes.[3] The study was done by means

[2] As to other possible determinants of joint involvement, this study found no correlation between the wife's education and joint involvement.

[3] The fact that the study includes all household decisions and not merely those on expenditures makes it less precise for our purposes. Furthermore, it does not distinguish in its summaries between task allocation (who does what) and influence.

of schedules with the opening question: "Who in your family usually (most of the time) actually does the following things which I will read to you?" The five status areas were based on occupation and education.

For *all* the household *tasks* and *decisions,* the results support our curvilinear hypothesis. Joint sharing of responsibility includes only 24.8% of all modes of decisions at the bottom level; it goes up to 28.2, 27.9, 28.3% for levels 4, 3, and 2, and falls to 25.7% at the top level. The author concludes: "The transition from the traditional to the companionship form of family is not equally noticeable in different strata of society. In general, it is more evident in middle-status families, and less evident in high- and low-status families" (16, p. 37).

Our second hypothesis with regard to the role of the wife is also confirmed by Olsen. "The amount of responsibility taken by the wife increases inversely with status level, being least in the high area and greatest in the low area" (16, p. 20).

(3) Wolgast (24) studied the role of the spouses in economic decisions concerning savings, household goods, automobiles, and money and bills, based on a survey of a cross-section sample of families in all parts of the United States.

Economic decisions are most commonly made jointly by husband and wife (24, p. 16). This comes out in response to direct questions. Internal evidence with regard to buying plans shows even more reliably that buying intentions have been discussed by the couple, because there is high agreement in the answers of husbands and wives questioned separately.

Division of labor and autonomy increase with income. In answer to the question "who in your family usually decides . . . ," answers indicating autonomy, "wife only" or "husband only," increased with income. Control over household items by the wife increased from 24% in the under $3,000 group to 31% in the $10,000 and over group. Concern with savings becomes increasingly the husband's task with higher income ("wife only" responses decreased from 36% for families with $3,000 to 9% for families with $10,000 and more). "Higher income is positively, though not strongly, related to husband's autonomy in car-purchasing decisions" (24, p. 8). "With advancing age, and perhaps increased length of marriage, joint decisions decline and one member or another is increasingly likely to decide alone."

This study confirms our hypothesis of the greater autonomy in the upper classes but the same was not true in the under $3,000 income group. However, the question on household goods specifically inquired about "big items for the house" (furniture, appliances, etc.). One would expect more consultation about such unusual purchases in the lower-income classes. Our hypothesis about the generally greater autonomy in those classes was postulated on the supposition that a greater percentage of all the purchases were routine expenditures on necessities. Similar reasons may account for the failure of this study to confirm still another expectation, the relatively greater role of the lower-class wife in expenditures.

In contrast to Wolgast, two sources do support the last mentioned hypothesis:

(4) Van Bortel and Gross (1) in an interview study of 26 upper-lower- and 24 upper-middle-class homemakers found that lower-class homemakers had more of a voice in financial planning than middle-class homemakers.

(5) Sharp and Mott (18) found that in Detroit low-income families the wife was twice as likely as her husband to handle household bills. In families with income of $8,000 and over, either spouse performed this task about as frequently as the other.

Finally, several English studies of working-class families (21, 25) reveal that household purchases and bills were handled by the wife with little consultation with her husband.

The final study to be examined is by Sharp and Mott (18). The income classes are divided by $2,000 intervals from those with incomes under $2,000 to those with $8,000 and over. Questions asked are: "What car to get," "Whether or not to buy life insurance," "How much to spend on food," "What house or apartment to take," "Where to spend a vacation," "If wife should go to work or quit work," "Who keeps track of money and bills."

The dominant role of the lower-class wife is apparent not only in "keeping track of money and bills" but with regard to each item. The relative proportion of "wife only" answers decreases consistently with rise in income for all items.

In still another respect, Sharp and Mott are consistent with our expectations. Those with incomes of under $2,000 show more division of labor and autonomy than the higher-income groups. However, the top income group, those with $8,000 and over, fail to manifest the return to autonomous decisions which we predicted.

On most of the items, the $8,000-and-over group gives a higher percentage of *joint* decisions. It is possible that a still higher income group than the 111 persons in the $8,000-and-over bracket of this study would, in fact, exhibit a greater autonomy. This was reported by Wolgast (24), whose top income category was $10,000 and over.

In conclusion, three generalizations were presented concerning decision-making on expenditures: the curvilinear hypothesis of class differences, the greater influence of the wife in the lower socio-economic classes, and the higher rate of joint involvement among the younger couples. There is enough support for these generalizations to warrant provisional acceptance and further study.

References and Supplementary Studies

1. BORTEL, DOROTHY G. VAN, and IRMA H. GROSS. *A Comparison of Home Management in Two Socio-economic Groups.* Michigan State College Agricultural Experiment Station Bull. 240, Ap. 19521.

2. BOTT, ELIZABETH. *Family and Social Network.* London: Tavistock Publications Limited, 1957.

3. FERBER, ROBERT. "On the Reliability of Purchase Influence Studies," *J. Marketing, 19* (Jan., 1955), 225–32.

4. FOOTE, NELSON N. "Matching of Husband and Wife in Phases of Development," in *Transactions of the Third World Congress of Sociology.* International Sociological Assoc., 1956. Pp. 24–35.

5. ——— and LEONARD COTTRELL. *Identity and Interpersonal Competence: A New Direction in Family Research.* Chicago: University of Chicago Press, 1955.

6. HEER, DAVID M. "Dominance and the Working Wife," *Social Forces, 136,* No. 4 (1958), 341–47.

7. HILL, REUBEN *et al.* "Intra-Family Communication and Fertility in Puerto Rico," *Rural Sociology, 20* (Sept.–Dec., 1955), 258–71.

8. HOMANS, GEORGE. *The Human Group.* New York: Harcourt Brace, 1950.

9. JOURARD, S. M., and P. LASAKOW. "Some Factors in Self-Disclosure," *J. Abnormal and Social Psychology* (Jan., 1958).

10. KARLSSON, GEORG. *Adaptability and Communication in Marriage.* Uppsala: Almqvist & Wiksells Boktryckeri Ab, 1951.

11. KENKEL, W. P., and D. K. HOFFMANN. "Real and Conceived Roles in Family Decision Making," *Marriage and Family Living, 18* (Nov., 1956), 311–16.

12. KOMAROVSKY, MIRRA. "Continuities in Family Research: A Case Study," *Am. J. Sociology, 62* (July, 1956), 42–47.

13. ———. *Women in the Modern World: Their Education and Their Dilemmas.* Boston: Little Brown, 1953.

14. MOGEY, J. M. *Family and Neighborhood.* London: Oxford University Press, 1956.

15. NEWCOMB, T. R. "Communicative Behavior," in *Approaches to the Study of Politics,* ed. Kimball Young. Evanston: Northwestern University Press, 1958. Pp. 244–65.

16. OLSEN, MARVIN E. *Distribution of Responsibility within the Family as Related to Social Stratification.* Grinnell College, 1956–57.

17. RABBAN, MEYER. "Sex-Role Identification in Young Children in Two Diverse Social Groups," *Genetic Psychology Monographs*, Aug., 1950.

18. SHARP, H., and P. MOTT. "Consumer Decisions in the Makeup of Family," *J. Marketing, 21* (Oct., 1956), 149–56.

19. SMARDAN, LAWRENCE EUGENE. "An Exploratory Study of Communication," Ph.D. dissertation, Cornell University, 1957.

20. STEINER, IVAN D., and JOAN S. DODGE. "Interpersonal Perception and Role Structure as Determinants of Group and Individual Efficiency," *Human Relations, 9* (Nov., 1956), 467–81.

21. TOWNSEND, PETER. *The Family Life of Old People*. Glencoe, Illinois: Free Press, 1957. Pp. 68–73.

22. VOGEL, EZRA FEIDEL. *The Marital Relationship of Parents and the Emotionally Disturbed Child*. Ph.D. dissertation, Harvard, April, 1958.

23. WILKENING, EUGENE A. "Joint Decision-Making in Farm Families," *Am. Sociological Rev., 23* (April, 1958), 187–92.

24. WOLGAST, ELIZABETH H. "Economic Decisions in the Family," *J. Marketing, 23* (Oct., 1958), 151–58.

25. YOUNG, MICHAEL, and PETER WILLMOTT. *Family and Kinship in East London*. Glencoe, Illinois: Free Press, 1957.

Discussion

RICHARD N. ROSETT

Both Becker and Komarovsky have suggested to me problems on which co-operation between an economist and a sociologist might lead to a clear gain for one or the other.

I have been working for the past few years on the problem of explaining the participation of married women in the labor force. Recall the model which Mahoney described as the model of consumer choice used by economists and which Watts mentioned in his discussion later in this conference. I have found, like Watts, that this simple model can be useful in work I am doing because it actually suggests testable hypotheses despite the fact that indifference curves are not directly observable. In using this model, Mahoney, Watts, and I have chosen to ignore the fact that it is not as obviously applicable to a family or spending unit as to an individual. The very special conditions under which a group can be thought of as having a utility function with the desirable properties that economists like to associate with utility functions, were shown by Paul Samuelson to be: (1) "as you take equal amounts of a good away from one [member of a spending unit], you must give increasing amounts to another if spending unit welfare is to remain constant," and (2) within a spending unit, there must be "optimal reallocation of income so as to keep each member's dollar expenditure of equal ethical worth."

I cannot speak for Watts or Mahoney, but I ignored Samuelson's warning that the indifference curves might cross over because the first condition seems so likely to be fulfilled for most families and because I hope that the second condition is fulfilled. I regard Komarovsky's paper as a tentative approach to the problem of whether or not my hope is justified. I would like to know the circumstances under which there is communication between the decision-makers which may lead to an "optimal reallocation of income." I do not mean to imply that I think this paper sheds any light on this question. There is no reason why it should. My intention is simply to suggest this as one area in which economics might benefit from something that is being done in sociology.

I am not in a position to criticize this paper, but I would like to ask a few questions about the hypotheses. It seems to me that such attributes as future-orientation and egalitarianism are observed primarily in communication between the spouses. Doesn't this make Hypotheses 1 and 4 tautological? I would like to see a careful definition of communication. Is a husband communicating if he bares his soul and his wife doesn't care? Or if he explains why one car is better than another and she doesn't understand? How does one actually measure communication? I don't mean to suggest that communication cannot be measured, but there are some problems here that worry me. For example, spouses with lots of experience at communicating may have become so efficient as to seem to communicate very little.

Becker's paper was especially interesting to me because when I first read it I was sharing an office at the Rand Corporation with Richard Nelson, who is working on a problem that seems at least formally similar to the one in which Becker is interested. At the risk of seeming more a matchmaker than discussant, let me suggest this as another area in which economists and sociologists might join forces. Nelson's work differs from Becker's primarily in that his model is normative while Becker's is descriptive.

Briefly, Nelson is interested in telling the Air Force how it should go about procuring new weapons systems. At present the procedure is typically as follows: A specification is drawn up by the Air Force and aircraft companies are requested to submit designs, cost estimates, and delivery-date estimates. The original specification may include the actual configuration of the weapon, or it may merely specify the required performance characteristics. The Air Force selects the single most promising estimate and contracts for the delivery of the new weapon.

Nelson is attempting to demonstrate that it would pay the Air Force in terms of lower cost and earlier delivery for a given weapon if it were to follow a policy similar to the process Becker describes as that by which occupations are chosen. The Air Force ought to arrange to make its commitments a little at a time. First, the specification ought to be as general as possible, given the end the weapon is to serve. Second, several contracts should be awarded, not for delivery of the weapon, but for research on the actual configuration of the weapon, perhaps up to the construction of a prototype. Thus at several points the Air Force should have an opportunity to choose between alternatives. Finally one of the companies would be awarded a contract for the production of the weapon.

How is this like the process of choosing an occupation? It seems to me that the physiologist, the engineer, and the philosopher all started with some specification of goals. Each made commitments a little at a time, always narrowing the range of alternatives. Each must be aware that many possible outcomes exist; few people are so firmly committed to one career that suicide is the only acceptable alternative. I have no wish to present a model of sequential decision-making under uncertainty here this morning, but I do want to suggest that Becker and Nelson might benefit from an exchange of ideas.

There is just one more point in Becker's paper on which I would like to comment. I regret the implied value judgment in the statement that the goal of this conference is "the development of an abstract model that will enable us to understand, explain, and perhaps predict. . . ." I would prefer to predict, explain, and perhaps understand.

Discussion

CAHALAN (to KOMAROVSKY): On the basis of the joint-interview study on which I reported yesterday, I have to disagree with the view that husbands and wives appear to agree on decisions when questioned separately. There is not even agreement on the facts. In our study of men's clothing, we ran some limited controls, questioning husband and wife separately and getting independent responses on ownership, which we wanted to measure as exactly as possible. In a fourth to a third of the couples, there was inconsistency about the presence of synthetic fabrics in the husband's wardrobe. This shows the unreliability of using only one informant. In estimating the aggregate market, if any reliance is to be put on data from a single member of the family, much depends on the relative competence of whichever one is used as the informant.

KATONA (to KOMAROVSKY): Although I might explain it differently, I would accept the fact that the middle class is more communicative and more egalitarian. At the recent meetings of the American Psychological Association, however, I heard three papers which differ from this view. Swanson and Miller reported on infant-care practices in the family and Bronfenbrenner on parental relations. The third was by David Riesman, who said the middle classes were until a few years ago the carriers of change, listening to dissent and adopting new practices, but recently they have become authoritarian and conservative. I was unfavorably struck by their discussion, yet in Germany in the '30's we learned that, contrary to the '20's, the middle classes were not propagators of change but followers of Hitler. If it is true that fundamental changes can occur within short time periods, you might be right for the period up until the early 1950's but wrong for the 1960's. They may become less communicative and egalitarian.

KOMAROVSKY: I would have to see their evidence. I would not dare say offhand if they are right or wrong. They open up a tremendously interesting question, deserving much thought and study. Meanwhile, the pedantic point to be made is that, as long as the middle class has the qualities we attributed to it, the predictions hold. If the qualities change, so will their consequences for communication.

DANIERE: I am much interested by your nonlinearity of income interaction, as I have found this in my own studies of consumption. It has shown up in a study we have done at Harvard on the financing of higher education. Planned expenditure on higher education goes up with income toward the middle-income levels, then the curve tends to flatten out, then becomes steep again.

I am now working on the consumer expenditure part of a Leontieff project, correlating expenditures item by item with income. We have found more interaction with other variables, for instance in clothing expenditure, in high- and low-income groups than in medium. You would expect an interaction with family size in ratio to family income, but it does not work that way; the relationship is curvilinear. Your first hypothesis seems to explain why. That is, what happens in the medium group is that you find more competent budgeters because they can aspire to more things—a new house, a better neighborhood. Therefore, food and clothing expenditures are controlled in order to attain their aspirations. Aspirations change with movement into the middle-income group. In the low-income group, it is impossible to aspire to such things, so income is used on food and clothing. In the high-income group, less of a dent is made on income by expenditures. In the medium group, competition is intensified among items of the budget.

FOOTE: There is more price shopping by middle-income people.

HILL (to KOMAROVSKY): Is it possible that you are working with a syndrome or complex of patterns that need to be distinguished from one another—a companionship syndrome of which the symptoms are communication, sharing of tasks and activities, joint decision-making? The syndrome may relate more closely to class than do these individual symptoms. If so, you might want to include individual symptoms in your hypothesis, to increase your chances of finding alternate statements of the syndrome.

KOMAROVSKY: Your question is related to another comment, as to whether there is really a distinction between egalitarianism and joint decision-making. I have thought it useful to distinguish authority from task specialization. While egalitarianism may tend to be associated with the sharing of tasks, "colleague-spouses" may have equal authority but each rule over a distinct sphere. To some extent then, authority and task specialization are independent of one another, and each may exercise an independent influence upon communication about expenditures.

HILL: I would agree that colleagueship may collect certain of these symptoms as companionship does. But as you have lined up your two-variable hypotheses here, do they not become tautological unless you are more specific on the combinations? Koenig ran into this trouble in a study of authoritarianism in the German family.

BILKEY: What criteria did you use to define class? It sounded economic—was it just income class? Was a dollar criterion used? During what period? What do you do regarding time sequences, including income changes?

Also, are you referring to relative position in the economy or to absolute? There is still argument about the absolute income hypothesis versus the permanent income hypothesis. With more people moving into the middle-income class, perhaps it is the absolute position that is more important. Their behavior may be a function of rising income and not of class.

KOMAROVSKY: The studies I have cited date from 1953 on and used criteria such as income, status based on rent, occupation, and education. You suggest a valid point regarding comparisons in time.

GLICK (to KOMAROVSKY): It would be interesting to examine data on duration of marriage and authoritarianism to see if a relationship exists. If there were a relationship, it might conceivably reflect changes in cultural norms over the generations. Perhaps what is needed is a check of cross-sectional data with longitudinal data to interpret the problem under discussion. Repetition of cross-sectional studies over several decades might or might not serve the same purpose as longitudinal studies of panels of respondents over the same period.

FOOTE (to GLICK): Burgess at Chicago has dealt with this question. In his study of marriages of 20 years' duration, comparing successful and unsuccessful husbands, he found that egalitarianism declined with the degree of economic success.

MORGAN: We need definition, not just terms. Social-class measurement must take account of many things—whether the wife is in the labor force, nonwhites, stage of life cycle. Too often middle class seems to include disproportionately the middle-aged and the two-income households. These confusing elements must be controlled or removed in defining social class, so as to avoid spurious correlations. Particularly as we go from studies of narrowly defined groups to national samples, variables like social class prove to be highly correlated with a number of these other variables. Perhaps we need not be this severe with our hypotheses, but a tight test would require that we remove the effect of these simpler variables to see whether there is something else that could be called social class which remains to affect the behavior in question.

KOMAROVSKY: I would certainly accept those important refinements for future studies.

KENKEL: I believe the concept of "differential social status" would prove less confusing than "social class." In any case, social status is an important variable, and differences will be found associated with it after age and stage of life cycle are controlled.

STANTON (to BECKER): Your description of the phases of occupational choice was, I thought, a very able job. But the way in which your findings were expressed raises an important issue, with respect to which I would like clarification. For example, you say that graduate students in physiology go into that field after being rejected for medical school and remain in it after a second rejection a year later has left them with an investment in physiology then too great to throw away. Is it fair to ask what percentage of graduate students in physiology has actually been twice rejected for medical school?

BECKER: In our very small sample, about 50 or 60%. No measurement on a large sample was really made.

STANTON: But how exact were you about numbers? Let me take another example: you say that success in an occupation is measured by the extent to which one's position protects him from the chronic problems of that occupation. Would it negate this rule if a third of all your subjects did not use this criterion? What is the relationship between the counting of cases and the kind of description of a model process which you employ?

BECKER: We generalized from philosophy and physiology students, but we were not studying physiologists. We were studying commitments. Each occupation has peculiar patterns of recruitment. We need to develop categories that take account of these. We did open up the way for research using occupational specifics.

STANTON: Can your model be standardized? Do you regard your model, or prologue to a model, as the kind that can now be tested by someone going out and counting positive and negative cases, so and not so?

BECKER: In principle, yes, although some of the right data are hard to get. The task is not how to standardize interviews or questionnaires which go direct to the point of inquiry, but to standardize observation. In many occupational situations in which questions are not easily answerable, the answers may be easily observable.

DuBois: Please elaborate your notion of "decision." Do people make decisions and then decide to stick to them?

BECKER: I did not focus on decision-making, but on how to account for a consistent line of activity. Decisions as such rarely account for this. I watched five boys change their views again and again in the course of their surgical experience.

HILL (to BECKER): I believe occupational choice is different from consumer choice. Consumer behavior requires fewer commitments; it offers the opportunity to shop around. Occupational decisions are more like mate selection. Both the job and the mate can answer back; they can refuse to be chosen. The range of selection is not so wide. Occupational choice is not just sequential—there are other differences too.

BECKER: You are right. We need more distinctions like those of Westoff, for example, irrevocability. Many distinctions are needed as to what kind of decision is being made, whether among occupations or among specialties within an occupation, for example. The subtypes are important even after a commitment is made, as in the case of the dance musician who can easily change his subspecialty, depending on the economic situation of the dance business.

KATONA: You must recognize that embarking on one decision automatically leads to many future decisions or forecloses another decision. There are sequences of effect, of the house purchase on the car purchase, for example, and so on. So I wish to contradict Hill. I like Becker's view: I agree with the analogy between occupational choice and consumer decisions. Embarking on certain policies often makes it impossible to make any further choices. That is why in a book I wrote 15 years ago I introduced a distinction between *genuine* decisions and *habitual* decisions, that is, routine actions already settled.

BRIM: Hill probably meant much simpler decisions, but we can allow no further comments, unless written out and submitted to the editor.

LEICHTER: The paper by Becker raises a general point of much relevance to discussion throughout the conference, which should be further emphasized. His discussion of occupational career choices implies that any model of household decision-making should include the time span, recognizing the sequential process of commitment. Attention has been mainly on the time span prior to a decision or an act based on a decision, especially where the focus has been the process rather than the outcome. But an equally important area for study is the family interaction that occurs after selection of a particular alternative action, as in the earlier example of advertisement reading after car purchase. Some of the most vivid and significant interaction within a family comes then, and this may be of the greatest importance in the process of learning to make future decisions.

Certain methodological problems in using retrospective data may be turned to advantage, if distortions of memory and selective forgetting are used as indices of the process of re-evaluating alternatives after decision and action. Negative evaluations of selected alternatives and positive evaluations of rejected alternatives arise after choice has been made and have to be dealt with in the household.

Similarly, the division of labor and the amount of communication between husband and wife may vary meaningfully during the period after choice of an alternative; dissatisfaction, regret, remorse, blame, and recrimination enter then. Different forms of consensus and changed marital relationships may emerge from repeated decision-making.

MORGAN: Hill raised the question whether Komarovsky was not using a group of variables which might be called "companionship," including communication, sharing of decision-making, and joint rather than separate performance of tasks. In the light of the difficulty with the problem of the definition of power in the family and of the various kinds of communications, would it not be useful to focus on some dependent variable like the proportion of communication devoted to solving problems (making decisions), or even the proportion devoted to solving problems of a particular sort, i.e., those involving the allocation of household spending (rather than brand and style choices or child rearing)?

Such a dependent variable is more specific, less subject to measurement difficulties, i.e., less dependent on the total amount of communication, which may simply reflect verbal facility or lack of other forms of communication (nonverbal). A similar variable would be the proportion of family decisions that involve use of money as against discipline of children, social relations, or pure household mechanics, though such a variable would be more interesting to family sociologists than to economists.

The Family as a Set of Mutually Contingent Careers[1]

BERNARD FARBER

Generally, in the development of family typologies, the sociologist has an image of the social and economic system in which a family operates and then raises the problem of the kinds of family appropriate to this social system. For example, Burgess, viewing contemporary society as one of increased horizontal and vertical social mobility, regarded interpersonal forces as increasingly important in holding the family unit together. His typology opposed an ideal-typical *institutional* family, held together entirely by pressures external to the nuclear family, to an ideal-typical *companionship* family, held together entirely by forces within the nuclear family (2).

Similarly, Miller and Swanson, noting a tendency toward large-scale organization of economic and governmental institutions, devised a typology based on the kind of family life appropriate to development toward large-scale organization. The historical movement implied in their typology is from the traditional patriarchal family, associated with rural life, to the companionship family, associated with an entrepreneurial economic system, to a colleague family, associated with a highly bureaucratized economic system (10).

An alternative approach to the problem of typology is to regard the nuclear family as a kind of small group and to focus upon the means by which the family group maintains its integration under

[1] By invitation of the editor, the original discussion of the papers by Becker and Komarovsky has been extended and systematized. It now refers only to Becker's paper.

various social conditions. By this alternative approach, kinds of family behavior developed to meet conditions not only of economic organization in urban society but also of illness, family life cycle contingencies, and other critical problems can be explained.

This paper describes the family as a set of mutually contingent careers. The career frame of reference facilitates the development of propositions not apparent in other views of the family. On the basis of the description of the family as careers, a research model of the family is developed. The research model described in this paper was constructed to co-ordinate a number of hypotheses in the study of family integration. An attempt is made to state the model in its most general terms.

THE FAMILY AS MUTUALLY CONTINGENT CAREERS

Concepts of career, success, and career contingencies have been used in describing occupational decision-making. It is suggested that these concepts are applicable to the study of family life. Each of these concepts is examined below.

A *career* can be regarded as "a progression of statuses and functions which unfold in a more or less orderly though not predetermined sequence in the pursuit of values which themselves emerge in the course of experience" (6, p. 31). A person's life career would be a general description of the course of his progression through the various statuses he has occupied. This life career can be analyzed into special careers—occupational career, domestic career, recreational career. These special careers, in turn, could be analyzed into subcareers. The special careers refer to the course of the individual's development within specific institutions (e.g., the family, the economic agencies, and the school).

Success in an occupation is achieved when a person attains a position in the social structure that "best" solves the characteristic problems of that occupation. Moreover, as Becker has said, "success is achieved by moving from one to another of the positions that the social structure of the occupation makes available" (1). Successful family life can also be described as that in which the characteristic problems of family living have been solved "satisfactorily." There is, however, no objective position in a hierarchy of families which corresponds to the successful family. Rather, as studies of marital prediction have indicated, the successful family is defined in terms of the character of interpersonal relations themselves.

The *career contingencies* of an occupation have as their counterpart in family life critical events that upset expectations, norms, and values at any time.

The concepts of career, success, and career contingency thus seem transportable to family life. If the family is viewed as a set of careers, a marked shift in the domestic career of one family member should affect the careers of the other family members. To the extent that the other family members adjust their careers in a predictable manner in response to this stimulation, the family exists as a system of mutually contingent careers.

In the family as a set of mutually contingent careers, the end of the grouping is assumed to be the facilitation of career development of each member. If the career patterns of each member of the group are co-ordinated with the others in the family, the career of the individual member will be advanced through (a) an efficient division of labor, (b) constant reinforcement of personal norms and values by significant others, (c) existence of a nonthreatening arena for relaxation and discussion, and (d) reinforcement of motivation through personal obligations toward other family members. Thus, for all members, career facilitation will take place when there is high family integration at any time.

In the model, the unit that describes the state of a career at a given point in time is the person's role. For example, in her domestic career in the family of procreation, a woman will develop through a series of roles—wife without children, wife-and-mother with preschool children, wife-and-mother with preadolescents, etc.

A *role* is regarded as a patterned sequence of intended *actions* or deeds to be performed by a person in an interaction situation. The organizing of the actions is a product of person A's perceptual and cognitive behavior upon observing B. B performs one or several acts which A observes and defines (on the basis of the intentions he imputes to B) as B's role. A then expects certain further actions from B. Having defined B's role, A organizes certain acts which he regards as appropriate to reciprocate to B's role; these acts are conceptualized by A as A's role.

If roles are regarded as a patterned sequence of intended actions, they must be regarded in terms of the various ends of the individuals. The contention here is that there are two aspects of roles, the social-emotional and instrumental (12).

Social-emotional aspects of roles entail the development of procedures to protract the social relationship; these procedures include (a) the timing of communication of significant information pertaining to crucial issues (e.g., involving problems of empathy, verbal facility, ability to delay gratification until "appropriate" time, and degree of personal identification), (b) effective release of physiological tensions, and (c) reinforcement of mutual interest in the members of the group (e.g., obviously affectional behavior, sympathy, and encouragement) or, more generally, (d) competence in interpersonal relations (8).

In the instrumental aspects of the role, strategies are developed for the purpose of acting consistently in accordance with an end. The strategic aspects of the role relate to cultural entities defined as hierarchies of preferences of the individuals.

It is assumed here that roles are not fixed, but as situations change, the roles played must also undergo change. In the uncertainty of contemporary society, with a continued trend toward independence of the nuclear family, each family is faced repeatedly by changing situations, demanding decisions, which will affect the future course of family life. Choice of the number of children; choice of residence; choice of occupation of husband, wife, and children; choice of recreation; choice of friends; choice in the accumulation of material goods; and choice in the education of children are only a few of the foreseeable indeterminacies of contemporary life (8). Each of these events has to be faced at the time it arises. The decision therein provides a stimulus for each shift in roles of the family members (7). The stimuli for role changes, of course, come not only from the parents, but also from children as they develop in the course of their biological growth.

The careers of A and B seem to develop in response to both critical events and mutual adaptation. An event occurs so that either through planning or by accident, B finds that he must now institute acts m and n instead of a and b. A must now devise a Role 2' to reciprocate appropriately the action of B, which A now conceptualizes as Role 2. In the time that has passed, B's career has developed from Role 1 to Role 2 and A's career has developed to Role 2'. If, however, the careers of A and B are to be mutually contingent, B would now have to shift his Role 2 to Role 2" in order to meet the new stimuli of A's role. This continual role change (or career development) could go on, with successive events stimulating other series of role shifts.

If A did not establish a role appropriate to B's actions, A's and B's roles would not be integrated to co-ordinate the development of future roles of A and B. In terms of careers, failure of A to reciprocate appropriately the actions of B would not give support to B's career. This may lead, in turn, to a mutual elaboration of hostile or defensive reactions. There then would be no orderly change in the relationship. Both A and B would find tension, anxiety, and frustration generated in developing their somewhat independent careers in the same family. Thus, A's and B's domestic role at any particular time might be said to be in a state of tension, i.e., prediction of B's career line on a basis of knowledge about A's would not be possible.

The family with complete consensus, if it did exist, would be one in which all values were similarly ordered or ranked by all its members. For any given decision to meet a critical event, alternative means might be questioned or devised, but the ends would be agreed upon. Within the family, hence, there would be a mutual support of value ordering. The community of values would then provide during crisis a strong sense of identity among the family members and, therefore, a strong motive for reciprocating roles appropriately would exist. For example, there would be a high probability that the husband's career line could be predicted on the basis of knowledge about the wife's and vice versa. (This assumes equal authority for husband and wife.)

By the means-ends scheme assumed, at a given point in time, commitment to values differs from commitment to roles. Two individuals can agree on a given ranking of ends and yet each might be unwilling to commit himself to roles which the other expects of him to attain these values. The reverse may be true. Two individuals may develop roles which the other expects, but may do this to attain different ends. *Family integration* as the extent to which the careers of its members are mutually contingent at any given time should therefore be described in terms of *both* role integration and consensus (3).

The verbal description above relating to integration and careers does not indicate various relationships that would sensitize an investigator to seek particular kinds of problems in interaction. The verbal statement does not permit efficient description of the relationship between family integration and such elements as past career development, anticipated career development, preference hierarchy of careers, divergence among family members in their conceptions of actual or ideal careers, and the problem of time span in career development. Moreover, the verbal statement does not easily accommodate the handling of more than one subcareer at a time. In order to facilitate the handling of these elements, a symbolic model was constructed.

The aim of the symbolic model is to explain how certain factors, which can be described in supplementary statements concerning each element in the basic symbolic model, influence family integration at a given point in time. Ultimately, the model is intended to indicate conditions under which maximum integration could occur, given the particular preference hierarchy of careers of the members. Hence, the model would account for both decisions based on a high degree of commitment and "decisions" involving submission or default. In applying it currently in our own research, we are merely trying to determine factors and decisions that seem to maximize marital integration in families with mentally retarded children.

There are two levels of generality in the model: (1) The symbolic level, describing the interaction of family members as participants in a small group. The elements of the model at this level are so general as to include all stable small groups. (2) The cultural level, describing the particular roles and positions prevalent in a given society at a particular time. Empirical hypotheses are developed by relating the description of the group at the symbolic level to the description at the cultural level.

MODEL AND THEORY OF GAMES OF STRATEGY

A basic element in the model is a description of the degree to which the family constitutes a coherent system of interpersonal relations. *A system is regarded here as existing to the extent to which a set of elements exerts such influence on one another that various predictions can be made of future interaction of the elements.* Predictability is here regarded as an essential element in assuming the existence of a system.

In the study of institutions as regularized patterns of interaction, it is often assumed that in the long run, through a tendency toward consistency, norms and values have tended to become systematized and therefore predictable. Unpredictability, from such a viewpoint, would result if incompatible patterns were superimposed upon one another.

The position taken here is that the continuity and stability of rules assumed in the view of the family as a regularized system of interaction exists in contemporary urban society only in a general way. Within these general rules, however, the individual families must develop their own systems of interaction to cope with the many contingencies of modern life. The family group is regarded as engaging in collective behavior, and the amount and kind of system in their interaction is regarded as problematic. Thus, a major problem for research is to determine how consistent patterns of interaction are developed in particular families. The general rules pertaining to marriage and family life constitute rules of the game. These consistent patterns of interaction can be regarded as strategies for creating systematic interpersonal relations. As an aid in investigating and evaluating this development of consistent strategies of interpersonal relations, the theory of games of strategy seems to present a workable methodological framework (5).

One interpretation of the application of the theory of games to social science is that it *represents* social activity. Von Neumann and Morgenstern so argued in their work on the theory of games (11).

A second possible interpretation of the theory of games is that there are classes or sets of decisions or choices that must be made in groups facing various circumstances. These circumstances can be described as the strategies of Nature. A large number of combinations of choices is possible. Without objective cues as to the relative desirability of any particular choice, ordinarily the "best" any group can do is to utilize subjective probabilities. To minimize the use of subjective probabilities, this second kind of application of the theory of games aims to provide objective cues for persons or groups wishing to maximize rewards. Under a given set of circumstances, if the person or group wants to make a rational choice, he can utilize those strategies that have been evaluated as "best." Thus, problems for research are two: (a) in terms of a given criterion, to evaluate strategies used in the past; and, afterward, (b) to experiment in the use of these strategies.

When the theory of games is applied to the situation in which the investigator attempts to determine the "best" strategies, the investigator is not concerned with the problems of the actors' perceptions of probability and utility of each strategy. The investigator merely makes the assumption that the actor has made his choice on the basis of maximum subjective probability and utility. The problem of the investigation is to determine whether the strategies estimated to be "best" by the actor actually do provide the most utility in the long run.

One consequence of this kind of application of the theory of games is that utility no longer is subjective but is objective. A second consequence is that probabilities also can be viewed objectively.

In the discussion of decision-making models and theory of games, an assumption is often made that the researcher or actors can specify the number of utility units attached to a given strategy and the probability of the successful completion of this strategy. This assumption implies an amount of information possessed about utility and probability that seldom exists in a social situation. Instead of making the assumption of full information in a decision-making situaton, let us assume that the researcher or actor has only a vague notion concerning the utility and probability regarding a strategy.

If utility and probability are regarded as having numerical values, a distinction can be drawn between vague and precise numbers. A precise number is one which falls on a unique point of a continuous line extending from negative to positive infinity. A vague number then refers to a range of points on a continuous line. There can, however, be degrees of vagueness. A partially vague number can have the limits of its range precisely defined by two unique points. For a highly vague number, the limits of the range itself would be vague. As vague numbers, ranked numbers not merely can refer to order, but also can represent a series of undefined ranges on a continuum. Viewed from this perspective, ranked numbers are not discrete. Instead, they refer to values on a measurement continuum where precise information on the size of the units is missing.

If ranked numbers are regarded as approximations of measurements with continuous precise numbers, results of arithmetic operations performed on ranked numbers are approximations to results based on precise numbers. In ranking numbers, we assume, in a practical sense, that items being measured are equidistant on an "order" continuum. As a first approximation, this assumption may be adequate.

Inasmuch as the amount of information about a given strategy determines the preciseness of the degree of probability and utility accruing from a given strategy, an aim of the research can be to increase preciseness of statements of probability and utility to the actors. In terms of the research process, the aim of the research is to move from a position of highly vague probability and utility statements to precise numbers.

The vaguest statements that can be made concerning the utility (or probability) of a series of items is that the utility of certain items is greater than the utility of other items. In doing this, the researcher makes no estimate of a unique point denoting the size of the utility number or of the possible range of vagueness. By using rank-order numbers, perhaps the researcher can start with only a vague approximation of numbers and, through repeated iterations, made possible by replications and progressive refinement of studies, increase the preciseness of utility and probability statements.

From a theoretical point of view, the concept of the vague number makes possible the construction of mathematical models without the assumption of the actors' (or researcher's) possession of full information on utility and probability regarding a strategy. Thus, we can take a strategy with a success probability of rank 1 and a utility of rank 3 and compare it in actual payoff with a strategy of success probability of rank 3 and a utility of rank 1. The probability of the successful execution of these strategies would depend upon the conditions facing the actor (or the strategies of Nature).

The probability of successful execution of a strategy can be viewed from two perspectives: the all-or-none probability and the estimated degree of fulfillment. The all-or-none probability has to do with the probability that the state of Nature will permit the strategy of utility rank i to be successfully executed. The degree of fulfillment pertains to the estimate of the extent to which Nature will permit the strategy of utility rank i to be executed.

For each strategy considered, there exists a series of all-or-none probabilities. Each of these all-or-none probabilities pertains to a particular degree of fulfillment. The degree of fulfillment with the highest probability of occurrence is the best estimate of how much of the strategy will be effectively executed.

The best estimate of degree of fulfillment of a strategy seems appropriate to social life, in that most social situations are not all-or-none affairs but are rewarding over a range of units. The value of any strategy is then:

$$\frac{\text{probable rank in degree of fulfillment}}{\text{utility rank}}$$

By the assignment of appropriate numbers to the ranks, a ratio can be determined. If we are interested only in the strategy of the highest utility rank, then the ratio is always smaller than one. More generally, if the strategy of the highest utility rank is given a number equal to the maximum possible degree of fulfillment, the maximum value of the ratio equals one and the minimum, zero. (This is a limitation of the model discussed in this paper.)

Three research problems arise: (a) What are the factors in determining the probable fulfillment rank? (b) What are the factors in determining the probable fulfillment rank for each strategy? and (c) What are the factors that determine the probability of occurrence of specific fulfillment ranks within each strategy? These three problems concern appropriateness of norms, the likelihood of future integration given particular sets of conditions, and the relative appropriateness of different career patterns for maintaining high family integration.

THE SYMBOLIC MODEL

In the model described below, let us assume the following:

(1) The concept of closed system is not a part of the definition of a human group. Instead, the group has an arbitrary boundary defined on the basis of a particular problem or interest. We can then regard *system* as a property of which a group may have more or less. The extent to which a system exists is regarded as the degree to which change in one element produces a predictable change in the other elements.

(2) A particular group has the property of a perfect system so that a change in one element produces a predictable adjustment of all other elements. We are thereby describing the group as a dynamic system.

(3) The positions of the participants in the system at any given time are described in terms of their means (roles) and ends (values). A description of the system as a static entity would thus be given in

terms of integration of means and ends (or roles and values) of the elements.

(4) The system, being perfect in addition to being a closed system, is completely rational. Each element moves at an appropriate rate to a different position which interferes with no other element in the system. There is thus a perfectly co-ordinated movement of elements in the rational system.

(5) In the perfectly rational dynamic system, *at any given time,* there would be no conflict of means or ends of the elements so that all roles and values would be integrated.

The description of the hypothetical group as a completely rational, dynamic entity and as a completely rational, static entity creates the basic relationship for the model: The extent to which there is systematic, orderly movement of elements varies directly with the degree of their integration.

The model is described in symbolic form below:

(1) K denotes the extent to which movement of elements is systematic. $(O < K < I.)$

(2) Movement of elements is defined in terms of career, the units of a career being roles. The development of a career is thus defined by changes in role.

(3) A refers to Role A; B to role B; F to Role F; and G to Role G.

(4) $d(A \to B)$ refers to change in role from Role A to Role B; similarly, $d(F \to G)$ refers to change in role from Role F to Role G.

(5) i and j refer to individuals (elements) in the group.

(6) $d(A \to B)''_i$ is a utility function and refers to the career line (or career development or change in role) preferred for individual i by both elements in the group, i and j; similarly $d(A \to B)''_j$ refers to the career line preferred for individual j.

(7) $d(A \to B)'_i$ refers to the probable fulfillment of the career or actual career line of individual i and $d(F \to G)'_j$ refers to the probable fulfillment or actual career line of j.

(8) t' refers to the probable or actual time for $d(A \to B)'$ and t'' to the preferred time, within tolerance limits of the elements of the group, for $d(A \to B)''$.

(9) T refers to the extent of integration of means, e.g., roles of the elements, so that they do not conflict. As a measure of the extent of rationality, T refers to the inverse of the degree of tension generated between roles. (The concept of tension will be discussed later in connection with solutions implicit in the model.)

(10) C refers to the integration of ends or goals of the elements. As a measure of the extent of rationality in group interaction, C refers to the consensus on values pertinent to the decisions made by the elements as members of the given group under consideration. The specific values to be taken into consideration would depend upon the kind of group.

(11) I refers to the extent to which means and ends of the members of the group are integrated at a particular time.

(12) $d(A \rightarrow B)'_i$ is the stimulus career line or the change in roles which generates a change in the system. The career line, $d(F \rightarrow G)'_j$, then refers to the systematic career line or the change (or development) in roles required by j to maintain a desirable relationship with i. A desirable relationship is one which would continue to facilitate the development of career lines of i and j in a direction of high utility to both i and j. (Because in interaction, career lines can be both stimulus and systematic with respect to other career lines in the group, this distinction may in many respects be a methodological fiction.)

In addition to the assumptions listed above, the following conditions are assumed to be present:

(a) i and j agree on perception of actual and preferred career lines for i and j.

(b) i and j are of equal status.

(c) $t' = t''$.

(d) $d(A \rightarrow B)' = d(A \rightarrow B)''$ (which defines an orderly rate of movement).

Where individual j attempts to take a completely systematic career line in response to the development of i's career, $d(A \rightarrow B)' = d(F \rightarrow G)''_j$ and the group is integrated to the extent that $d(F \rightarrow G)'_j$ approaches $d(F \rightarrow G)''_j$ so that if:

$$\frac{d(A \rightarrow B)'_i}{d(A \rightarrow B)''_i} = I$$

and

$$\frac{d(F \rightarrow G)'_j}{d(F \rightarrow G)''_j} = K,$$

$$\frac{d(A \rightarrow B)'_i}{d(A \rightarrow B)''_i} = \frac{d(F \rightarrow G)''_j}{d(F \rightarrow G)'_j} K = I. \quad \text{(Equation 1)}$$

If the assumption is made in Equation 1 that $d(A - B)'_i$ lies between o and $d(A - B)''_i$ and $d(F - G)'_j$ lies between o and $d(F - G)''_j$, the extent to which a rational system K exists can thus be defined by multiplying Equation 1 by the term:

$$\frac{d(F \rightarrow G)'_j}{d(F \rightarrow G)''_j}.$$

This yields:

$$K = \frac{[d(A \rightarrow B)'_i \quad d(F \rightarrow G)'_j]}{[d(A \rightarrow B)''_i \quad d(F \rightarrow G)''_j]}. \qquad \text{(Equation 2)}$$

Equation 2 is the statement of the extent to which the group as a dynamic entity exists as a rational system.

By definition, at any given time, the group as a static entity exists as a rational system to the extent that the means and ends of the elements in the group are integrated. In terms of the symbols described above (9 and 10 in list):

$$K = I = \frac{1}{2} \left[\frac{T_{actual}}{T_{maximum}} + \frac{C_{actual}}{C_{maximum}} \right], \qquad \text{(Equation 3)}$$

where the subscript "actual" refers to the integration existing in the group at a given time and the subscript "maximum" refers to the integration that would exist in a completely rational system. The constant $\frac{1}{2}$ is introduced in Equation 3 so that K will describe the mean integration resulting from the factors of consensus and role integration. The plus sign $(+)$ is to be interpreted as "in combination with" rather than as additive.

Equations 2 and 3 are related in that, in a logical sense, they are a tautology. Equation 2 defines the integration of a group at a given time (or period of time) in terms of its historical process; Equation 3 refers to the integration of a group in terms of the roles and values at that time. Equations 2 and 3 can thus be equated to form the basic model:

$$\frac{d(A \rightarrow B)'_i \quad d(F \rightarrow G)'_j}{d(A \rightarrow B)''_i \quad d(F \rightarrow G)''_j} = I \qquad \text{(Equation 4)}$$

The terms in the equation can be expanded and qualifications added as required in a specific research problem. To evaluate choices made by a sample of families over a period of time, the content of the terms in the model at time a can be used to predict the content at time b.

Solutions Generated by the Model

Implicit in the model are three ways of handling data pertaining to problems of family development and integration. The three methods depend upon the locus of the initial question of the investigator. These methods can be called (a) the maximum likelihood solution, (b) the disarray solution, and (c) the maximum utility solution.

(a) The maximum likelihood solution is generated by raising the question of what is the probable organization of roles and values at time t_2 if a particular organization of roles and values exists at time t_1. According to this solution, at a particular time, the state of the group is reflected in the relationship between the relative utilities of the various sets of careers on the one hand, and the probabilities of their occurrence on the other. This career development should then be reflected back again in the organization of roles and values at a later time t_2. The research procedure is first to describe the state of integration at time t_1 and assume an ideal line of development of sets of careers (or of a single set of careers), second, to describe the various alternative conditions which the family will be facing in the period between t_1 and t_2, and then, third, to determine the probability of high integration at time t_2, given the alternative conditions.

In trying to determine the way in which various conditions will affect family integration at time t_2, the investigator must first hypothecate the basis for a lack of integration at time t_1. The diagnosis of the potential lack of integration at time t_2 can be as follows:

(1) Diachronic tension in the organization of roles: If at time t_2, person i takes role a, which is appropriate to Career A pattern at time t_1, but j takes role a_2, which is appropriate to Career A pattern at time t_2.

(2) Career conflict tension: If at time t_2, i takes role b_2, which is appropriate to Career B pattern at time t_2, but j takes role a_2, which is appropriate to Career A pattern at time t_2.

(3) Dysfunctional (or "noise") activity in the organization of roles: If at time t_2, i takes role b′ which is not appropriate to Career B pattern of roles at any time (and which may be dysfunctional to any orderly career pattern), person j takes a role b″ which is appropriate to b′ but not to Career B at time t_2. We are assuming that persons i and j prefer a B career pattern to other career patterns.

(4) Unilateral tension in the organization of roles: If, at time t_1, i acts in a role dysfunctional to any orderly career pattern, but j acts in role b_1, which is appropriate to Career Pattern B at time t_1.

(5) Role-value inconsistency: The value hierarchy of person i is consistent with Career Pattern A but the role taken by i is inconsistent with Career Pattern A; the value hierarchy of person j is consistent with Career Pattern A, but the role taken by j is consistent only with that taken by i (and not with Career Pattern A).

(6) Disagreement over values: At time t_1, person i has a value hierarchy consistent with Career Pattern A and acts in role a_1; person j has a value hierarchy consistent with Career Pattern B, but acts in a role complementary to role a_1 of i.

(7) Individualization: At time t_1 person i has a value hierarchy consistent with Career Pattern A and acts in a set of roles a_1; person j has a value hierarchy consistent with Career Pattern B and acts in a set of roles b_1.

The state of a family at any given time can be described in terms of combinations of the above possibilities. The task of the investigator is to determine whether some cultural conditions introduce one or more combinations of the above situations into family life while alternative conditions do not. Then, given the conditions present that affect the integration of roles and values at time t_1, the investigator can use this theoretical formulation of family diagnosis to predict the probability of high integration at time t_2. The propitiousness of conditions for family development can thus be determined.

In the discussion above of tension in the system of roles, "noise" activity, and unilateral tension, social-emotional aspects of role are involved. Two kinds of questions can be raised concerning the development of social-emotional aspects of role: First, have the family members at time t_1 developed affectional behavior, a sense of timing, and procedures for tension release to enable them to sustain family relations past time t_2? Second, what is the probability, given the most likely set of conditions, that social-emotional aspects of roles effective for protracting family relations will develop by time t_2? In terms of career contingencies, a major problem is to describe the various kinds of affectional relations, timing procedures, and mechanisms of tension release which are appropriate to high integration of strategic roles and values at time t_1 and then at time t_2.

(b) Another solution is called a disarray solution because under conditions of complete disarray or equal probability of all sets of careers, there is complete uncertainty as to appropriateness of norms.

The disarray solution generates a series of problems related to uncertainty. In the maximum likelihood solution, we started with the degree of integration at a particular point in time. In the disarray solution, we start with the alternative career lines that are being considered. In order to specify our problems clearly, we shall not concern ourselves with the distinction between utility and probability. Instead, we shall assume that probability is equal to utility. This would mean that at any given time, all families are perfectly integrated. This ideal situation provides an occasion for studying the nonfamily conditions that influence the probability that norms relevant to Career Pattern B will prevail in the period t_1 to t_2. We assume that the sets of careers reflect prevalent norms.

If we define "functionalism" as the development of norms appropriate for adaptation to particular conditions, then the disarray solution would indicate the strategies (or sets of careers) which are most fitting to the conditions. Here we regard careers in both their social-emotional and instrumental aspects. Thus, if we find that the collections of careers associated with the companionship family and the colleagueship family are each associated with some kinds of metropolitan living, and the collection of careers associated with the traditional or institutional family associated with rural living, we can assert that particular family norms are associated with urban living conditions. Similar statements can be made with respect to other living conditions, such as different industrial conditions; religious, ethnic, social class, and social-mobility conditions; or ecological distribution.

(c) The maximum likelihood solution focuses upon the state of integration of the family at a particular time and the disarray solution upon the probability that certain career patterns will develop under particular sets of conditions. The maximum utility solution, however, starts with the hypothesis that certain specified career patterns have a greater objective utility than others.

In evaluating strategies, the investigator makes the assumption that all families under study seek fulfillment of all preferred careers of each member of the family. However, according to the maximum utility solution, if there is a contradiction in careers either between family members or within careers of a particular family member, career fulfillment by the other family members will be impeded.

With the contradictions in careers, the family members have three alternatives: they can act independently of other family members, or they can believe that their careers are frustrated, or they can change their career line to remove contradictions. In the first two alternatives, family integration would be impeded; in the third, family integration would be maintained. The research procedure is to (1) determine, either through observation or theory, sets of career patterns that are not contradictory and regard these as having more utility than other career patterns studied, (2) estimate the degree of success that is most likely to occur for all career patterns considered, and (3) empirically evaluate the utility of the strategies by examining degree of family integration associated with each strategy at a particular time. It would remain necessary to determine whether each of the putatively integrative strategies was effective regardless of the severity of the conditions that the family faced. These conditions, along with the contradictions in careers, would impede family integration.

Actually, the disarray solution is not a legitimate solution of an equation. It is merely a way of extending the model to problems concerning norms. The two major solutions are the maximum-likelihood and the maximum-utility solution. The maximum-likelihood solution is based on static concepts, whereas the maximum-utility solution is concerned with consistency of changing parts. The consistency with which the maximum-utility solution is concerned is both consistency of sets of careers between members of the family and the consistent organization of each set of careers of the individual members.

Application of the Model

In the study of the severely mentally retarded child and his family, the model was applied in two ways. Both applications were based on the maximum-utility solution. The different applications resulted from variation in the description of careers.

In the first phase of the analysis, the description of careers was made in terms of family life-cycle development (4). In this phase of the analysis, the focus was on effects of various conditions upon marital integration. Since the family life cycle stems from biological growth and cultural factors, career development is essentially a passive conformity to expectations. A basic assumption was that because of the retarded child, the life cycle of the family tended to be arrested. The age and sex of the retarded child and the religion and social status of the family were found to affect the severity of the impact of the retarded child on his parents' marriage.

In the first phase of analysis, the careers of the parents were regarded as a function of the probable career development of the severely retarded child. Insofar as the life career of the severely retarded child would be highly restricted if he continued to live at home, the probable development of the parents' careers was relatively fixed. If A is regarded as the probable pattern of parental domestic careers, p(A), the probable degree of fulfillment of strategies is fixed. The degree to which integration is inhibited would be determined by the kind of development most preferred in the subculture. Let us regard u(B) as the pattern of domestic careers of greatest utility in the subculture of the family studied. Since p(A) is fixed, the more achievement expected in the normal family to define the content of u(B), the less is the integration of the family. Thus, achievement expected in connection with the retarded child's sex, the family's social status, and the family's religion would determine the impact of the child on family integration.

In the second phase of the analysis, the focus was on strategies used by the family to maintain its integrity (5). The family was regarded as involved in a game of strategy against "Nature" as it imposed conditions of varying degrees of potential severity of impact (as found in the first analysis of the data). In the second phase of analysis, the choices made in the various careers of the family members could be regarded as "moves" and the organization of these moves as "strategies." In accordance with the requirements of the model, the moves of each parent were required to be consistent not only with the other moves of that parent, but also with the moves of the spouse. According to the model, only if these interpersonal and intrapersonal consistencies were maintained could there be a payoff of high marital integration.

The problem in the research was to determine whether certain combinations of choices would provide a consistency in career lines. The assumption was that the existence of career choices consistent with one another would produce a high integration of roles and values at any particular time. This high integration would also suggest a high predictability in specific decisions within each area of activity.

The content of the several careers was described in terms of the structuring of family life in middle-class American society. It was assumed that the wife's role evolves around the home, whereas the husband's role is primarily aimed at relating the home to the community. That is, the wife is generally responsible for the internal relations of the family, whereas the husband is responsible for keeping the family as a going concern in relation to the rest of the community. Insofar as this division of roles occurs, the wife is in the position of balancing the demands of the husband with those of the children. Successful mediation by the wife of the husband's and children's needs and demands would be necessary for the smooth co-ordination of activities within the family.

Generally, the task of the husband in achieving high marital integration is to adapt his family role in such a way as to minimize contradictory demands made on his wife. Theoretically, minimizing the demands of the husband can be accomplished in one of three ways: (a) by instituting a sharp division of labor, (b) by a coalition between husband and wife in giving priority to social-emotional tasks in structuring family life, and (c) by a coalition between wife and husband in giving priority to achieving goals in the community social structure. These three strategies can be described in terms of persons whose demands and needs are given priority in family life. The strategies are described below:

(1) *The child-oriented strategy. The parents agree that the most important task in family life is the maintenance of the family unit as an on-going concern vis-à-vis all other social groupings.* For the husband, this goal would imply that he must concentrate on securing the artifacts and economic and moral stability required for family continuity. Inasmuch as family continuity presupposes the presence of normal children to provide this continuity to the group, the husband would place a high valuation on children. The consistent pursuit of these goals by the husband would not place the wife in the position of having to mediate between the husband's demands within the family and her activities aimed at fulfilling her own ends for the children. Essentially, through a sharp division of labor, both parents would structure their family life around the needs and demands of the normal children. Because it is assumed here that parents try to reproduce their own norms and values in their children, boys would be valued especially for their potentialities for achievement; girls would be valued more or less intrinsically.

(2) *The home-oriented strategy. The husband minimizes the importance of the task of relating the family unit to external groupings and emphasizes the internal structuring of the family.* Severe conflicts between demands by the husband and children would be obviated by the husband's joining forces with his wife in the social-emotional patterning of family life. Because by occupational role and tradition, the husband is also the instrumental leader in the family, through common interests or high personal identification with the wife, the husband here would be *the* central figure of the family. Because the husband takes on a social-emotional task, the division of parental labor in the family would be minimized; both parents would concentrate on structuring congenial interpersonal relations in the home. (This orientation assumes that there is present a minimum economic and moral stability regarded as sufficient by the husband and wife.) With the de-emphasis on achievement in the middle-class social structure, both boys and girls would be valued "intrinsically" and their mental health stressed.

(3) *The parent-oriented strategy. The husband and wife agree that the demands of the children be subordinated to those pertaining to the husband's role.* The husband's demands are associated with problems of achievement in the middle-class structure in the community. The primary tasks of the wife become those of (a) reinforcing such goals as the attainment of artifacts and social contacts symbolic of success in middle-class society and (b) developing necessary skills to collaborate with her husband in his work or social contact in the community. To compensate for the wife's assumption of achievement functions, the husband would have to perform some of the social-emotional tasks ordinarily performed by the wife. Hence, such partnership norms as companionate practices in family life would be developed. Inasmuch as family life would be built around achievement, personal development and social skills would be emphasized. The children, too, regardless of sex, would be expected to learn the social skills necessary for middle-class advancement.

In terms of the model, the hypothesis would be expressed as follows:

(1) A = child-oriented set of careers; B = parent-oriented set of careers; C = home-oriented set of careers; and D = all other sets of careers.

(2) The theoretical utility of any set of careers = u.

(3) Assume that the probable degree of fulfillment of strategies varies directly with their utility rank.

(4) Let I = the degree of integration at time t_1.

(5) By definition, where M is the set of strategies with the highest theoretical utility rank:

$$I_a = \frac{p(A)}{u(M)}; \quad I_b = \frac{p(B)}{u(M)}; \quad I_c = \frac{p(C)}{u(M)}; \quad I_d = \frac{p(D)}{u(M)}.$$

(6) From discussion of family types above,

$$u(A) = u(B) = u(C) > u(D).$$

(7) Therefore,

$$\frac{p(A)}{u(A)} = \frac{p(B)}{u(B)} = \frac{p(C)}{u(C)} > \frac{p(D)}{u(A) \text{ or } u(B) \text{ or } u(C)}$$

or

$$I_a = I_b = I_c > I_d.$$

The findings pertaining to the relationship between the use of child-oriented, parent-oriented, and home-oriented strategies and marital integration were as follows:

(1) When parents who used consistent parent-oriented, child-oriented, or home-oriented strategies were compared with those who did not, the parents who utilized one of the three consistent orientations were found to have a higher marital integration than the others. However, the difference in marital integration between parents who used one of the three strategies hypothecated as integrative and those who did not was greatest for families faced with unfavorable circumstances as defined by the results of the first phase of analysis.

(2) For each level of favorableness of circumstances of potential disruptive effect on the marriage, parents of children in institutions who used the putatively integrative strategies had a higher marital integration than similar parents who used other strategies. Similarly, parents of retarded children at home who utilized the hypothetically integrative strategies tended to have a higher marital integration than those who did not.

(3) Generally, among those families using the putatively integrative strategies, the difference in mean marital integration between parents with a retarded child in an institution and parents with a retarded child at home *increased* with the decrease in favorableness of circumstance. As a result, for families faced with unfavorable cir-

cumstances, the mean marital integration of parents with a child in an institution was substantially higher than that of parents with a retarded child at home. In contrast, parents who did not utilize one of the putatively integrative strategies showed no consistent difference in degree of marital integration between families with a retarded child at home and those with a child in an institution.

The model of the family as mutually contingent careers has been presented in this paper in terms of its implications for research. It is an attempt to formulate a criterion for evaluating a crucial problem in contemporary family life. At the same time, it aims at describing mechanisms of family development that are pertinent to the furtherance of the life careers of family members. In this paper, however, there was no attempt to formulate implications of the view of the family as mutually contingent careers for directions in the actual development of norms and values in family life (9), nor were supplementary research models introduced.

References

1. BECKER, HOWARD S. "The Implications of Research on Occupational Careers for a Model of Household Decision-making." Pp. 239–254 above.
2. BURGESS, E. W., and H. J. LOCKE. *The Family: From Institution to Companionship*. New York: American Book Co., 1953.
3. FARBER, BERNARD. "An Index of Marital Integration," *Sociometry*, 20 (1957), 117–34.
4. ———. "Effects of a Severely Mentally Retarded Child on Family Integration," *Monographs of the Society for Research in Child Development*, No. 71, Vol. 24, 2 (1959).
5. ———. "Family Organization and Crisis: Maintenance of Integration in Families with a Severely Mentally Retarded Child," *Monographs of the Society for Research in Child Development*, No. 75, Vol. 25, 1 (1960).
6. FOOTE, NELSON N. "The Movement from Jobs to Careers in American Industry," in *Transactions of the Third World Congress of Sociology*. International Sociological Assoc., 2 (1956), 30–40.
7. ———. "Matching of Husband and Wife in Phases of Development," in *ibid.*, *4*, 24–34.
8. ——— and L. S. COTTRELL, JR. *Identity and Interpersonal Competence*. Chicago: University of Chicago Press, 1955.
9. FRANK, L. K. "Research for What?" *J. Social Issues*, Supplement Series, No. 10, 1957.
10. MILLER, D. R., and G. E. SWANSON. *The Changing American Parent*. New York: Wiley, 1958.
11. NEUMANN, J. VON, and O. MORGENSTERN. *Theory of Games and Economic Behavior*. Princeton, New Jersey: Princeton University Press, 1957.
12. PARSONS, T., and R. F. BALES. *Family, Socialization and Interaction Process*. Glencoe, Illinois: Free Press, 1955.

VI. Further Considerations

Explaining Consumer Behavior— on What Level?

F. STUART CHAPIN

Although it is a commonplace in science, the fact that the search for explanation of human behavior goes on at different levels is not steadily kept in mind in empirical research. It may therefore be useful to consider some examples of this exploratory process in relation to the subject of our common interest.

Let me illustrate with the case of the dread mental malady called schizophrenia. Dr. Ian Stevenson says, "This disorder affects close to half a million persons in hospitals and perhaps five or ten times that many who remain at home. . . . And even these statistics tell us nothing of the terrible suffering of these persons whose sickness cuts them off from happy contact with other people" (9, p. 62). Osborn says, "The category 'schizophrenia' recognizes four types of behavior, including apathy and carelessness, silliness and bizarre ideas, negativism and mutism, and paranoia, which covers delusions of persecution and grandeur . . ." (7, pp. 39–40).

Explanations of causation have been offered at three levels of phenomena: the researcher at the psychosocial level explains schizophrenia as arising from early damage to the personality of the child, brought about by the attitude and behavior of the mother; at the biological level, explanation is given in terms of a predisposition to the disorder derived from hereditary factors; and more recently, a biochemical explanation is made in terms of a chemical upset in the brain. This explanation at the lowest level leads to such treatments as that by Dr. Stig Akerfeldt of Sweden, who adds a dyestuff to a small amount of blood serum.

No doubt each level of research on the problem of what causes schizophrenia has its merits. But what I want to stress at this point consists of two different arguments about the adequacy of explanation at different levels. The first point is the so-called "reduction fallacy"; and the second point is the fallacy of the "so-called reduction fallacy." Let me now explain my explanation.

Some social scientists have insisted that adequate explanation of human behavior should always be obtained at the level of individual and social relations. They have contended that the attempt to seek explanation of such a complex phenomenon as human behavior could not be adequate on the biological, and especially on the biochemical, level. To seek explanation on the latter or lowest level is a fallacious venture. Such a position now seems untenable in view of recent discoveries in the treatment of schizophrenic behavior. Reduction to the biochemical level seems an extreme method, and yet the late Dr. Manfred Sakel had early success in using insulin shock treatment. He reasoned that insulin is a body product which works biologically as a natural corrective ability of the body itself. It stimulates in a natural way the innate self-regulatory defenses of the body to correct distorted metabolic biochemical functions. More recently, other biochemical treatments have been spectacularly successful. Their success may suggest that more realistic explanation of consumer behavior can be found at levels of explanation nearer to that on which the human behavior takes place.

This is analogical reasoning, a form of thinking which is far from rigorous logic, and which has often misled explanation. Among primitive peoples, this form of analogical reasoning was prevalent in their magical practices. For example, if you wished to injure or warn an enemy, one primitive way was to make a small doll or image of him and then stick sharp points into this image, thus causing sickness and suffering to your enemy. Or better still, obtain a strand of his hair and burn it. With our emancipation from magical ideas has grown distrust of all analogies in scientific research. Certainly the physicist, who does work of such high precision, with its aftermath of successful prediction, would presumably be the first to shun analogical reasoning. But let us see what Einstein said on this matter:

> It has often happened in physics that an essential advance was achieved by carrying out a consistent analogy between apparently un-

related phenomena. . . . We have often seen how ideas created and developed in one branch of science were afterwards successfully applied to another. The development of the mechanical and field views gives many examples of this kind. The association of solved problems with those unsolved may throw new light on our difficulties by suggesting new ideas. It is easy to find a superficial analogy which really expresses nothing. But to discover some essential common features, hidden beneath a surface of external differences, to form on this basis a new successful theory, is important creative work (3, pp. 286–87).

Einstein's discriminating analysis could be illustrated in the recent development of information theory, which has led to new knowledge, often based on convergences among engineering research, physics, cybernetics, psychology, and sociology.

Although social scientists have long since exploded the myths of magical practices, we are still like primitive peoples in our readiness to be misled by merely verbal distinctions, and this source of error is particularly dangerous when we attempt to explain human behavior in terms of its own level. Let us look at a few more examples. The principle to be illustrated is one of simple semantics: wrong words are used for essential concepts, and these become misleads to real understanding and hence to successful outcomes of research.

The history of medicine and surgery is replete with examples of wrong leads to practice which are given by concepts and terms of past explanations (5, pp. 170–73). Between 1864 and 1866 about 45% of patients died from amputations. The patient would be well for a day or two, and yet even in the most favorable cases, pus appeared in the surgical wound. But at that time the mere presence of pus was considered a sign of healing. It was called "laudable pus" because in those patients who lived some days after the operation, pus appeared and was regarded as a favorable indication. Most patients only lived shorter times after surgery; they quickly died of blood poisoning. This belief in "laudable pus," which had persisted from the time of Galen in A.D. 131, misdirected thinking into a false lead to adequate understanding.

Joseph Lister, the great surgeon of those times, had noted that when an occasional wound healed without pus formation, there was no putrefaction. He had observed that a simple fracture of a bone was not accompanied by the formation of pus, but that in a compound fracture, in which the broken bone projected through the skin, there was infection. At first he thought that the contamination was carried by the air and failed to realize that the real source of infection was on the surgeon's hands and instruments. He therefore tried to control infection by spraying the air with carbolic acid. At that time, it was thought that the atmosphere was full of "putrid exhalations," so his idea of sterile air was a natural if ineffective idea. Later he learned to sterilize the surgeon's hands and instruments, and immediately the usual infections disappeared. In this example, we see that erroneous concepts of the cause of infections from surgical operations were promoted by wrong leads to explanations, which were implied in the use of such terms as "laudable pus" and "putrid exhalations."

Let us turn to another example nearer home, an explanation of industrial unrest and violence given just after World War I. In 1918, Ordway Tead published his book *Instincts in Industry*. It represented an early lead to a behavioristic explanation of industrial unrest. It was based on McDougall's *Social Psychology,* published in 1908. In this book, McDougall explained human behavior in terms of instinctive reactions. It seemed natural to Tead to take the concept of "instinct" as a new lead to better understanding. Even Park and Burgess (8, p. 494) in 1924 mentioned Tead's work on "instinct" as an example of ". . . seeking to apply the new science of human nature to the problems of society." Note in passing the use of the concept "human nature" in this quotation from Park and Burgess, with its latent implications of biological inheritance of human traits, in sharp contrast to our contemporary and much more realistic concept, "human behavior." At any rate, the lead word "instincts" fortunately had too short a life to do much damage to effective explanation, since in 1924 L. L. Bernard, in his book *Instinct: A Study in Social Psychology* completely demolished the argument for human instincts as causal explanations of behavior.

These examples show how explanation may be erroneous because wrong words and concepts were used as leads. Often, however, these semantic fallacies are further complicated by the principle that the wrong words sometimes carry with them an emotional charge that makes them easily accepted and then even more misleading. Explanation of criminal behavior was held back for a long time by use of the concept "moral imbecile"; and understanding of poverty was blocked by use of the concept "the worthy poor." It will be noted that lurking in the background of such concepts as "moral imbecile" and "worthy poor" are implications of invidious comparison, whereby the user of the term satisfies his own needs for security and social status.

In many contexts, the use of emotive terms or adjectives expresses the emotional needs of the speaker, rather than describing the object or subject of his remarks. Thereby the discriminating listener can learn a great deal about the speaker—information that is unwittingly revealed by the speaker's use of adjectives. Just as revealing are certain forms of total overt behavior, such as the purchase of a Cadillac, or an elaborate television set on time payment, or an expensive house by contract for deed. Far too often such behavior is exhibited by those who have little pecuniary strength, persons whose stability of employment and income fail to justify any appraisal that their purchasing decisions are sound. It is a case of "keeping up with the Joneses" or, to use Veblen's colorful term, of conspicuous consumption, as when someone indulges in unnecessary and lavish entertainment of visitors.

Symbols of prestige and status are often bought at too high a price, and the unfortunate thing is that such behavior among the "leisure classes" has set the model that motivates much unsound consumer behavior by others. In a variety of ways, stereotypes of the kinds used in the foregoing examples tend to get in the way of advancing our knowledge of the matter we investigate, because the chief characteristic of stereotyped thinking-behavior is to define first and only afterward observe. Too often we as scientists get entangled in the prejudiced language of our subjects. What is needed is a new breakthrough into a language other than our self-imposed choice of wrong words. This breakthrough is already present in the opportunity to devise mathematical models which parallel the events of the real world about us.

Langmuir says, "The essential characteristic of a model is that it shall resemble in certain desired features the situation that we are considering" (6). He proceeds to explain that the mathematical equations that state the laws of physics are themselves a kind of model. It is first assumed that there is some correspondence between the things that we measure and the symbols used in the equation. After solving the equation to obtain a statement of new relations, we then attempt to establish some similar correspondence between the new relation and the data obtained from an experiment. "If we succeed in this operation we have demonstrated the power of the mathematical equation to predict events."

Now it should be evident that the development of mathematical models subsumes measurement of some sort and that these measurements must be made on some kind of units of observation. How is all this related to the problem of explaining consumer behavior? The answer has been stated briefly by Kenneth J. Arrow in his essay, "Mathematical Models in the Social Sciences." Here, in commenting on the present trend to reject the individual as the unit of observation for measurement (where the units are on some external scale of reference) and to substitute the household as the unit of observation, Arrow says, "In fact, even in economics, the unit of the theory of production is not really the individual but the firm, which is an operating organization of individuals." Then he proceeds to make a statement of considerable interest to researchers of consumer behavior. He says, "Similarly, the unit of consumption is really the household, not the individual" (1, p. 134).

In the light of my earlier description of misleads to fruitful research results due to choice of the wrong word or concept, is it not possible that some of our frustrations in research on consumer behavior have been due to our conceiving of the individual as the unit of observation rather than using the household as the unit of observation?

The family and the household are real units of observation. Some basic needs of human beings are met only in the family, making it a small, unitary social system, having its own independence and integrity. This unity is important in the modern mechanized society with its anonymity and mobility.

This family unity is also manifested by an increasing overlap of years in the three generations of grandparents, parents, and children. In a study of one American family from 1635 to the present day, I found that in the 1600's, grandparents often did not live to see their grandchildren born. But as the expectation of life increased, grandfathers overlapped their grandchildren by two years in 1712, by three years in 1772, by 10 years in 1843, and by 27 years in 1941. This overlap, if not complicated by too much family-member mobility, should support the continuity of family traditions and hence family unity. In this one family, at least, the homes of the grandparents in each three-generation overlap were often the central rallying points. How far this pattern characterizes the general population, I do not know, but it would be strange if the pattern did not extend to many other families.

Since the papers presented at this conference have developed the matter in detail, it would be redundant for me to attempt any further elaboration of the virtues of the household unit. I shall therefore confine the remainder of my discussion to some principles that seem to me important for the consumer researcher in the practice of his trade.

First, I should like to stress the principle that the mathematical model is not usually the first, but the last, stage of our search for explanations of consumer realities. The beginnings of our research consist of homely verbal statements. We describe in words of the common language the relationships which we observe, or which we suspect exist. From such humble beginnings, we may devise primitive models in the form of heuristic diagrams and heuristic equations. Next we may proceed to empirical equations fitted to the data of our observations. Do you know that among aborigines so primitive as to have no written language, there exists nonetheless a systematic grammar of which they are entirely unaware, but which underlies their spoken language? Anthropologists have proved that this is the case (4, p. 17). Similarly, in our time and in our more sophisticated life, there underlies the verbal logic of our argumentation potentially discoverable mathematical equations. When discovered, these equations may in first instance take on only an empirical form, until by subsequent refinement of measurement and theory, they take on true mathematical form. In other words, mathematics is itself nothing but another language. It is the language of science, to be sharply contrasted with folk languages, commonly known as English, French, German, Italian, Russian, and all the rest.

Some years ago I became interested in the study of poverty as a form of individual and social disorganization, as a sort of disease of society. Many people now think that we have eliminated poverty and that it cannot recur. I have reason to doubt this complaisance and would suggest that we have only banished poverty. The old adage, "the poor we have ever with us," is still true when we look at levels of deprivation other than mere physical existence. I can formulate the principle I have in mind by stating a paradox: the higher the standard of living goes, the more ways there are of being poor. This is so because, while the needs for food, clothing, and shelter are for the most part now provided, at the same time our *wants* grow apace with every new invention. This is particularly so when your "ownership" of a Cadillac is merely "a legal fiction," as is most certainly the case when the purchase is by installment payments. Hence the social problem of poverty, like so many of our other problems, is not so much *what we think it is,* as that it actually is *only what we think!*

In pursuit of our study of poverty (2), we began at the lowest level of privation, the level of the families receiving poor relief from public and private sources. For the years 1915 through 1935, we obtained data by months showing the number of relief cases (single individuals and families, i.e., households) on the relief rolls of the city of Minneapolis. This yielded a time series of 240 observations, a time series that exhibited these familiar patterns of movement: first, a long-time secular trend; second, superimposed on this trend, a cycle of change related to prosperity-depression changes; and finally, superimposed upon these more basic curves, the seasonal fluctuations from lows each summer to high relief loads each winter. Our objective was to discover, if possible, some correspondence, perhaps a cause and effect relationship, if only indirect, between changes in fundamental economic indices as independent variables and changes in relief case load as the dependent variable. The first step was to fit an equation to the rising secular trend of the observed relief load. This was done; the empirical equation of a second degree polynomial obtained was: $Y = 100 - 3.5t + 0.264t^2$. This described one aspect of mass behavior, the presumed effect of changes in prosperity-depression cycles. Then the curves of secular trend and seasonal fluctuations were smoothed and adjusted by applying the techniques of time-series analysis used in the 1930's, to reveal the net movement of the current business cycle. So much for the processing of the dependent variable. We then examined 12 indices of economic changes, 6 regional and 6 national, and correlated each with our adjusted relief index. Eleven of these economic indices were discarded. Our final choice of the New York bank debits index as the independent variable was made on the evidence that it correlated negatively with the relief index on a six month lag, in a range of $-.527$ to $-.683$, the highest correlations obtained. This meant that low values of the New York bank debits index tended to precede high values of the relief index by six months and that consequently we might predict the Minneapolis relief case load six months in advance of the event. For the six months of December, 1932, through May, 1933, our predictions of the monthly magnitudes of relief loads, made six months in advance of the events, were within $\pm 2\%$ of the actuality. Thereafter, with the advent of the Civil Works Administration program, which took over half of the direct relief load and placed these persons on work relief, our predictions were increasingly in excess of the actuality, and further efforts to predict broke down. But this is not the point I wish to make.

The question I sought to answer was this: What is the practical meaning of the parameters, i.e., the constants 100, and -3.5 and 0.264, the coefficients of the last two terms in the equation, $Y = 100 - 3.5t + 0.264t^2$? In a second degree polynomial of the form $Y = a + bx + cx^2$, the constant, a, is the cut-off on the Y-axis. Hence the empirical constant 100 may be interpreted to mean the normal relief load in prosperous times. The factor, $+0.264t^2$, may then represent the tendency of the numbers of relief cases to pile up exponentially, because of higher fuel costs in winter, increasing unemployment, more frequent illnesses, the exhaustion of family savings, and financial losses. The factor, $-3.5t$, would then represent such checking factors to relief-load increase as use of family savings, borrowing from the finance company, taking in lodgers, aid from relatives, use of credit, and borrowing on life insurance. No doubt further research to test these hypotheses would have led to new equations in which the parameters would themselves be the dependent variables of new functions and in which the itemized accelerating factors or checking factors would perform as new independent variables. In some such manner as this, we could give more scientific meaning to our as yet purely empirical equation and thus provide a more rational explanation of the human mass behavior expressed in the climbing relief load. Note finally that the unit of observation throughout this analysis was the family or household unit.

Of course, this entire study of the time changes in the numbers of cases receiving poor relief was done without benefit of the recent mathematical devices of stochastic difference equations, Markov chains, and all the rest. It was done on an empirical level of analysis. It does indicate, however, the advantage that the use of a quasi-scientific language has over the old folk-language concept of the "worthy poor." Even a quasi-scientific language is more nearly purged of emotive misleads than the plain folk language. The folk language has the disconcerting property of reverting to its emotive or expressive function in the very situations in which we most depend on the exercise of language in its representative function.

REFERENCES

1. ARROW, KENNETH J. "Mathematical Models in the Social Sciences," in *The Policy Sciences*, ed. D. Lerner and H. D. Lasswell. Stanford, California: Stanford University Press, 1951.
2. CHAPIN, F. S., E. JACOBSON, and SARAH STONE. "Predicting Relief Case Loads for Minneapolis by Empirical Procedures," *J. Am. Statistical Assoc.* (Dec., 1933), 414–22.
3. EINSTEIN, ALBERT, and L. INFELD. *The Evolution of Physics*. New York: Simon & Schuster, 1951.
4. GOLDENWEISER, A. A. *Early Civilization*. New York: Knopf, 1922.
5. HAGGARD, H. W. *Devils, Drugs and Doctors*. New York, 1929.
6. LANGMUIR, I. *Science News Letter*, Jan. 2, 1943, pp. 3–4, 14–15.
7. OSBORN, F. *Preface to Eugenics*. Rev. ed. New York: Harper, 1957.
8. PARK, R. E., and E. W. BURGESS. *Introduction to the Science of Society*. Chicago: University of Chicago Press, 1924.
9. STEVENSON, IAN. "Schizophrenia," *Harper's Magazine, 215* (Aug., 1957), 59–65.

Durable Goods Purchase Intentions, Purchases, and the Consumer Planning Horizon[1]

F. THOMAS JUSTER

Since the end of World War II, a substantial research effort has been devoted to the analysis of consumer spending and saving behavior.[2] The emphasis has been split: There have been studies concerned primarily with the predictive value on both aggregate and atomistic levels of consumer buying plans, expectations, and attitudes, and studies concerned mainly with understanding the process by which households arrive at spending or saving decisions.[3] This paper attempts to provide insights into certain characteristics of the purchase-planning process. Questions of predictive value are discussed only to illuminate particular aspects of the planning process and the planning horizon.

All data discussed in this paper are obtained from mail questionnaires sent out by Consumers Union of the United States, the prod-

[1] This paper constitutes an elaboration and refinement of data and concepts that have been presented in Chapter II of *Consumer Expectations, Plans, and Purchases: A Progress Report,* published as Occasional Paper 70 by the National Bureau of Economic Research. The author is indebted to the National Bureau for permission to publish these results and to the Relm Foundation, Ann Arbor, Michigan, and the Carnegie Foundation for financial contributions to the project of which this paper is one part. Thanks are due Stanley Besen for assistance with the statistical calculations.

[2] The scope of this research effort can be seen from the annotated bibliography compiled by J. N. Morgan (1).

[3] This dichotomy is somewhat overstated, since the ultimate usefulness of a more complete understanding of decision-making and of consumer behavior is the ability to make better predictions. The difference really seems to resolve itself into a question of the weight that should be applied to predictive accuracy as a specific criterion by which to judge the fruitfulness of one line of empirical investigation versus another.

uct testing and rating organization. Consumers Union (CU) has sent annual questionnaires to subscribers for the past 20 some years; summary tabulations (based on a sample of 5,000 responses) are available from 1946 to the present, and some detailed data are available for years later than 1951. These questionnaires have included a wide variety of topics—magazine reading habits, automobile repair experience, opinions on the contents of *Consumer Reports* (CU's monthly publication), personal characteristics of subscribers (income, occupation, geographical location), actual purchases of selected major durable goods over the past year, and purchase intentions for these goods in the year ahead. The questions about purchase intentions and income have been asked almost every year; other questions of significance for our problem have been included sporadically.

It should be clearly understood at the outset that these data are gathered from a sample that is thoroughly atypical in many respects.[4] The median income for this group is usually about double the population median; almost half the group are college graduates, and about a third are employed in professional occupations. Furthermore, membership in Consumers Union is itself a distinguishing characteristic.[5] Despite these biases—perhaps in part because of them—it has been shown that the aggregate purchase intentions of the CU sample are very closely related to purchases of durable goods by the United States population and could have been used to predict such purchases quite accurately over the period 1948–1955 (5). This paper will touch on some of the reasons for this unusually good prediction record, although the major focus is placed on other problems.

PATTERN OF AGGREGATE INTENTIONS AND PURCHASES: SPECIFIC COMMODITIES

Our point of departure will be an examination of buying intentions and actual purchases for a number of specific commodities by the CU sample. We have data of this kind over the period 1951–1956,

[4] The sample is clearly atypical with respect to the U. S. population. Since it is in addition a self-selected sample—only about 20% of CU members answer the questionnaire—it is also likely to be atypical of the CU member population. (See 5.)

[5] It appears to be true that many of the members who return questionnaires do so regularly. About half the people in a recent survey indicated that they had filled out a questionnaire in the previous year. Since almost one-third of the sample consisted of first year members who could not have answered previous questionnaires, it would seem plausible that the respondents divide into a fairly sizable "permanent" component and a "high turnover" component.

with one year (1953) missing. Most surveys have found that the frequency of buying intentions (per cent of the sample planning to buy) is substantially lower than the frequency of purchases. For example, the Survey of Consumer Finances reports such data for a random sample of the population covering about six items, ranging from new cars to washing machines; with the occasional exception of new automobiles, the fraction of the sample reporting purchases is always higher than the fraction with buying intentions—two or three times as high for many items. Some of the usual explanations have been that (1) the planning horizon for many items does not extend over a 12-month period and thus all relevant plans are not obtained if the Survey is conducted annually; (2) such unforeseen events as breakdowns or excessive repair bills induce people to buy when they had not planned to do so; (3) many people do not bother to plan—particularly for relatively inexpensive items—and simply buy on impulse.

From the CU data, it seems clear that these generalizations apply mainly to widely owned items like cars, refrigerators, and television sets, i.e., the "standard" durables. They do not necessarily apply to "prestige" durables like air conditioners, dishwashers, and garbage-disposal units, where ownership is (at present) not widely diffused throughout the economy and where purchases are generally made by people with higher than average incomes. Table VI.1 shows this tendency rather clearly; ratios of the frequency of purchase plans to the frequency of purchases are always below unity for the standard items, always above unity for some "prestige" items, and close to unity for others.

It is interesting to note the general tendency in some of the "prestige" durables for the ratio to decline over time. Air conditioners and garbage-disposal units have this characteristic to a marked degree; certain other prestige durables fail to exhibit a clear tendency of this kind if we exclude the 1950–1951 period, when purchases were abnormally high, relative to plans, because of the Korean War.[6] There also seems to be some relationship between the cost of the item and the over-all ratio of plans to purchases, although this relationship is not consistent throughout. Vacuum cleaners—the least expensive of the standard durables—generally have a lower ratio than the other items in this category, and used cars have a lower ratio than new cars. On the other hand, automobiles generally show

---

[6] The tendency for 1950–1951 ratios to be relatively high runs throughout the data in Table VI.1.

TABLE VI.1

RATIOS OF THE FREQUENCY OF BUYING INTENTIONS TO THE
FREQUENCY OF ACTUAL PURCHASES, CONSUMERS UNION SAMPLE

Item	*Ratio * during*				
	1950–51	*1951–52*	*1952–53*	*1954–55*	*1955–56*
New auto	NA	NA	NA	.64	.69
Used auto	NA	NA	NA	.44	.50
Total auto	.78	.58	.59	.58	.64
Refrigeration	.73	.58	.70	.81	.68
Electric range	.73	.88	.86	.88	.68
Washing machine	.88	.61	.76	.70	.68
TV set	NA	.73	.77	.74	.79
Vacuum cleaner	.88	.56	NA	.69	.57
Movie camera	1.56	1.02	.89	.97	.98
Clothes dryer	1.42	.95	1.14	1.11	.98
Dishwasher	1.83	1.37	1.29	1.34	1.42
Room air conditioner	2.18	1.56	1.12	1.05	1.08
Garbage-disposal unit	2.33	1.64	1.58	1.37	1.12
Home freezer	1.93	1.43	1.77	1.94	1.60
Hi-fi components	NA	1.23	1.12	1.44	1.13

* Purchase intentions and purchases for a comparable period are not obtained from identical people and in some cases do not cover an identical time span. Purchase intentions are obtained from the questionnaire sent at the beginning of a period; purchases are obtained from the succeeding questionnaire, provided that the commodity has been included on both questionnaires. Unless two successive mailings are made on the same date, the time span will be different. For the data shown in Table VI.1, the largest difference between the two periods is three months.

Source: Basic data from Consumer Purchases Study, National Bureau of Economic Research.

a low ratio relative to standard household-equipment items despite their considerably higher cost even after allowance for trade-in. There does not seem to be any obvious explanation for this.

In passing, two other propositions should be noted. On balance, the aggregate amount that CU members plan to spend on durables (other than cars) is about equal to their total expenditures on these items; the average ratio of purchases to plans, weighted by prices, varies between .87 and 1.15, depending on the number of items and the period.[7] Excluding the 1950–1951 period where purchases were abnormally high because of the (unforeseen) Korean War, the ratio varies between .87 and 1.01.

In addition, it is clear from Table VI.1 that the CU sample is

[7] The number of commodities is not the same for all periods because of variations in the question asking about purchase intentions and purchases. In order to make the calculations in Table VI.1, an item had to be included for two consecutive years, since purchase intentions are obtained from one questionnaire and purchases for a comparable period from the next. In general, the list shown in Table VI.1 gives higher ratios than the expanded list used for some of the later periods, since the marginal items all have ratios lower than unity.

extremely successful in predicting their own purchases. If the ratio of intentions to purchases were always the same, one could make a perfect prediction of purchases from buying plans. That is, if buying plans increased by 10% between two periods, purchases would also have to increase by 10% if the ratio of plans to purchases is to remain the same. Consequently, differences between the ratios for successive periods are a rough measure of errors in prediction, although one cannot tell (from this table) the nature of the divergence between plans and purchases. Table VI.2 summarizes the relationship

TABLE VI.2

LINK RELATIVES OF PURCHASE INTENTIONS AND ACTUAL PURCHASES
FOR THE CONSUMERS UNION SAMPLE, SELECTED PERIODS
(per cent of preceding period)

| | Commodity Groups | | | | | |
| | New and Used Autos | | Household Equipment | | Total Durables * | |
Change between	Plan	Actual	Plan	Actual	Plan	Actual
1950–51 and 1951–52	53.5	72.3	67.9	85.4	60.7	78.9
1951–52 and 1952–53	115.8	114.3	107.9	100.5	111.8	107.4
1952–53 and 1954–55 **	134.4	135.3	130.5	130.4	132.4	132.8
1954–55 and 1955–56	102.7	98.0	98.5	106.3	100.6	102.2

* Estimated as the arithmetic average of the other two categories; this conforms roughly to the ratio between actual expenditures on these two categories by the population at large.
** Data for 1953–54 are not available, because the buying-intentions question was not asked in the 1953 survey.
Source: Basic data from Consumer Purchases Study, NBER.

between aggregate changes in plans and in purchases for the CU sample. The figures in the table are weighted link relatives, showing indices of plans and purchases based on the level in the preceding period. For example, the figure of 53.5 for new and used auto plans between 1950–1951 and 1951–1952 means that the fraction of the sample planning to buy autos in the later period was 53.5% of the fraction planning to buy in the earlier period. Similarly, the fraction of the sample purchasing autos in 1951–1952 was 72.3% of the fraction who purchased in 1950–1951.

The relationship between plans and purchases is extraordinarily close and suggests (although it does not prove) a relatively high degree of plan fulfillment. The high degree of accuracy for the aggregates is reflected in the individual items. About one-third of the predicted changes for individual items are within 10% of the actual change, and half of these are within 5%. Another third of the predicted changes are within 20% of the actual, with the remaining third on the extremes. A recomputation to correct for one rather systematic bias—a tendency for actual purchases to fall moderately whenever plans show a drastic decline—would put half the predicted changes within a range of 10% of the actual changes, reducing the extreme errors to about a quarter of the total observations.

VARIATIONS IN PLANS AND PURCHASES WITH INCOME

On the basis of the discussion above, one might expect to find a very close relationship between plans and purchases of specific items by individual households. Although we cannot verify this supposition directly, certain characteristics of the data indicate that a close relationship on the individual level is not probable, despite the aggregate results. Of perhaps greater interest, we also find some very systematic patterns in the relationship between income and both purchases and purchase plans. These patterns of behavior are strikingly different for different kinds of commodities; they are also systematically different for buying plans and purchases and seem to be quite sensitive to the length of the time horizon implied by the buying-plans question.

Our examination of this set of problems will be facilitated by use of an income-elasticity concept. In its ordinary usage, income elasticity is a ratio of the proportional change in quantity purchased to the proportional change in income. Thus, an income elasticity of 1 or unity means that a 10% rise in income results in a 10% rise in quantity purchased. If income elasticity is less than 1, a change in income results in a less than proportional change in purchases, and vice versa if greater than 1; when income elasticity is negative, a rise in income is associated with a fall in purchases. In our usage, the income elasticity of buying plans or purchases is defined as the proportional change in the fraction of the sample with buying plans or purchases compared to the proportional change in relative income position.[8] The latter is simply actual income divided by the median income of the entire sample.[9]

[8] It should be noted that the fraction of households who plan to buy or do buy a particular item is equal to the average plans or purchases per household of the item because no multiple plans are included in the data.

[9] The relative income position variable is used in preference to income primarily because it appears to provide a more stable elasticity measure over time. There also seem to me sound analytical reasons why this should be the case; e.g., those discussed by J. Duesenberry (2).

To begin with, it will be useful to classify durable commodities into three categories: (1) automobiles, both new and used; (2) "standard" household durables like refrigerators, ranges, and TV sets; and (3) "prestige" household durables like air conditioners, garbage-disposal units, and dishwashers. The latter two categories are rather arbitrary; they overlap to some extent because goods in the prestige category at any one time are in a continual process of being transferred to the standard category.[10] The distinction between the two is nonetheless meaningful; one might define standard durables as those whose demand is primarily replacement and secondarily new acquisition. Prestige durables would be those whose demand consists mostly of sales to newly acquiring households.

The basic data consist of the fraction of households in each income group who report plans or purchases. We have computed weighted regression equations relating both buying plans and purchases to relative income position. The weights consist of the number of people in each income class. The equations take varying forms, depending on the type of function that seemed to provide the best fit to the data.[11] Because the number of income classes was quite small (9 at most), statistical tests were not used to determine the equation form or the closeness of fit. Straight line relationships were used where it seemed at all reasonable or where the data provided a bad fit for any simple function. The degree to which the computed equations fit the data is noted in the discussion.

All computed relationships, regardless of the original equation form, are plotted on double logarithmic scales. This convention facilitates the discussion of elasticity, because the elasticity is numerically equal to the slope on such scales.

---

[10] This would be especially true during a period when real disposable income per family is rising, as has generally been the case during the period under discussion.

[11] The following equation forms were used:

P = fraction of planners or purchasers
Y = relative income position (income ÷ median income)

1.0	$P = a + bY$
1.1	$\log P = a + b \log Y$
1.2	$P = a + b \log Y$
1.3	$P = a + bY + cY^2$, where $b > 0$ and $c < 0$
1.4	$\log P = a + b \log Y + c (\log Y)^2$, where $b > 0$ and $c < 0$

Equations 1.0, 1.1, and 1.2 are all straight lines on natural, double logarithmic, and semi-logarithmic scales, respectively; 1.3 and 1.4 are parabolic on natural and logarithmic scales, respectively.

INCOME-BUYING PLANS RELATIONSHIP

Buying plans for automobiles show very consistent relationships to relative income position. Four periods are available for new and used cars combined; only two periods permit comparisons of new and used cars separately. Figures VI.1 and 2 show computed relationships for the available periods.[12]

FIGURE VI.1

ESTIMATED PERCENTAGE OF CONSUMERS UNION SAMPLE PLANNING
TO BUY AUTOMOBILES, BY RELATIVE INCOME POSITION, SELECTED YEARS

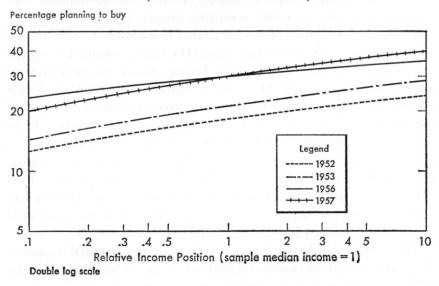

The stability of these relationships, with respect both to time and to the level of buying plans, seems quite remarkable. The income elasticity for total automobiles is almost identical, at every income position, for three of the four periods; the 1955–1956 periods shows a somewhat smaller elasticity than any of the others, but even here the differences are quite small. Consequently, the factors responsible for changes in automobile buying intentions over the period had about the same force in all income groups. Unfortunately we do not have data for the 1954–1955 period when automobile sales were extraordinarily high. One might expect that income elasticity for this period would have been relatively low, because the largest in-

12 All these regressions were fitted as straight lines on semi-logarithmic scales, and all would show a very close relationship between the original data and the computed regression.

creases in intentions were probably in the lower-income groups. If so, the proportional change in purchases relative to income would have been smaller than in other years.

FIGURE VI.2

ESTIMATED PERCENTAGE OF CONSUMERS UNION SAMPLE PLANNING TO BUY NEW AND USED AUTOMOBILES, BY RELATIVE INCOME POSITION, SELECTED YEARS

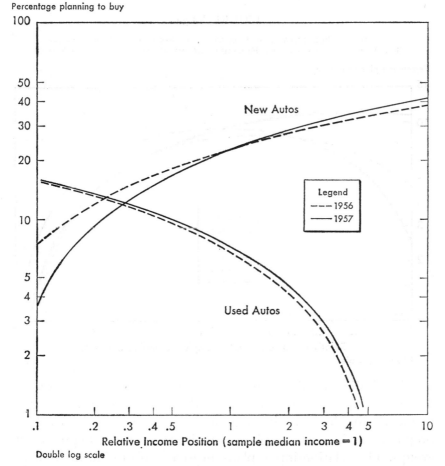

Percentage planning to buy

New Autos

Legend
--- 1956
——— 1957

Used Autos

Relative Income Position (sample median income = 1)

Double log scale

The two regressions we have on new cars and used cars separately are also very similar. Income elasticity for new cars is about double that of total cars—it tends to be larger relative to the total at low income positions and smaller relative to the total at high incomes. Used cars have negative elasticity throughout, with the curves becoming strongly negative at high relative income positions.[13]

[13] All these functions follow the original data closely and show no systematic tendency to deviate even at extreme income values, although it seems probable that in-

These results can be summarized as follows: The negative income elasticity of used auto plans indicates that as income rises plans to buy used cars decrease. In the upper-income groups, the proportional decrease in plans caused by any given increment in income is larger than it is for the same increment in income in the low-income groups. In the case of new autos, the income elasticity of plans is

FIGURE VI.3a

ESTIMATED PERCENTAGE OF CONSUMERS UNION SAMPLE PLANNING TO
BUY VACUUM CLEANERS, BY RELATIVE INCOME POSITION, SELECTED YEARS

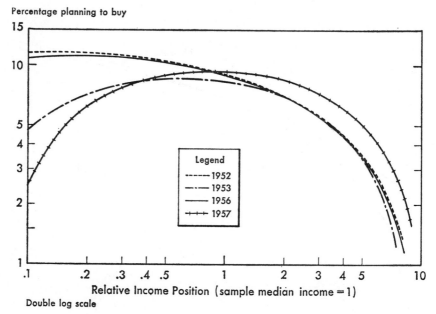

positive, indicating that plans to buy increase as income rises. The flattening out of the curve illustrates the fact that a given increment in income in the lower-income groups is accompanied by a larger proportional increase in plans than is true for the higher-income groups. The relationship of plans for total autos to income indicates an income elasticity that is almost constant and also rather small in

creased detail in the lower-income classes would result in the income–used-car relationship's becoming parabolic—with a peak at a relative income position of around .3 or .4. (The income groups below $3,000 a year are very poorly represented in the Consumers Union sample.) It is also likely to be true that many CU members with less than $3,000 income per year are "out of place," either in the sense that their normal incomes (permanent income in the Friedman sense) are much higher or in the sense that their incomes are derived from property of one kind or another (and pensions). Although the entire CU sample is atypical by definition, the lower-incomes parts are probably more atypical than the rest.

magnitude, as the line is not very far from being horizontal. In effect the changes in elasticity for new and used cars at both the upper and lower extremes of relative income have canceled each other out, resulting in close to a straight (and almost horizontal) line for the total.

FIGURE VI.3b

ESTIMATED PERCENTAGE OF CONSUMERS UNION SAMPLE PLANNING TO BUY RANGES, REFRIGERATORS, AND WASHERS, BY RELATIVE INCOME POSITION, SELECTED YEARS

Percentage planning to buy

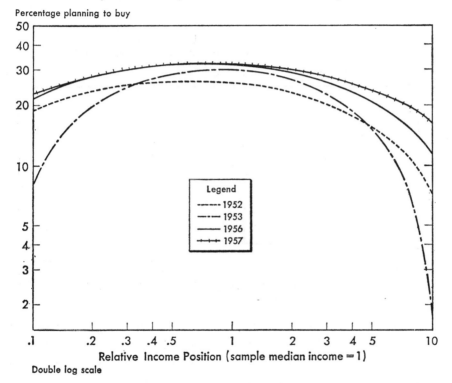

Relative Income Position (sample median income = 1)

Double log scale

Moving to the household equipment category, we find a quite different and less stable pattern of relationship between income and buying plans. The "standard" durables shown in Figure VI.3 are all parabolic, i.e., first rising, then reaching a peak and declining. Although these curves fit the original data less well than was the case with automobiles, the tendency for buying plans to fall off sharply in higher relative income positions is unmistakably clear in the basic data. The category of ranges, refrigerators, and washing machines also shows a consistent tendency for buying plans to increase as income rises toward the median. This tendency is weak for vacuum cleaners and hardly existed at all in the 1951–1952 period. The peak frequency of buying plans for these items is never at a relative income position higher than the median and is ordinarily quite a bit below that point. There does not seem to be any systematic relationship between the shape of these functions with respect to either the time period or the level of intentions.

The remaining "standard" durable for which data are available—TV sets (Figure VI.4)—shows the least relationship of any com-

FIGURE VI.4

ESTIMATED PERCENTAGE OF CONSUMERS UNION SAMPLE PLANNING TO
BUY TELEVISION SETS, BY RELATIVE INCOME POSITION, SELECTED YEARS

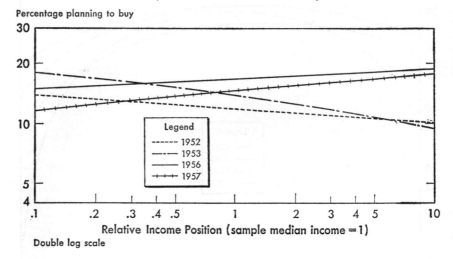

modity. This is the only case in which computing a regression might not be warranted, because the original data show considerable deviation from the line of best fit. The only conclusion that seems to emerge from Figure VI.4 is that there is no persistent relationship between plans to buy any TV sets and relative income positions; two of the periods show small positive elasticities and the other two show small negative ones. These elasticities could easily be reversed in direction by minor changes in weights.

What may be happening here is a combination of circumstances that affect households in different income positions in divergent ways. Replacement (or upgrading) demand for TV sets has probably been growing throughout this period. In 1951, most people owned sets that were only a few years old; hence the average age of the outstanding stock must have been quite low compared to other standard durables. By 1956, there must have been substantial numbers of relatively old TV sets. At the same time, many middle- and upper-income households are in the process of acquiring "second" TV sets, and others in these income brackets are in the market for color sets. Replacement demand—to judge from the other standard durables—generally seems to result in a negative income elasticity at high relative positions, probably because high-income households do not make plans for the replacement of items they already own provided the items are in reasonably good working order.[14] The "second set" factor should result in a positive income elasticity at high relative income positions, if, as seems plausible, households are more likely to plan the purchase of an item they do not already possess but are thinking of acquiring. In the case of TV sets, the combination of second-set and replacement demand may tend to cancel out, leaving nothing but random variation in the buying plans of higher-income households.

The behavior of plans to buy "prestige" durables fits into this framework. Figure VI.5 shows the income–buying-plans relationship for room air conditioners and a combined category of dishwashers, dryers, and electric ironers. Income elasticity is generally positive, except at very high relative income positions for some periods, and is strongly positive at low and middle incomes. There is a pronounced tendency, especially for air conditioners, for elasticity to fall over time in any given relative income position. This is due to a rapid rate of expansion in the air-conditioner buying plans of lower-income households while upper-income households remain at roughly the same level. In the 1956–1957 period, elasticity for air conditioners actually becomes negative at moderately high income positions.[15] A similar movement shows up in the combined category, although here the curves do not show any tendency to flatten out because of an increase in plans for the lower-income groups in later periods. However, the maximum points on the computed curves are

[14] Relative costs would also have some influence, because a higher-income household is less likely to have a purchase plan when the item in question is comparatively inexpensive. Ranges, refrigerators, and washing machines tend to run in about the same price range, so one would not expect any difference on this count. For vacuum cleaners, whose cost is lower, we find a tendency for income elasticity to be more sharply negative with higher income (see Figure VI.2). Replacement demand for TV sets may have the same pattern as vacuum cleaners.

[15] Figure VI.4 may exaggerate this effect somewhat, to judge from the original data. The level of buying plans falls very sharply in the second highest income class and then rises in the highest one. The computed parabola is more heavily influenced by the former than by the latter because of the weights.

reached at lower relative income positions in the later periods than in earlier ones; at median income, therefore, elasticity is always smaller for later periods. In addition, the decline in elasticity in the high-income groups is more pronounced in later periods than in earlier ones.

It is also clear that, for comparable income positions, elasticity is always higher for prestige durables than for standard durables

FIGURE VI.5a

ESTIMATED PERCENTAGE OF CONSUMERS UNION SAMPLE PLANNING TO BUY DRYERS, DISHWASHERS, AND IRONERS, BY RELATIVE INCOME POSITION, SELECTED YEARS

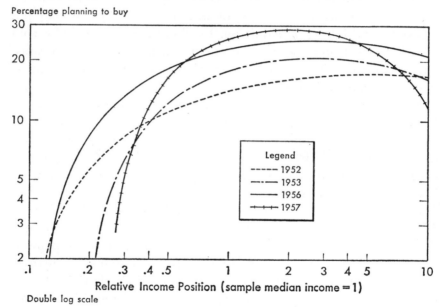

Percentage planning to buy

Legend
----- 1952
--·-- 1953
——— 1956
+++ 1957

Relative Income Position (sample median income = 1)

Double log scale

(with the exception of TV sets, as discussed above). Elasticities for standard durables become negative in all periods by the time we reach the median income position, and usually much before that position. For prestige durables, some elasticities are positive throughout; where they became negative, it is only at income positions higher than the median—usually quite a bit higher.

All these data are consistent with the notion that households are more apt to form purchase plans for goods they do not already have than for goods that they own but intend to replace whenever necessary. Put most simply, purchases that are replacements for existing items are more likely to be "surprises," in the sense that households unexpectedly face the necessity of immediate replacement. If the household does not own an air conditioner, it obviously cannot be "surprised" into replacement forced by unexpected breakdown,[16] and purchases are more likely to have been preceded by a reportable plan.

FIGURE VI.5b

Estimated Percentage of Consumers Union Sample Planning to Buy Air Conditioners, by Relative Income Position, Selected Years

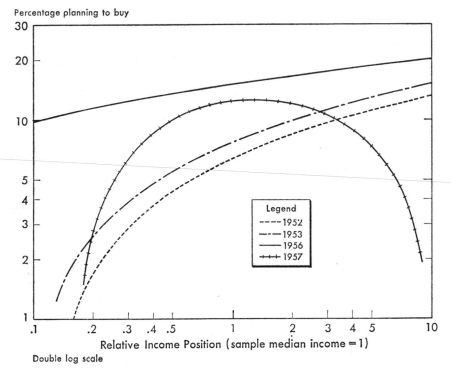

Percentage planning to buy

Relative Income Position (sample median income = 1)

Double log scale

Legend
---- 1952
—·— 1953
——— 1956
+++ 1957

In general, it seems plausible that the buying-plans–income relationship goes through the following phases. When an item is first introduced, it is likely to show very high income elasticity. Few low-income households are potential purchasers because the item is outside their experience, knowledge, and interest.[17] If the commodity becomes an important component of the socially desirable "way of life"—for any reason—it may reach the mass market of middle- and

16 The *timing* of the replacement is the unexpected part of the process. Either wearing out or breaking down is clearly expected to take place at some point in the future.

17 It may also be financially beyond reach because of its cost, but this factor is in addition to the considerations sketched above.

relatively low-income households. If so, income elasticity will fall through time as the rate of usage expands rapidly in these income classes. Eventually saturation will set in and replacement demand becomes an increasingly important part of total demand. At this stage the income elasticity of buying intentions becomes parabolic, because the high income households who already have the commodity and will replace it when necessary do not generally have replacement plans with a specific time horizon.

INCOME-PURCHASES RELATIONSHIP

Most of the differences that we have discussed above for the income–buying-plans relationships are also apparent when we look at the relationship between income and purchases. In contrast, however, the income-elasticity measures for purchases are generally posi-

FIGURE VI.6

ESTIMATED PERCENTAGE OF CONSUMERS UNION SAMPLE THAT BOUGHT
AUTOMOBILES, BY RELATIVE INCOME POSITION, SELECTED YEARS

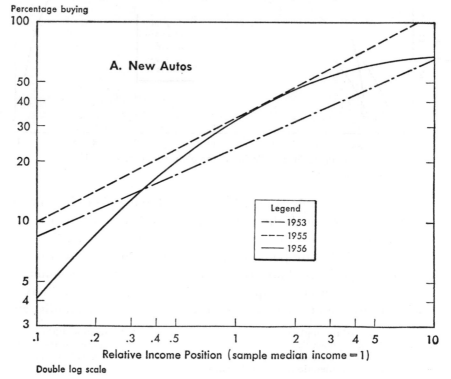

Percentage buying

A. New Autos

Legend
---·— 1953
--- 1955
——— 1956

Relative Income Position (sample median income = 1)

Double log scale

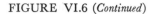

FIGURE VI.6 (*Continued*)

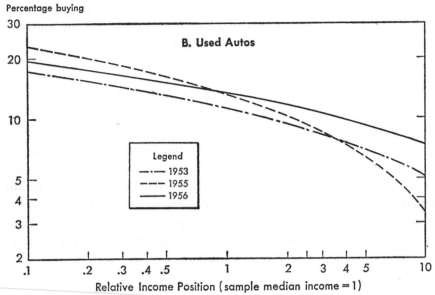

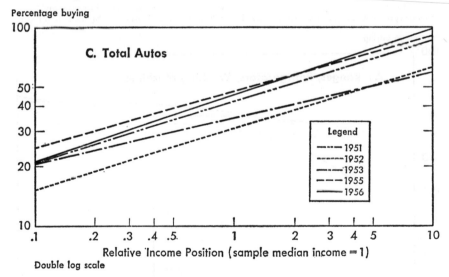

tive throughout.[18] Differences between "standard" and "prestige" durables show up primarily in terms of the numerical value of income elasticity rather than in algebraic sign or in the location of peak frequencies. For the prestige durables, elasticity tends to be quite high—usually greater than .50 and frequently greater than

[18] There are a few exceptions to this generalization, all for two standard durables.

unity. For standard durables, the elasticity measures are usually close to zero and are occasionally negative. As was true above for buying plans, the relationships between income and purchases of automobiles follows a distinctive pattern of its own.

Automobiles

The income-purchases regressions for automobiles are shown in Figure VI.6. The elasticities are positive throughout for new cars and for the total, and negative throughout for used cars. All these regressions are extremely good fits to the basic data. In terms of magnitudes, it is interesting to note that new-car elasticities are generally about double that for the total—a ratio similar to that found when the buying-plans–income regressions were examined for these items. Further, income elasticity is always higher for purchases than it was for buying plans; this generalization holds for every relative income position in every year for which we have data. Our results

FIGURE VI.7

ESTIMATED PERCENTAGE OF CONSUMERS UNION SAMPLE THAT PURCHASED
STANDARD HOUSEHOLD DURABLES, BY RELATIVE INCOME POSITION, SELECTED YEARS

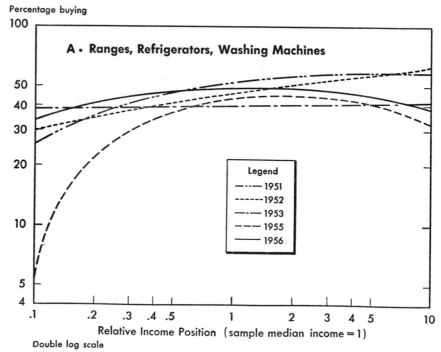

Percentage buying

A · Ranges, Refrigerators, Washing Machines

Legend
— · — 1951
------ 1952
— ·· — 1953
— — — 1955
——— 1956

Relative Income Position (sample median income = 1)

Double log scale

FIGURE VI.7 (*Continued*)

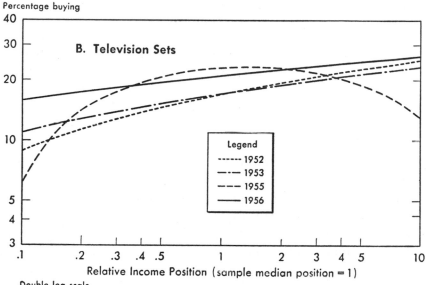

B. Television Sets

Percentage buying

Legend
······ 1952
—·—· 1953
——— 1955
———— 1956

Relative Income Position (sample median position = 1)

Double log scale

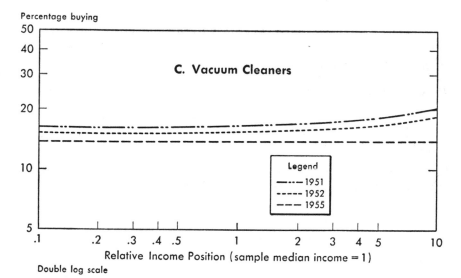

C. Vacuum Cleaners

Percentage buying

Legend
—·—· 1951
······ 1952
——— 1955

Relative Income Position (sample median income = 1)

Double log scale

indicate that lower-income groups are relatively more likely to have buying plans and not purchase than upper-income groups, and the latter are relatively more likely to purchase without reporting a buying plan. Since elasticity is measured by the slope of the function, higher plans relative to purchases in the lower-income groups tend to reduce the slope of the plan function, relative to that of the purchase function. Despite these tendencies, almost every income group shows a higher *absolute* fraction of purchases than of buying plans.[19]

Standard Household Durables

Turning to the household equipment items, we find roughly comparable, though not as consistent, results. The elasticities of the purchases-income regressions are ordinarily quite low for the standard durables. Some of the data behave quite erratically (particularly for vacuum cleaners), but this results chiefly in a tendency for the extremes of the regression lines to provide a poor representation of the actual observations. Despite the fit, the general character of these relationships is adequately portrayed by Figure VI.7.

If we exclude the lowest relative income positions, where the plotted relationships represent extrapolations, none of the elasticity measures is higher than about 0.40, with most falling between 0.15 and zero. Again excluding the extremes, the elasticity is almost always higher for the purchases-income relationship than it was for buying plans—given comparable relative income positions. The explanation of this tendency has already been noted in the case of autos. The only exceptions to this generalization show up for the TV-set category, where the regressions are generally less meaningful because of the wide scatter shown by the original data.

Prestige Household Durables

These items show a very consistent pattern. The purchases-income elasticities are always positive and are generally well above 0.50. Almost half the elasticities computed are above unity, and only two observations (out of 19) fall below the highest elasticity found for the standard durables—again, excluding extreme relative income positions for the latter. All the elasticity measures in this category are higher for the purchases-income regression than they were for buying plans, frequently being two to three times as high.[20]

---

[19] These considerations bear on aggregate predictive value only to a limited extent. The fact that lower-income classes are relatively more likely to plan and less likely to purchase than higher-income groups would indicate that individual plan fulfillment is lower than if no bias of this kind existed. However, from the viewpoint of aggregate predictions, what matters is whether or not changes between two time periods in the frequency of buying plans and purchases are systematic for every income position. If they are (and the evidence leads one to believe so), then the bias is irrelevant for aggregate prediction.

[20] This is only true, strictly speaking, if we exclude extreme positions on the income scale. The buying-plans–income regressions frequently show very high elasticities at low-income positions because of the parabolic shape of these regressions.

Figure VI.8 (A, B, C, D) shows a fairly consistent tendency for the income elasticity of purchases to decline over time, given relative income position. The latest period (1956–1957) shows elasticities in the higher-income groups beginning to flatten out and even becoming negative at very high incomes; data for this period are better fitted by parabolas than by straight lines. This pattern is particularly noticeable for air conditioners, garbage-disposal units, and the combined category of dryers, dishwashers, and ironers. Generally, the data behave very much like the buying-intentions–income relationships discussed earlier.

The results shown in this last section seem to be thoroughly in accord with general preconceptions about the relationship between income and purchases. Perhaps the most striking over-all result is the degree of consistency between the income-elasticity characteristics for purchases and those relating to plans. For both purchases and plans, the income elasticity is consistently lower for standard durables than for prestige durables, given comparable relative income positions.

The material presented thus far has been concerned with the buying-plans–income and purchases-income patterns considered separately, although in the first section we compared aggregate plans and purchases for comparable periods. It is worthwhile to look briefly at a direct comparison of the income patterns, using selected cases that can be regarded as typical.

Figure VI.9 shows these relationships for air conditioners, as a typical prestige durable, and for the combined category of ranges, refrigerators, and washing machines as representative of the standard durables. The frequency of purchases exceeds the frequency of plans throughout for the latter; the income elasticity of purchases is also higher than that of plans throughout. In the case of air conditioners, the frequency of purchases is smaller than that of plans in low relative income positions and larger in high ones. Again we find that the elasticity of purchases tends to exceed that of plans, with the exception of very low relative income positions. The probable reasons underlying these relationships have been discussed earlier, e.g., the relative importance of replacement versus new-acquisition demand for standard and prestige durables.

In the automobile category (Figure VI.10), new cars behave somewhat like prestige durables, and used cars like standard durables. The major differences are that buying plans for new cars do not show the absolute decline at very high incomes that is characteristic of prestige durables, nor do they show as much tendency for plans to exceed purchases at low incomes. The first of these differences is

FIGURE VI.8

ESTIMATED PERCENTAGE OF CONSUMERS UNION SAMPLE THAT PURCHASED PRESTIGE HOUSEHOLD DURABLES, BY RELATIVE INCOME POSITION, SELECTED YEARS

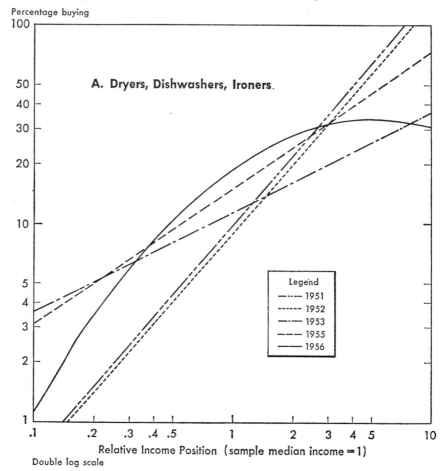

possibly due to the cost of new cars relative to the other prestige durables. Even very high-income families usually seem to make re-portable plans to buy new cars, although they apparently do not make or report plans for less expensive items. (The gap between automobile plans and purchases does tend to grow somewhat at very high incomes, however.) No good explanation appears for the second difference; it may reflect the very heavy emphasis in *Consumer Reports* on the testing and rating of automobiles, which would result in CU subscribers' having unusually high purchases, but no reason emerges why this does not show up in buying plans as well.

FIGURE VI.8 (*Continued*)

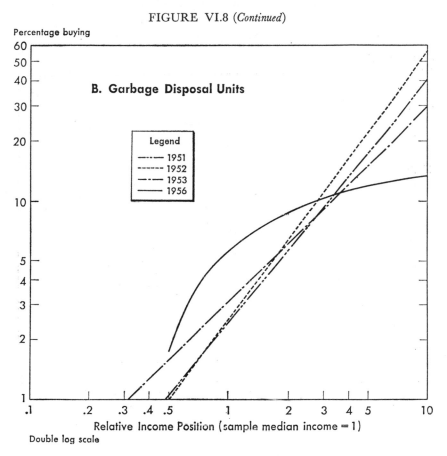

Percentage buying

B. Garbage Disposal Units

Legend
—·—— 1951
—----— 1952
—··— 1953
——— 1956

Relative Income Position (sample median income = 1)

Double log scale

Actually, one would probably expect plans to buy new cars in the relatively low-income groups to exceed purchases of new cars by a greater extent than plans to buy other prestige durables exceed purchases, since many prospective new car buyers in these income groups must wind up buying used cars.

CHARACTERISTICS OF THE PLANNING HORIZON

The data that we have discussed above seem to suggest that household planning is predictably different for certain classes of commodities. Planning seems to be most closely related to purchases in the automobile category, both as regards the consistency of the computed income relationships and the degree to which the regression functions fit the data. It also seems to be a plausible hypothesis that consumer plans to purchase what we have labeled standard durables

FIGURE VI.8 (*Continued*)

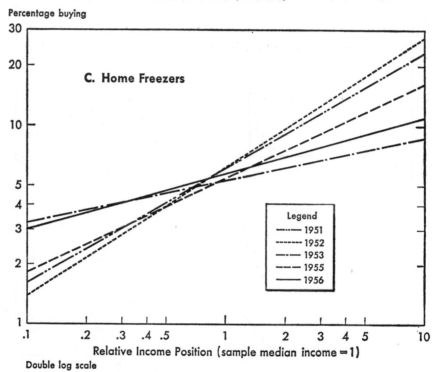

Percentage buying

C. Home Freezers

Legend
——·— 1951
------- 1952
—·—· 1953
——— 1955
——— 1956

Relative Income Position (sample median income = 1)

Double log scale

—refrigerators, washing machines, etc.—are primarily a reflection of replacement needs plus some nonpostponable acquisitions for newly formed households.[21] In addition, one might argue that, under contemporary United States conditions, fluctuations in the rate of purchase (and of buying plans) for standard durables are probably less influenced by expectational variables and "buying moods" than fluctuations in the rate of purchase (and buying plans) for the prestige durables or for automobiles.

All the buying plans that we have discussed thus far consist of re-

[21] This is overstated somewhat, since the formation of new households is itself postponable, and the acquisition of secondhand items is an alternative to purchases of newly produced ones.

sponses to a question having the time horizon of approximately one year. The exact wording of the buying-plans question has varied slightly over the period, though probably not enough to make much

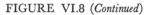

FIGURE VI.8 (*Continued*)

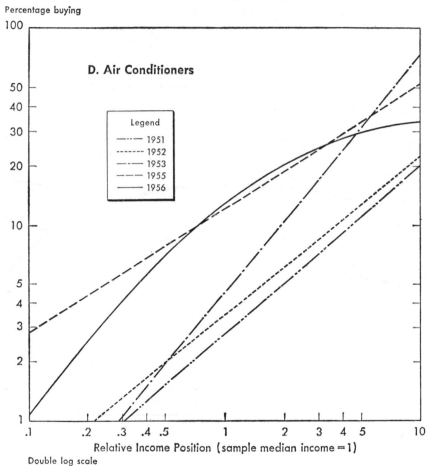

Percentage buying

D. Air Conditioners

Legend
— ·· — 1951
········· 1952
— · — 1953
— — — 1955
——— 1956

Relative Income Position (sample median income = 1)

Double log scale

difference.[22] The October, 1957, questionnaire contained a substantial change in the buying-plans question. Respondents were asked a dual question: (a) "Which of the following products do you plan to

[22] The question usually has read "Which of the following products do you plan to buy over the next twelve months or so?" The vague "or so" phrase has always been included in the questionnaire and may have a substantial impact on the income characteristics of the responses. It is perfectly conceivable to me that this question is interpreted by many people as meaning s'omething like "the next 12–18 months," which would give very different kinds of answers from "the next 12 months." This problem comes up later.

buy within the next 6 months?" and (b) "Which of the following products do you plan to buy later [than 6 months]?"[23]

Responses to these two questions have proved to be quite interesting. Briefly, the six-month question showed, along with a quite low

FIGURE VI.9

Estimated Percentage of Consumers Union Sample That (1) Planned to Buy and (2) Bought Typical Standard Durables and Typical Prestige Durables, by Relative Income Position, 1956

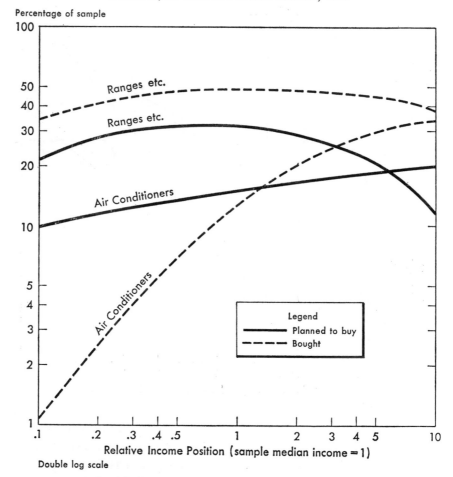

Percentage of sample

Relative Income Position (sample median income = 1)

Double log scale

level of buying plans, considerably higher income elasticity than had been found for any of the previous years' (12 months or so) ques-

[23] The phrase in brackets was not included; it seemed clear from the arrangement of the question that respondents would interpret it in the manner suggested by the brackets.

tions. For all commodities except vacuum cleaners, the six-month plans showed positive elasticity throughout the entire range of relative income positions. The combined "6 months" and "later" buying-plans question showed both a very high *level* of intentions com-

FIGURE VI.10

ESTIMATED PERCENTAGE OF CONSUMERS UNION SAMPLE THAT (1) PLANNED TO BUY AND (2) BOUGHT AUTOMOBILES, BY RELATIVE INCOME POSITION, 1956

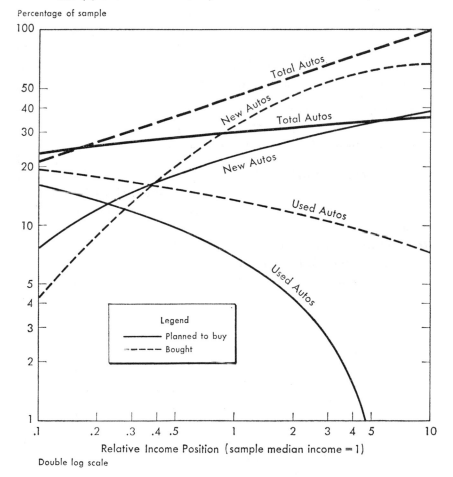

Percentage of sample

pared to any previous year and, for most commodities, a considerably *lower* income elasticity measure than had been computed for previous years, "lower" in this sense referring to lower positive elasticity or greater negative elasticity.[24] All the income elasticity measures

[24] Exceptions to this generalization are found in the lowest relative income positions. Most of the "6 months plus later" functions are parabolic; the extremes of the

TABLE VI.3

INCOME ELASTICITY OF BUYING PLANS, FOR CONSUMERS UNION SAMPLE,
SELECTED PERIODS

Income Elasticity at Median Income for

					"6 Months	
					and later"	
		"12 Months or So" Horizon			"6 Months"	Horizon
					Horizon	
Commodity	P-6	P-7	P-10	P-11	P-12	P-12
New automobiles	NA	NA	+.290	+.363	+.517	+.137
Used automobiles	NA	NA	−.563	−.541	−.115	−.303
Total automobiles	+.135	.143	+.091	+.144	+.362	.046
TV sets	−.070	−.138	+.050	+.092	+.127	−.082
Air conditioners	+.459	+.457	+.148	+.119	+.568	+.033
Ranges, refrigerators,						
washing machines	−.098	−.045	−.069	−.043	+.095	−.200
Vacuum cleaners	−.270	−.138	−.264	−.038	−.036	−.254

Source: Basic data from Consumer Purchases Study, NBER.

for the "6 months plus later" buying plans show negative elasticity at some point in the income scale. For commodities where elasticities had previously been negative for the "12 months or so" horizon, they are usually negative at a lower relative income position and fall more rapidly thereafter; where elasticities had been positive throughout for the 12-month horizon (automobiles), they now become negative at high relative income positions. Table VI.3 summarizes these data, showing elasticities at median income for a number of commodities during selected periods.

The general pattern of the results is obvious, although there are some observations in this table that do not conform. Unfortunately, we do not have really good data for any of the prestige durables for the "6 months" or "later" horizons. The only item in this category that was included in the October, 1957, questionnaire happened to be air conditioners, because none of the other items for which we have previous data were listed. There is a very strong seasonal factor in plans to buy air conditioners, doubtless leading the seasonal fluctuations in purchases.[25]

relative income scale sometimes show very sharp rises and falls, with concomitant very high income elasticity at low incomes and very low (high negative value) elasticity at high incomes. Extrapolations on both ends frequently tend to be too extreme.

[25] The six-month question included the period from October to March. The later category for air conditioners contains about eight times as many plans as the six-month category—the highest ratio found for any of the durable goods listed. This does not necessarily throw off the "6 months plus later" plans, but it makes the six-month

The most consistent feature of these data is the behavior of the six-month plans relative to the twelve-month ones. There is no commodity where the income elasticity for any twelve-month horizon is as high as its elasticity for the six-month horizon, although the difference is trivial in one case. The consistency is not quite so striking when we compare the twelve-month horizon with the longer ("6 months plus later") horizon. Here we find five observations (out of 24) in which the elasticity for the longer horizon is larger than the elasticity for one of the twelve-month horizons.

Looking at the over-all results, the following interpretation is suggested. The six-month buying plans generally consist of rather definite commitments that have been thought about in enough detail to make it fairly certain that they will be carried out unless some unforeseen (and economically important) event takes place. This notion is buttressed by a comparison of elasticities for the six-month *plans* with the twelve-month *purchases*. The magnitudes of the two elasticities are frequently quite close to each other, and both are quite different from elasticities for either the twelve-month or the longer-horizon plans.

In every case above—with the possible exception of air conditioners—the similarity of elasticities for the six-month plans and purchases is quite evident.[26] Although we cannot verify this directly, it is almost certainly true that the six-month plans would also show a higher fulfillment ratio than the longer horizon plans (3). It was pointed out above that the dissimilarity in income elasticities between twelve-month plans and purchases almost certainly meant a relatively low plan-fulfillment ratio, although this proposition could not be proved conclusively from the data. By the same token, the similarity that we find here augurs for a relatively favorable fulfillment ratio.[27]

Given our findings for the shorter horizon plans, what then can be said about what "12 months or so" plans actually represent? Clearly, they are something of a mixed bag. The "12 months or so" plans necessarily have included the six-month plans, although we do not know what fraction of the total would normally consist of the short

plans impossible to interpret relative to the other items where there is no seasonal problem. Actually, we find that the income elasticity for the six-month plans is higher than anything calculated previously and about three times as high as the elasticity in the two previous years.

[26] We have noted above the reasons why air conditioners present special problems.

[27] Plan fulfillment in the CU sample is now being examined. A report will be issued sometime during early 1961.

range, more definite plans. But they also include rather more uncertain, indefinite, or longer range plans that may not really be buying plans at all in any narrow sense of the term. It is perfectly possible that these longer range plans really measure and reflect "buying mood" or some kind of "optimism coefficient." It seems evident that they do not represent merely whim, wish, and hope in various proportions, partly because the internal structure is reasonably consistent through time and partly because the plan frequencies are usually *lower* than the actual purchase frequencies of the CU population.

TABLE VI.4

INCOME ELASTICITIES FOR PURCHASES AND BUYING PLANS,
CONSUMERS UNION SAMPLE

Income Elasticity at Median Income for

	Purchases (Past 12 Months)			Buying Plans		
				"Within 6 Months"	"12 Months or so"	
Product	A-6	A-7	A-10		P-6	P-7	P-10
New automobiles	NA	+.441	+.604	+.517	NA	NA	+.290
Used automobiles	NA	−.235	−.197	−.115	NA	NA	−.563
Total automobiles	+.309	+.230	+.332	+.362	+.135	+.143	+.091
TV sets	+.204	+.156	+.107	+.127	−.070	−.138	+.050
Air conditioners	+.809	+.209	+.762	+.568	+.459	+.457	+.148
Ranges, refrigerators, washing machines	+.152	+.017	+.022	+.095	−.092	−.045	−.069
Vacuum cleaners	+.010	NA	+.014	−.036	−.270	−.138	−.264

Source: Basic data from Consumer Purchases Study, NBER.

Further, it is by no means evident that the variations over time in the six-month plans would turn out to be more closely related to variation in actual purchases over time. Even assuming, as seems almost certain, that shorter range plans have a significantly higher fulfillment ratio than longer range ones, it might be possible for their aggregate prediction record to be worse. The time-series correlation between buying plans and purchases depends on (1) the percentage of households who report plans and their fulfillment ratio (the fraction of the planners who actually purchase); (2) the percentage of households who do *not* report plans and their *nonfulfillment* ratio (the fraction of nonplanners who actually purchase); and (3) the variation in buying plans over time. It has been shown that buying plans have predictive value over time if the fulfillment ratio of the planners is higher than the nonfulfillment ratio of the non-planners, i.e., if relatively more planners actually buy than nonplanners, assuming that the fulfillment and nonfulfillment ratios are independent of the percentage of planners.[28]

From the argument above, it seems to follow that the larger the difference between the fraction of planners and of nonplanners who buy, the greater the aggregate predictive value of the buying plans. It thus seems to follow that the six-month plans should have a better predictive record. However, suppose we have a situation in which the percentage of short horizon planners, A, remains relatively stable through time because the plans are closely related to, e.g., demo-graphic variables, the percentage of long horizon planners, B, fluctu-ates considerably through time because B really measures some kind of "buying mood" complex, and the percentage of "A" nonplanners who buy (the nonplanner, nonfulfillment ratio) is positively related to the percentage of "B" planners. It would then follow that B would furnish better aggregate predictions, despite the fact that "A" planners have both a higher fulfillment ratio and a larger difference be-tween the actions of planners and nonplanners than do "B" planners.[29]

Given the lack of experience with the shorter horizon buying plans, a conclusive test of the above propositions will not be possible for some time. We do have one piece of indirect evidence that bears on the problem. Over the period 1949–1957, it has been shown that the aggregate predictive record of buying plans for the Consumers Union sample is somewhat better than that of the Survey of Consumer Finances (6). It is possible that one explanation for this is the vagueness of the CU buying plans question! The Survey asks about plans for a twelve-month forward period—actually a bit less, because they ask about a calendar year period and some households are not interviewed until March. In addition, the Survey asks about the degree of certainty accompanying the plans. The series of questions asked by the Survey is probably more confining than the CU buying-plans question, which simply asks about "buying plans" over

[28] This statement is a translation of Arthur Okun's formal analysis (7).
[29] Okun (7) does not take up this problem directly, although he does specify conditions under which predictive value at the individual level would fail to result in predictive value at the aggregate level. This question is discussed in my paper presented at the same conference (6).

the "next 12 months or so"; if it is, this greater degree of precision might be a reason for worse aggregate results.

In addition, experimentation with the Survey data seems to suggest that the aggregate predictive value of the "definite" buying plans is lower than that of the "definite" plus the "probable" and the "possible" plans.[30] This evidence is certainly not conclusive, although it does provide some straws in the wind. Additional evidence along these lines has been obtained from recent surveys of the Consumers Union sample, which have asked different buying-plans questions of different subgroups of the sample. Some of the results have been reported, but the question of major interest—fulfillment for the different questions—is still under investigation.

References

1. CLARK, LINCOLN, ed. *Consumer Behavior: Research on Consumer Reactions.* New York: Harper and Brothers, 1958. Pp. 93–219.
2. DUESENBERRY, J. *Income, Savings, and the Theory of Consumer Behavior.* Cambridge: Harvard University Press, 1949.
3. FERBER, ROBERT. "The Role of Planning in Consumer Purchases of Durable Goods," *Am. Econ. Rev., 44* (December, 1954), 854–74.
4. JUSTER, F. THOMAS. "Prediction and Consumer Buying Intentions," *Papers and Proceedings of the Am. Economic Assoc., 50* (May, 1960), 604–17.
5. ———. "The Predictive Value of Consumers Union Spending Intentions Data," in *The Quality and Economic Significance of Anticipations Data.* Princeton, New Jersey: Princeton University Press, 1960. Pp. 263–89.
6. ———. *Consumer Expectations, Plans, and Purchases: A Progress Report.* Occasional Paper 70. New York: National Bureau of Economic Research, Inc., 1959.
7. OKUN, ARTHUR. "The Value of Anticipations Data in Forecasting National Product," in *The Quality and Economic Significance of Intentions Data.* Princeton, New Jersey: Princeton University Press, 1960. Pp. 407–51.

[30] See Okun (7). My own experiments with Survey data confirm this impression.

Index

Index